Cheap Chow
CHICAGO

3RD EDITION

A LaBan
and
Andarshia Townsend

CHICAGO
REVIEW
PRESS

Library of Congress Cataloging-in-Publication Data
Is available from the Library of Congress.

Cover and interior design: Mel Kupfer
Cover photograph: Allison Leach©/Photonica

Revised edition
Published by Chicago Review Press, Incorporated
814 North Franklin Street
Chicago, Illinois 60610
ISBN 1-55652-433-1
Printed in the United States of America
5 4 3 2 1

To my frequent dining companion Eric.

A LaBan

If it wasn't for one person's persistence
and dedication, I wouldn't be here today.
I dedicate this book to my mother,
Dr. Florence "Nkechi" Townsend.
I'd also like to thank God for giving me
the gift to write in the first place.
Warm thoughts also go out to the
journalism department of Columbia College,
my alma mater, and Whitney M. Young High School,
where this whole writing obsession began.

Audarshia Townsend

Contents

Introduction

You're so busy, right? You're trying to balance long hours at work with maybe a family or a social life or school or something and wouldn't it be easier just to go out and grab something to eat? But you're so busy trying to do it all that you rarely have the time to sample any new places to eat.

And then there's the money thing. All that eating out begins to add up after a while, doesn't it? Not necessarily. *Cheap Chow Chicago* is a way of helping you through a busy time. It's a way of acquainting you with the endless opportunities that exist in your own backyard to eat well for less. *Cheap Chow Chicago* points you in the direction of myriad dining establishments where the food is, at minimum, pretty good and always relatively cheap.

The concept here is "Taste for Less." *Cheap Chow Chicago* uses a two-tier price-rating system to deliver to readers satisfying meals, including tax and tip (but not appetizers and desserts, alcohol, or cappuccino) for either:

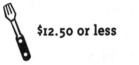 **$12.50 or less**    **$20 or less**

Restaurants are organized by themes ranging from ethnic to a focus on a Chicago neighborhood to a type of food—for example, ribs or vegetarian—to a type of dining—all-you-can-eat or late night—or just whatever we felt like writing about. To enhance the dining and guidebook experience, each chapter has an informative and chatty lead-in editorial designed to capture the designated theme.

So you may be asking yourself, "What gives them the right? What do they know? And why should I spend my hard-earned money on this book and take their advice? And, after reviewing some 300 restaurants, how much do they weigh?"

Well, *Cheap Chow* was a successful (at least financially) monthly newsletter for three years before it became a book, and we're now publishing updates. A LaBan has honed her talents as food editor at the now-defunct, hip Wicker Park 'zine *Chicago's Subnation* and, more recently, at *NewCity* and the *Chicago Reader*. Audarshia Townsend is a nightlife and dining writer for the *Chicago Tribune* as well as several other local publications. Together we bring an insightful and lighthearted approach to Chicago's dining scene.

You know, people find out you review restaurants and they want to ask you all kinds of questions. Challenge you. "What's your favorite cheap restaurant?" We hear that all the time. You know, that's proprietary information—it's worth money. As restaurant writers, we cringe when people just want to pump us for free advice. Hey, here it is—all of it. Buy this book. Or if you can't do that, here's our short list. Copy this page and save the, we think, very reasonable cover price:

THE BEST OF *CHEAP CHOW CHICAGO*

That's Italian   Anna Maria's. Forget all those expensive trattorias in Lincoln Park or downtown. A once nondescript storefront has spiffed itself up and still houses an extraordinary kitchen.

Soul Satisfied   BJ's Market & Bakery. The South Side's award-winning soul-food restaurant cranks out some mighty portions of mustard-fried catfish, greens, and smothered chicken—without the grease.

Late-Night Bites   4 Taste. This hip little appetizer lounge makes eating cheap chic with its hot and cold portions of roasted duck breast, Australian beef tenderloin, and apple-stuffed raviolis with smoked chicken.

Latin Fling   Rinconcito Sudamericano. Chicago's premier establishment for Peruvian cuisine, this unpretentious storefront in Bucktown more than makes up for its humble ambiance with quality meals.

Stick to Your Ribs   Hecky's. Hands down, the best ribs in the Chicago area.

Go Fish   The $7.95 sushi deluxe at Shiroi Hana. Nine pieces and a maki roll, accompanied by the inevitable miso soup and hot towels. A small price to pay for the nightly wait.

Where Everybody Knows Your Name   J. T. Collin's Pub. Almost the perfect neighborhood bar where you can lounge with friends or comfortably alone with a room full of strangers. Great chicken flat bread.

A Room with a View   The Signature Room on the Ninety-Fifth. The $13.95 pig-out buffet makes this one of the Mag Mile's hidden gems.

Oktoberfeast, Ja!   Resi's Bierstube. Cheap sausages served in a classic bier garden.

A FEW NOTES ABOUT USING THIS BOOK

This book does not purport to identify every budget restaurant in the city. This is the new and updated version of *Cheap Chow Chicago*—Version 3.0, if you will, with all new restaurants, new chapters, new reviews, and updated pricing. But no, we still haven't eaten at every dump, dive, diner, and cheap buffet out there. There's simply not enough space in the week, the year, or our stomachs. For those of you who are competitive, who righteously want to point out a place we missed, feel free. You could be an excellent source for some good finds.

The bottom line is, this book is just indicative of what's out there. It's here to point you in the right direction. It doesn't feature every restaurant; it certainly doesn't have write-ups on many of those eateries you should know about anyway if you get out at all. Feel free to explore on your own. Read the competition—we do. Also, talk to those who consider themselves adventurous eaters and go out a lot.

Once you get there, realize we know how to spell! But, each restaurant has its own ambiance, its own flavor, its own way of spelling dishes on their menus. So, the spellings in each review are true to these nuances, to help preserve the ambiance, you know.

In spite of all efforts to keep up to date on pricing or even places being in business, things change. We've done a good amount of research on each chapter's subject matter and restaurants, but if you've got to know for sure whether that risotto is still $9.95, give the place a call. Who knows, maybe the place isn't even serving risotto anymore. In some hopefully isolated and very sad situations, the place might not be serving anything anymore (as in no longer in business). It happens to even the best of places. If you're the anxious type, phone first.

Keep in mind, these are restaurant reviews, so they are, after all, a matter of opinion. Reviews are also done from the angle of the average eater (there were no free meals here, and restaurants were reviewed after "mystery shopping"), but they are subjective. Although we've rarely written about a place we think is just terrible (what's the point in wasting the space?), we're not averse to pointing out the warts. You might expect some for $12.50 or less. Remember, this is a value deal here. If you're expecting Le Français, you'd better drive to Wheeling.

Regardless, you may disagree with the book. Go ahead and express yourself. If you've got particularly strong opinions about something, feel free to write us a note. Why stop there? If you're really adamant, feel free to write your own book. There's nothing stopping you. Have fun.

Latin Fling

SALSA SAVINGS THAT YOU CAN'T BEAT... CHA, CHA, CHA!

ateline, 1492—In Italy, there is no such thing as tomato sauce, the Irish aren't able to enjoy potatoes with their meat in shepherd's pie, and Mexicans have never heard of a burrito with cheese. Five hundred years ago, however, with the arrival of Columbus and subsequent Iberian explorers, menus changed globally as the world became truly well-rounded. An exchange of flavors from the old to the new accompanied the movement of ships as the indigenous ingredients of the Americas mixed with the spices and foodstuffs of Europe and Asia to create new dishes in the Old World and completely *nuevo* cuisine in the New World.

The Spanish explorers' first port of call was the Caribbean, where Columbus, and ultimately the rest of Europe, first tasted four of the five most economically important New World crops: maize, sweet potatoes, chili peppers, and manioc. (The fifth, the potato, was later unearthed as the Spaniards moved south into the Andes.) The Spaniards added cattle, pigs, and other livestock to this picture, and a new cuisine was cooked up in the tropical kitchens of Puerto Rico, the Dominican Republic, and Cuba.

> "Tita knew through her own flesh how fire transforms the elements, how a lump of corn flour is changed into a tortilla, how a soul that hasn't been warmed by the fire of love is lifeless, like a useless ball of corn flour."
>
> —Laura Esquivel, *Like Water for Chocolate*

In 1519, the Spanish left Cuba and moved inland into Mexico and Central America where they encountered the culinary traditions of highly developed Indian civilizations. The Aztecs introduced Cortés to chocolate, beans, corn tortillas, tamales, and deep-fried insects (one of the Aztecs' primary sources of protein). In turn, the Spaniards brought the Indians beef, chicken, pork, dairy products—and voilà . . . the burrito supreme was born.

As the Spanish influence spread farther south, many Peruvian traditions managed to coexist with, rather than be subverted by, the Spanish invaders. The world outside the Andes mountains is indebted to Peru for the potato and the tomato (although the world chose not to take advantage of the Incas' other major food source, the guinea pig).

Chicago is home to a broad range of Latin cultures, and it is estimated that one in every four Chicago residents is either Mexican, Puerto Rican, Cuban, or of another Latin or South American nationality. Today, there are primarily four Latin wards in the city: the Southwest Side's Mexican "barrio" neighborhoods of Pilsen and Little Village and the predominantly Puerto Rican communities of West Town and Humboldt Park. Other Latin groups tend to be spread throughout the city, with smaller concentrations of Cubans in Logan Square and the Far North Side Edgewater community. Given such a strong presence, Chicago is able to offer some fine examples of Cuban, Peruvian, Central American, and, of course, Mexican cuisine. That means plenty of opportunities to grab a cold Dos Equis, a Xingu, or a Negra Modelo and journey off on your own culinary voyage of discovery. *Mucho gusto*!

AMBASSADOR CAFÉ

3605 N. ASHLAND AVENUE, (773) 404-8770

A fine example of Cuban cuisine, the Ambassador is a homey little place with autographed pictures of the Cubs covering the walls. The specials are posted in Spanish (you'll have to ask for a translation if you *no hablas*), and a display case full of flan, plain or coconut, greets you as you sit down. Boasting the Famous Cuban Sandwich—ham, turkey, and pickles on flat rectangular bread that tastes like a French baguette—the Ambassador also offers a good number of meat entrées (particularly pork), chicken, and a large selection of fish and seafood. All dishes, except seafood, are priced under $10 and are served with white rice, fried sweet plantains, and black beans. Start your meal with one of the tropical fruit shakes and end it with sips from a tiny cup of thick, sweet Cuban coffee.

Open daily. BYOB. Street parking available.

CAFÉ BOLERO & GRILL

2252 N. WESTERN AVENUE, (773) 227-9000

Cuban food incorporates the cuisine of the Spanish conquistadors who "discovered" the island with the influences of the black slave population that supported the colonists. Marked by a neon sign that can be seen all the way to Logan Square and matches the blue neon bar inside, Café Bolero is an airy little café that serves fine examples of these hybrid island dishes. If you don't know a fried plantain from a tamale from a stuffed yucca, you might try ordering from the tapas section of the menu and grazing your way to awareness (tapas are $2.95–$7.99). Combination platters, including a Vegetarian Combo Plate, are available for $9 and under. Entrées start at $8.50 and are served with rice, black beans, and sweet plantains. Good-sized sandwiches run $4.95–$5.99. Three kinds of flan are available for dessert: de leche (plain), de mamey (tropical fruit), and de coco (coconut). A sidewalk patio with a shady trellis is a nice option on warm days.

Open daily. Full bar. Sidewalk seating. Free parking lot across the street.

CAFÉ 28

1800 W. IRVING PARK ROAD, (773) 528-2883

Café 28 serves traditional Cuban and Mexican dishes with flair in two cozy (some might say cramped) rooms decorated with warm colors and twinkling white lights. Standing-room-only crowds line up for this family-owned restaurant's interpretation of Cuban and Mexican dishes, including ropâ vieja ($10.95, literal translation, "old clothes"), beef slowly simmered in garlic tomato sauce until it falls apart; Cuban roast pork ($11.25), succulent slices topped with caramelized onions and mojo; and Mexican chicken pasilla ($12.95), grilled boneless breast of chicken with pasilla portobello mushrooms, jalapeño mashed potatoes, and grilled veggies. The *estilo nuevo* section, or "new style" dishes, of Café 28's menu, which includes options like citrus marinated salmon wrapped around julienned seasonal vegetables, almond-crusted halibut baked in a saffron cream, and beef tenderloin with saffron risotto, is, unfortunately, all priced in the budget-breaking high teens. Most entrées come with hefty sides of white rice and black beans.

Open daily. Saturday and Sunday brunch. Street parking available.

EL NANDU

2731 W. FULLERTON AVENUE, (773) 278-0900

At El Nandu, "La Casa de Las Empanadas Argentinas" (the House of Argentinian pastries), stuffed, flaky empanada pastries ($1.95–$2.00) are the name of the game and come with a variety of stuffings, including:

Criolla—ground beef with onion, tomato, olives, raisins, and hard-boiled eggs

Ticumana—diced steak with onion, tomato, olives, and hard-boiled eggs

Pollo—chicken with white cheese and tomatoes

Jamon y Queso—ham and white cheese

Queso—white cheese

Camarones—shrimp with white cheese

Pescado—cod with white cheese

Maiz—corn with white cheese

Espinaca—spinach with white cheese and hard-boiled egg

If you've got room after all those empanadas, entrées start at $9.45 (up to $14.95). Try the pollo con chimichurri, chicken breasts smothered in the signature sauce made from garlic, parsley, oil, vinegar, and spices; or the churrasco con queso y cebollas, a slab of tender charbroiled steak topped with a layer of grilled onions and white cheese. Argentinean slides flash on a screen during the week, while live Latin music throbs all weekend.

Open daily. Full bar. Music on weekends. Street parking difficult.

EL TINAJON

2054 W. ROSCOE STREET, (773) 525-8455

Dishes from the land of the Maya, which melded with Spanish influences to form Guatemalan cuisine, can be sampled at El Tinajon, a brightly decorated restaurant named after a handleless clay pot traditionally used to hold fresh drinking water. Guatemalan specialties accompanied by frosty mugs of Gallo (Guatemalan beer) include pepian antigueno, a spicy Indian stew with chicken, potatoes, and green beans; and jocon revolcado, pork stew made with tongue, heart, liver, and ears ($9.20). The menu has a number of other offerings that may seem similar to Mexican but are served with a Guatemalan twist, including chorizos, pork sausages prepared with Guatemalan spices and served with black beans, rice, tomato sauce, and salad. Vegetarian dishes, along with pricier red snapper and shrimp dishes, are also available.

Open daily. Full bar. Street parking available.

IRAZU

1865 N. MILWAUKEE AVENUE, (773) 252-5687

Head west on North Avenue and take a right on Milwaukee. At the intersection with Western, the neighborhood becomes more barren, populated by boarded-up warehouses that are rapidly being converted to expensive lofts but still offering little of the ambiance of chic Bucktown just east. Here on the edge of Bucktown and Humboldt Park, Irazu, a Costa Rican oasis, beckons. Originally a fast-food stand, Irazu has expanded for more seating. On a nice day, you can relax on the patio and sip a refreshing tropical fruit shake (15 different flavors, $2.45 with or without milk). Or, dig into a giant, spicy Central American-style chicken burrito ($5) or a cilantro-and-pepper-laden steak taco ($2.18). Specials, including pork chops with rice and beans, are $8.95. A new dining room is open, giving patrons an eat-in alternative to the patio.

Closed Sunday. BYOB. Patio. Street parking available.

RINCONCITO SUDAMERICANO

1954 W. ARMITAGE AVENUE, (773) 489-3126

Chicago's premier establishment for Peruvian cuisine, this unpretentious storefront in Bucktown more than makes up for its humble ambiance with quality meals. Take time to find out what excellent Peruvian food tastes like ("be patient, our food is made to order") and be prepared to haul home a big doggy bag—the portions are huge. Entrées start at $10.50, with most under $11—except seafood. Try the arroz con mariscos (Peruvian paella, $12.90) and don't miss the house specialty, aji de gallina ($10.50), shredded chicken in a nut cream with potatoes, Peruvian spices, and rice. There's a large selection of chicken, seafood, and other interesting dishes, including cau-cau (honeycomb tripe and potatoes, $10.80). Don't pass on the side dish of plantains. Go easy on the spicy stuff that comes with the bread. That's not guacamole! **Open daily. Full bar. Street parking possible.**

EL LLANO RESTAURANT

3900 N. LINCOLN AVENUE, (773) 868-1708

Fans of Las Tablas should head up the road for another taste of Colombia. Decorated with Colombian "artifacts," like cowboy hats, leather chaps, and a giant stuffed armadillo, St. Ben's El Llano offers tasty slabs of South American-style steaks, veal, pork, and chicken, as well as seafood, fish, and vegetarian platters. The restaurant serves many carnivores' favorite, churrasco ($12.95), a thin and tender N.Y. strip served with potatoes, yuca, and fried plantains and grilled with tangy chimichurri sauce, a mixture of olive oil, vinegar, parsley, oregano, onion, garlic, salt, and pepper, which is used by South Americans the way we lather ketchup on grilled meats here. The Antiquia Custome Dish ($12.95), a combo that delivers tastes of sausage, steak, fried plantains, rice, beans, and avocado, all of which is topped with a fried egg, is also a good bet. Some of the more authentic options on the menu include lengua en salsa ($9.95, beef tongue in gravy) and conejo asado o frito ($10.95, charbroiled or fried rabbit). Daily specials, including a daily soup ($4.95–$7.95), are a great option, particularly Saturday and Sunday's $19 Steak Combo for two—blood sausages, Colombian sausages, fried pork skins, pork ribs, two corn pancakes, two turnovers, fried sweet plantains, and potatoes. Spanish TV plays nonstop in the background. No decaf.

Open daily. Street parking available.

TORTAS U.S.A.

3507 N. ASHLAND AVENUE, (773) 871-8999

Long before Chipotle Mexican Grill tried to claim the fresh gourmet burrito market in Chicago, Tortas U.S.A. was dishing up $4.95, football-sized "Create Your Own Burritos." Now $5.38, they're spinach, tomato, or chile 'n' cilantro flour tortillas filled with cilantro lime rice and charcoal-broiled breast of chicken or marinated steak, topped off with fresh corn and chorizo, among some two dozen other toppings. In addition to its mix-and-match options, Tortas U.S.A. offers traditional steak, chicken, and veggie burritos, as well as tostadas, flautas, soft or hard shell tacos, and "super tortas," Mexican sandwiches that range from La Classica (breaded chicken with ham and sliced cheese) and La Asadera (grilled steak) to La Señora (breaded steak, cheese, ham, and sliced pork butt) and La Pesquera (fried fish, dressing, and lemon). Served in season, super shakes, or licuades, include strawberry, pineapple, guava, cantaloupe, banana, mango, and chocomilk, and can be pumped up with vitaminices, including protein and carbo powders. Finish it all off with an array of custards such as coconut, eggnog, vanilla, and even kahlua—but sorry, no chipotle.

Open daily 7 A.M. to 5 P.M. Small parking lot next door.

Where's the beef? South American steak houses offer budget options for budget carnivores. **Las Tablas**, for example, specializes in slabs of Colombian-style, thin tender steaks and chicken, marinated and served on butcher blocks with potatoes, plantains, fried yuca, and tangy chimichurri sauce, as well as assorted fish and seafood. Those trying to eat cheap can still sample the churrasquito ($11.95), the smaller but ample charbroiled New York strip. A marinated chicken breast, the Pollo al Ajillo, a number of rib eye and flank steaks, red snapper, king fish, and beef tongue are all also somewhat doable at prices that range from $11.95 to $13.95. Just north, **Tango Sur** is a small storefront Argentinian steak house serving parrilla (barbecue), various cocinas (entrées), and pastas con salsa Argentina (pastas served with Argentinan tomato sauce). Some of the beef options push the price barrier, but there are still a good number of chicken and veal entrées, and a breaded beef dish topped with two fried eggs, that make the cut and let you enjoy the food of the Pampas. Pastas can be ordered with estofado ($2.90), a beef stew in a tomato-meat sauce that goes great with any pasta.

LAS TABLAS
2965 N. LINCOLN AVENUE, (773) 871-2414
Open daily. BYOB. Parking in the lot accessed from the alley on the west side of Lincoln.

TANGO SUR
3763 N. SOUTHPORT AVENUE, (773) 477-5466
Open daily. BYOB. Street parking difficult; valet.

Square Deals

Make a Logan Run

In the late 1800s, Chicago's boulevard system, the "Emerald Necklace," was put in place. The sweeping boulevards were designed to create wide green spaces at a time when large families commonly lived in small apartments. The boulevards gave urban dwellers the opportunity to escape, to expand and breathe open air. They helped preserve the neighborhoods that were lucky enough to be part of the system, and the sweeping expanses bordered by classic graystones are still draws for homeowners and real-estate investors in neighborhoods like Logan Square.

Logan Square has been a melting pot and an integrated neighborhood since the nineteenth century. In its earlier days, the community was dominated by Jewish merchants centered around Kedzie Avenue between Armitage and Diversey. Swedes and Norwegians also populated the neighborhood—and apparently didn't get along very well. Evidence of past Scandinavian residents, in the form of statues and of dedications to various Svens and Björns, is still scattered throughout Logan Square and Humboldt Park.

Logan Square continued to be a destination for immigrants through World War II. In the 1960s, however, the makeup of the neighborhood began to change. The upwardly mobile lures of suburbia, as well as race riots that burned Chicago's West Side, resulted in White Flight, and many of Logan Square's longtime residents bolted for the suburbs. At the same time, with gentrification projects like Sandburg Village driving prices higher on the lakefront, large numbers of Hispanics found themselves being pushed west, and many settled in Logan Square.

The 1990 census found Logan Square to be the fifth largest of Chicago's 77 neighborhoods, and the population has continued to expand from the 90,000 counted in that census nearly a decade ago. Ethnically, Logan Square has a little bit of everything, including 16 different groups of Hispanics. Puerto Ricans and Mexicans are the two largest groups, while Cubans, the Hispanic group that has lived in the community the longest, now own many of the businesses. Socially, the community remains diverse with blue-collar workers, students and artists, and, increasingly, yuppies who are moving back into the rapidly regentrifying neighborhood.

Today, Logan Square encompasses an area defined by the Bloomingdale viaduct on the south (four blocks south of Armitage), Fairfield and Western on the east, Hamlin (3800 West) to the west, and a floating northern border that meanders between Diversey and Belmont. According to the Chamber of Commerce, from the Logan Square stop on the O'Hare rapid transit line, it's 12 minutes downtown to Marshall Field's and 14 minutes to O'Hare; by bus or car, it's five minutes to the Kennedy and 10 to the Eisenhower. The housing stock is sound with gracious lines. Logan Boulevard remains spacious and green. All of this contributes to the neighborhood's increasing popularity.

Logan Square's culinary community reflects the area's lively ethnicity and ongoing regentrification. Late-night option and longtime neighborhood tenant **Abril**, for example, features generous portions of traditional Mexican favorites, margaritas, and atole, a warm cornstarch-based drink. Kids eat free on Wednesdays, and there are candy-filled piñatas hung nightly.

Café 911 is owned by a former policewoman who dishes up hearty servings of Mexican and Puerto Rican dishes to many of her former colleagues. On the southern end of the neighborhood, offering some of the most southern gastronomic options, is **El Nandu**, an Argentinian restaurant that serves nine different flaky empanadas. If you've still got room left after the appetizers, order a steak or a breast of chicken smothered in chimichurri, a traditional sauce made from garlic, parsley, oil, vinegar, and spices.

The artistic element of the neighborhood is dished up by **Lula Café**, a coffee house with surprisingly large breakfast, lunch, and dinner menus featuring global dining options. The opening of a cozy trattoria or supper club seems to be a mark of full-swing gentrification, and Logan Square's step in that direction is represented by the **Boulevard Café & Lounge**, which serves "traditional and eclectic American" dishes, including a daily special meat loaf.

If you're looking for an introduction to Logan Square, take advantage of two annual summer events. The Taste of Logan Square is held in August at Logan and Kedzie. Proceeds go to local community youth groups. The Logan Square Historic Mansion House Walk, an opportunity to see some of the city's premier architecture, is also held every September. For more information, call the 35th Ward Office at (773) 276-3535.

ABRIL
2607 N. MILWAUKEE AVENUE, (773) 227-7252
Open daily until midnight, Friday and Saturday until 3 A.M. All major credit cards accepted.

THE BOULEVARD CAFÉ & LOUNGE
3137 W. LOGAN BOULEVARD, (773) 384-8600
Tuesday–Thursday 5 P.M.–2 A.M.; Friday and Saturday 5 P.M.–3 A.M.; Saturday and Sunday brunch 11 A.M.–2 P.M. Closed Monday. Major credit cards accepted. Reservations recommended.

CAFÉ 911
2523 N. MILWAUKEE AVENUE, (773) 489-9111
Open daily until 10 P.M. Visa and MasterCard.

EL NANDU

2731 W. FULLERTON AVENUE, (773) 278-0900

Monday–Wednesday 11:30 A.M.–10:30 P.M.; Thursday–Saturday 11:30 A.M.–2 A.M.; Sunday 4:30–10:30 P.M.. Live music Thursdays–Saturdays. All major credit cards.

LULA CAFÉ

2537 N. KEDZIE AVENUE, (773) 862-4277

Monday–Thursday 7 A.M.–10 P.M.; Friday 7 A.M.–11 P.M.; Saturday 8:30 A.M.–11 P.M.; Sunday 8:30 A.M.–10 P.M.

French Connection

SOME OF THE BEST THINGS IN LIFE ARE BRIE

We'll always have Paris . . . and its stuffy haute cuisine restaurants flaunting their haughty Michelin stars. But there's more to French cuisine than a tiny medallion of veal drizzled in some sublime but sparse sauce and garnished with a single sprig of parsley and exactly two baby carrots. *Non*, the real France, *la France profonde*, offers heartier fare as diverse and varied as the country itself. As different as the beaches of Normandy are from the glittering sands of the Côte d'Azur, regional French cuisine reflects not only the geographic but ethnic diversity of a country that has blended the influences of Germany, Scandinavia, Italy, Spain, and Africa since before the reign of Charlemagne to long after the time of de Gaulle.

> "I've discovered something: if I give the dish a name, or translate the repulsive name it already has into French, my family can't tell my cheap concoction from gourmet fare. I've decided the key to successful food presentation is arrogance."
>
> —Linda Henley,
> *The Cook's Journal*

Nobody knows the truffles I've seen. . . . The French were seemingly less successful than their European neighbors—the Spanish, English, and Portuguese—in the mad dash to colonize the world. Although they were able to occupy troublesome territories in Africa and southeast Asia, the French were summarily booted out of North America and most of the Caribbean after losing the French and Indian War in the mid-1700s. In spite of their sometimes abrupt departure, the French did make a lasting impact on a number of regional and national cuisines. In Indochina, French influences helped Vietnamese dishes develop into the most subtly sophisticated in Southeast Asia, and in Northern Africa, the impact of the French helped push desert dishes from the sustaining to the sublime. In the Western Hemisphere, French influences not only had an effect on the foods of the Caribbean but also contributed heavily to both the evolution of the Creole dishes of cosmopolitan New Orleans and the Cajun of the backwoods bayou.

The French had an influence on the Chicago area long before the doors of Le Français opened. In 1673, *Che-kau-kou*, a Native American word meaning "Wild Onion," was discovered by French voyageur Louis Joliet. A year later, Père Jacques Marquette stepped ashore at Grosse Pointe bluff, looked at marshlands, and declared, "*Merde*, this land is worthless." Although Père Marquette established a campsite at the present location of Damen Avenue and the Chicago River, it wasn't until 100 years later that trader Jean Baptiste Point du Sable, the son of a French merchant and a Haitian woman, became the first official non-Indian resident of Chicago.

Today, Chicago boasts a number of *nouveau* bistros serving regional French cuisine (along with other international and regional flavors that evolved under French influences—Vietnamese, Moroccan, Caribbean, Cajun, and Creole) that Parisians would be happy to frequent at twice the price. Oh *merci* me, some of the best things in life are brie. *Bon appétit*!

LA CRÊPERIE

2845 N. CLARK STREET, (773) 528-9050

The *grande dame* of Chicago bistro dining, La Crêperie has been around for some 30 years. Fans flock here for the delightful dinner crêpes and sinful dessert crêpes. Large pillows of buckwheat crêpes are folded in squares around broccoli and cheese, spinach creme, ratatouille, chicken curry and rice, or other fillings ($3–$8). Dessert crêpes sport descriptions like crème de marrons, Grand Marnier, and Suzette de la Germain for $3–$6.50. Non-crêpe entrée items include orange roughy or steak frites, both $8 à la carte. The original smoky front room contains a dark bar that's frequently haunted by accordion music.

Closed Mondays. Full bar. Patio dining. Brunch. Street parking difficult; parking lot across the street.

LE LOUP CAFÉ

3348 N. SHEFFIELD AVENUE, (773) 248-1830

So maybe you aren't one of the lucky sun worshippers on the sparkling beaches of the Côte d'Azur or French North Africa, but at Le Loup you can eat like one. Entrées, big enough for "howling appetites," are a little on the expensive side, starting at $10.95 for the vegetarian dishes, crêpes, and ratatouille. A number of the chicken dishes, including poulet breton ($13.95), poulet Louisiana ($12.95), and chicken couscous ($14.95), look and taste almost exactly the same, but since they taste good and you get a huge plate of whichever one you choose, does it really matter? Also available are cassoulet (duck, veal sausage, and white beans for $14.95) and boeuf bourguignon (beef stew for $12.95). Be warned: All of these push the limit in terms of price. As an added benefit, the back of the menu provides a detailed treatise on "The Wolf Society," which you can review as you relax amongst the numerous wolf posters and bumper stickers claiming that "Red Riding Hood lied." There's a nice, predator-free patio to enjoy during the summer.

Open daily. BYOB. Year-round patio. Street parking difficult.

THE RED ROOSTER WINE BAR & CAFÉ

2100 N. HALSTED STREET, (773) 929-7660

Located in the heart of booming Lincoln Park, the Red Rooster is a quiet oasis of French provincial cuisine. The quaint, cabin-like bistro is the sister restaurant and next-door neighbor to the fancier Café Bernard. A good portion of the menu, which is chalked up on the wall, offers a variety of hearty French options that will allow you to stay under the "fork & knife" limit. Try the mustard chicken, a quarter poulet with vegetables, for the right price of $8.75. Or, be a little adventurous and sample the smoked chicken and apple sausage over angel hair pasta with tomato coulis for $7.95. Other good bets are the pork scaloppini ($9.50), the duck à l'orange ($9.75) and spinach fettucini with sea scallops ($9.75). Remember, you're responsible for the consequences to *l'addition* (that's your check) if you should be driven to savor your meal with a glass of *vin*.

Open daily. Full bar. Valet; street parking difficult.

SINIBAR

1540 N. MILWAUKEE AVENUE, (773) 278-7797

Formerly within the restaurant Thyme, Sinibar has reopened on its own in Wicker Park. While the décor is Moroccan coffee shop with Berber wall hangings and stuffed leather beanbag seats, Sinibar's menu is French bistro with an occasional Mediterranean element. A generous and tender steak frites with crisp, shoestring french fries is served au poivre with brandy peppercorn sauce ($13), bordelaise with caramelized onions and mushrooms ($14), and in its classic form with Paris mustard sauce ($13). Similarly, chicken frites comes in three versions, with grilled onions, in lemon and thyme, or with mushrooms and parmesan ($12). Pasta options include a spicy penne arabiata ($11) and a hearty, heaping bowl full of rigatoni with Italian sausage, mozzarella, and peas ($10). Starters include plump tomato and mozzarella on a bed of greens large enough to share and, curiously, beef and chicken satay. Save room for dessert, particularly the apple cinnamon crêpes with cinnamon ice cream, a fresh finish to a *trés agreeable* meal. Dance off your full stomach until the wee hours in Sinibar's lounge, open until 2 A.M.

Closed Sunday, Monday. Valet parking; street parking difficult; lot nearby.

JILLIAN'S BISTRO

674 W. DIVERSEY PARKWAY, (773) 529-7010

This hidden Lincoln Park treasure fuses regional French cooking with classic Southern cuisine. All entrées are under the knife and fork limit, but highlights include brie and basil quiche, Asian grilled tuna with sesame noodles, and sirloin steak. Seating is scarce and close, with about 10 tables in the dining area and about six stools at the bar. On chilly nights, the fireplace makes this a cozy place to be; in the summer, the outdoor patio is the area's best-kept secret. Sunday brunch is also one of Lincoln Park's best bargains: You get three courses (including an entrée, dessert, and a slice of cornbread) for $15.95.

Open daily. Full bar. Street parking difficult; lot nearby.

Heaven Can't Wait

Join the Local Ragin' Cajuns at the Magnificent Mile's Heaven on Seven

Years ago, I had lunch with a friend at the original **Heaven on Seven**, or the **New Garland Coffee Shop** as it was originally known. I still remember. . . . It was a cold day, so we hiked a few blocks through the pedway, the catacombs of Chicago, and made our way into a dingy, overheated elevator in the Garland Building. We exited on the seventh floor to a dingy, overheated coffee shop kind of joint (the kind with the long counter where your grandmother used to take you for a tuna sandwich and pie). We waited in a long line of overheated customers and then wedged ourselves into a small table, where we sat elbow-to-elbow, cheek-to-jowl, with our dining neighbors. We all shoveled Cajun food. I've got to admit, the place did have some charm.

The way people raved about it, you'd think Heaven on Seven was a missing piece of the Bayou that had floated conveniently into the Loop. The only problem was the place was rarely open for dinner. That was fine if you worked downtown and could squeeze out for lunch, but what about those fans of Louisiana fare who didn't work just a pedway away? Those who maybe didn't even work in the city? Tourists, whose visit to Chicago might only be completed by a bite of the Big Easy?

Well, for those who couldn't find their way to Wabash Avenue, the gates of Heaven are also open in the mall at 600 North Michigan Avenue. Nestled on the back side of the Eddie Bauer retail store, underneath eight wide-body movie screens, is the second Heaven on Seven, which is open nightly for dinner.

My coworker Alexa and I decided to check out the place at lunch. We joined the hordes of fans rampaging up the back escalator off Rush Street. And there it was, Heaven looking like a scene right out of an Anne Rice novel that had been somehow mixed up with a genteel suburban truck stop.

A window, graced with an iron trellis and shutters flung open, beckons coyly to the would-be ragin' Cajuns pouring off the escalator: "Y'all come right in now, hear." Unfortunately, heaven must wait, and so did we. After putting our name on the long list, we clutched our vibrator and waited for the electric hum that would signal our turn to step through the gates.

Once buzzed, we scurried past a wall-to-wall, floor-to-ceiling rack of hot sauce to the back room, which is graced with a stuffed, grinning 'gator (or is it a croc?) mounted above the diners. Chandeliers, supposedly reminiscent of a New Orleans ballroom but probably filched from a local funeral parlor, are draped with Mardi Gras beads. We were escorted to our table, which was stocked with no fewer than 22 different bottles of hot sauce, making it a tight squeeze for a two-top. The bottled brew ranged from your standard Tabasco to more exotic stuff like "Vampire," "The Bat's Brew," the curious "Ass in the Tub," and our favorite (although Alexa thought it tasted kind of odd), the "Hot Bitch at the Beach," a product whose label touted, "She's all natural and all mighty hot 'n' delicious . . . she's got the hots for you!"

We were hoping the food could live up to the condiments. We stoked our appetites with a couple of starters, although Alexa had to avoid the gumbo since she's allergic to shrimp. With so many options, such as openers like potato-crusted jalapeño peppers, sweet potato moss, fried Alabama rock shrimp, and andouille sausage sweet potato polenta, it was difficult to choose.

We skipped the lagniappe ("a little something extra"), sides like jalapeño cheddar corn muffins and parmesan-reggiano cheese grits, and moved straight to the main event. We agreed that the po'boy sandwiches—made of soft-shell crab, "angry" chicken, or catfish—were not for us. But at $9.95 a pop, there was nothing poor about them. We fig-

HEAVEN ON SEVEN, 600 N. Michigan Ave., 2nd Floor, (312) 280-7774, fax (312) 280-8884, is open daily for lunch and dinner. Entrées start at $8.95. Heaven on Seven also has other locations at 111 N. Wabash Ave., 7th Floor, (312) 263-6443 (the original location) and at 3478 N. Clark St., (773) 477-7818.

ured if we were going to spend $15 on lunch, we wanted a real meal.

I went for the "Southern Classics" and got the Louisiana crab cakes, which were tender and tasty. Alexa chose from the linguinis and ordered the Chicken Voodoo, which we both agreed had kind of a strange peanut-coconut flavor. Since I obviously got the better deal, she vowed to order the Louisiana Soul Deluxe next time. It's a Southern Sampler Plate with Mardi Gras jambalaya, red beans and rice, and other good spicy stuff. We resisted the blandishments of the various paraphernalia for sale— shirts, private-label hot sauce, etc.—and headed back to the office with a Cajun fried shrimp carryout for a coworker. As we drifted down the moving staircase, we were sure we heard a whisper from above "A bottle of heaven . . . you can take it with you . . . for $4.95."

3

The Empire Strikes Back

HIGH TEA, HAGGIS, AND PUB GRUB
AT PINT-SIZED PRICES

Even after having to play catch-up after their nearly century-late start, the British quickly made up for lost time to their continental cousins. Propelled by the voyages of Sir Francis Drake and, subsequently, the East India Company, the British managed to corner all the tea in China and had curried favor for the queen in India by the early eighteenth century. Even halfway around the world where they had kicked out the French, Dutch, and Native Americans, the redcoats were having their way in North America until they suddenly found the (tea) party over.

> "'Take some more tea,' the March Hare said to Alice, very earnestly."
>
> —Lewis Carroll, *Alice's Adventures in Wonderland*

Don't tread on me. . . . In spite of their ability to conquer and rule, the British were never really able to impose one aspect of Britannia on the colonies—traditional British cuisine. And, can you blame the colonials for resisting to the end? The British could take the furs of North America, the spices of the East, and diamonds of South Africa, but they couldn't force their new subjects to take bangers and mash, Welsh rarebit, or steak and kidney pie.

Not somebody to trifle with. . . . Two hundred years later, here in the Heartland, Chicagoans continue their ancestors' resistance to Cornish pasties, black and white pudding, and parsnips and brussels sprouts. Even the few establishments in town that specialize in authentic Irish, Scottish, and English dishes dilute their menus with American burgers, salads, and pastas, leaving a straight diet of beans on toast to mad dogs and Englishmen. But if you're set on pounding some mixed grill or corned beef and cabbage, opportunities do exist, although they are thankfully few and far between. God save the queen.

THE RED LION

2446 N. LINCOLN AVENUE, (773) 348-2695

Chicago's original English pub, the Red Lion derives its name from the heraldic device of Edward III, who ruled England in the mid-fourteenth century. And the Red Lion serves a traditional English repast that has probably been around since then. You can start it all off with Welsh rarebit ($3.95) or beans on toast ($3.95). If you're looking for a lighter bite, you can move on to the pasties and pies—that would be Cornish pasties, shepherd's pie, and steak and kidney pie ($6.95). For heartier fare, try the bangers and mash (sausages and potatoes, $7.25). Finish it off with a proper English trifle (poundcake, macaroons, fruit cocktail, custard, whipped cream, and sherry, $3.95) and a Black and Tan.

Open daily. Full bar. Patio dining. Street parking difficult.

THE DUKE OF PERTH

2913 N. CLARK STREET, (773) 477-1741

Chicago's popular Scottish pub, with the Midwest's most extensive collection of single-malt scotch, serves all-you-can-eat beer batter–dipped cod accompanied by peas and chips (that's fries to you Colonials) for $7.95 every Wednesday and Friday from lunch until midnight. In addition to the ubiquitous batter-fried whitefish, the Duke of Perth offers the delicacies of the Highlands, including the Scotch egg, a breaded sausage wrapped around a boiled egg with sweet chutney ($5.25); steak and kidney potpie ($7.95); shepherd's pie ($7.95); and sides of stovies ($2.25). American-style burgers sport names dedicated to Scotch heroes with accompanying tributes, including the William Wallace Cheeseburger ($7.50) for the brave heart who was "hanged, drawn, and quartered with his head then impaled on London Bridge." A patio with picnic tables is available for nice weather, and there's often live music on the weekends.

Open daily. Full bar. Patio dining. Live music. Street parking difficult.

ABBEY PUB

3420 W. GRACE STREET, (773) 463-5808

The Abbey Pub, one of the best-known Irish hangouts in town, offers traditional Irish food and music. There are a lot of places around town where you can go see a hot local band while you enjoy some standard bar food. But why subject yourself to greasy grill when you can savor Mixed Grill (Irish sausage, pudding, bacon, lamb chops, and fries for $8.95), exceptional shepherd's pie ($8.95), and other Irish delicacies while you listen to that same band at Abbey Pub? You can enjoy your chow while you listen to the tunes of Irish bands on Wednesdays and Thursdays; folk, blues, or rock on Fridays and Saturdays; and a weekly Irish jam session on Sundays. Monday is the weekly barn dance; Tuesday is an acoustic open stage. Cover varies at Abbey Pub, but is usually around $10. (For more, see the Abbey Pub in "Diversionary Dining.") Big screens in each room carry live broadcasts of Irish, English, and Scottish football—soccer for you Colonials—all World Cup games, and rugby matches.

Open daily. Full bar. Street parking available.

CHIEF O'NEILL'S PUB

3471 N. ELSTON AVENUE, (773) IRELAND (473-5263)

Chicago likes nothing better than a lively Irish pub, and this one packs the crowds in its large dining room, spacious beer garden, and roomy bar. Named for Francis O'Neill, Chicago's first Irish police chief who "had an intense passion for the traditional (Irish) music," the pub, with its imported décor, fixtures, and staff, highlights the best in live, traditional Irish music and traditional Irish cuisine, including garlicky Galway Bay mussels ($6.95), a lighter-than-expected cheddar cheese soup made with Guinness and baked with a cheese crouton ($3.95), plump, pink slabs of corned beef and cabbage ($7.95), hearty helpings of lamb stew ($8.95), braised beef tips ($9.95), fish and chips ($8.95), and all-day Irish breakfast ($8.95). Service is a little harried, so you'll need to relax for a while with a draft after your first two courses and enjoy the music before you have room for dessert. You'll find the music schedule at www.chiefoneillspub.com.

Open daily. Street parking available.

TOMMY NEVIN'S PUB

1450 SHERMAN AVENUE, EVANSTON, (847) 869-0450

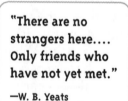

With Tommy Nevin's Pub, the owners of the Davis Street Fishmarket have attempted to bring the cheer of the traditional Irish pub to Evanston. "Pub Grub" offers the best of the Emerald Isles for $6.25–$9.95, including corned beef and cabbage, garlic and pepper roasted pork loin, shepherd's pie, Irish sausage rolls, and Irish lamb stew (available October 1 through April 30). Salads include smoked Irish salmon ($8.95), and fish and chips comes in three options ($9.95). A small New York strip is $14.95, served with your choice of a side of potatoes and vegetables. Chips and gravy are also available as a side; bread and butter pudding with whiskey vanilla sauce for dessert. On Sunday afternoons, an Irish band jams on Celtic favorites. Nevin's Live, the live-music venue adjacent to the pub, serves limited items from the menu until closing.

> "There are no strangers here.... Only friends who have not yet met."
>
> —W. B. Yeats

Open daily until 12:30 A.M. weeknights, 1:30 A.M. on weekends, and midnight on Sundays. Full bar. Street parking available; parking lot across street.

THE HIDDEN SHAMROCK

2723 N. HALSTED STREET, (773) 883-0304

In between English football, international rugby, and live bands, you can order from one of the most authentic Irish-oriented menus in town. Check out the bangers and mash (sausage, mashed potatoes, and baked beans, $5.75); Irish Fry, a traditional Irish breakfast with bacon, eggs, sausage, tomato, onion, mushrooms, and black and white pudding ($8.50); sausage and chips with beans ($4.50); or beer-batter fish fry made with Guinness ($7.50). Breakfast served only on weekends. *Slainte*, laddie.

Open daily. Full bar. Live bands Thursday through Saturday. Street parking difficult.

JOY OF IRELAND

CHICAGO PLACE, 700 N. MICHIGAN AVENUE, LEVEL 3, (312) 664-7290

This quaint Irish shop in Chicago Place offering lots of touristy Irish things also serves a not-so-touristy high tea ($16 per person) in a cozy tea room, which is graced with a half-dozen tables for just one or two that offer an impressive view of Michigan Avenue and a perfect rest stop after a few hours of shopping. Teas include Irish brands like Taylors of Harrogate, Fortum & Mason, Barry's, Brewley's, and Yorkshire Gold. Baked goods range from scones, coffee cake, fruit tortes, cookies, sweet bread, and brown bread (sold by the slice or the loaf). Joy of Ireland also serves a light lunch, including soups, salads, and plates of finger sandwiches such as smoked salmon and cucumber and cream cheese, and an assortment of cheeses, ranging from $7 to $9.50.

Open daily. Street parking difficult; parking lot nearby.

High Tea

INNOVATIVE EATERIES FOR THE FINANCIALLY FINICKY PALATE

Tea for two and two for tea. . . . Unfortunately these days in Chicago, finger sandwiches, dainty pastries, and the other accoutrements of high tea run a lot more than $2. In fact, you have to leave the confines of the city and the fancy downtown hotels to find a deal on high tea. For your best bet in the city, try **Joy of Ireland**, where high tea for one is $16 or, if it's tea for you and someone small, **The American Girl Café** (111 E. Chicago Ave., (877) 247-5223, reservations required) has two seatings daily at 2:30 and 4 P.M. ($16 including tip but not tax). The Mad Hatter Tea at **Seasons of Long Grove** (314 Old McHenry Rd., Long Grove, (847) 634-9150) makes the commute worthwhile. Tea-totalers don beribboned and flowered hats from a selection provided and then settle down for finger sandwiches, scones, biscuits, and pastries—all for $10.95, Thursday through Saturday at 2 P.M. It's a popular spot for young girls' birthday parties, and Seasons even serves a children's tea made with berries, raisins, hibiscus, and honey.

Quick Bites A FEW QUICK THOUGHTS

The Primavera Bar at the Fairmont Hotel, 200 N. Columbus Drive, (312) 565-8000, is the only place in Chicago that honors the old pub tradition of serving "yards" of beer; cold ones are literally served in yard-long glass tubes with a bulb on the end. Beers come in a variety of drafts from Bud to Guinness. A yard is $14 and a half-yard is $7.50.

Irish Ayes

Chicago's All-in-One Pub Crawl

I let off some steam every weekend in a coed soccer league, sprinting up and down the field, or the court if it's winter, while skilled players, most of whom are a decade younger than me, dribble circles around me. I may not be a great player, but I run hard.

I met Fergal through soccer. A young computer programmer, he came to Chicago from Ireland in the late 1980s, and we hooked up when he was looking for a team. After eight years, Fergal went back to Ireland. We're going to miss him on defense. Fergal was also a great source on what's "real" Irish in Chicago. Not much passed muster with Fergal—the Abbey Pub and a few other little places. So I'm wondering what Fergal would have thought of Fado.

Fado Irish Pub is astutely located in River North in an area that's visited by almost every traveler to our fair city, next to the Rock 'n' Roll McDonald's and under the benign gaze of two Chicago landmarks, the Rainforest Café's giant tree frog and the Hard Rock's guitar. To my pleasant surprise, no immense leprechauns or giant shamrocks loomed over the front door.

> **FADO IRISH PUB,**
> 100 W. Grand Ave.,
> (312) 836-0066,
> is open daily for
> lunch and dinner.
> Meals are priced
> $7.25–$16.95. Irish
> bands play Monday
> and Tuesday nights.

It was a little hokey, but Fado still seemed to be executed with an effort at good taste. The outside is designed to look like two traditional storefronts, one for "McNally & Sons" and the other "Ceol Agus Craic," which translates roughly as "music and fun." The inside showcases the historical gathering places of the Irish people. *Fado* means "long ago" in

Gaelic Irish, and the eatery has been decorated to illustrate "the story of Ireland's rich and celebrated pub culture."

Six different historical settings are featured. Upon entry, you see the massive wood tables and chairs of the fifth- and sixth-century Celtic chieftain. A stone dolmen, a monument marking the burial grounds of kings, wraps itself around this area of the bar, and crafted metals depict the work of Celtic blacksmiths who beat iron and bronze into weapons for the hunters and warriors.

You walk past a lattice screen on the bar that is reminiscent of the huts inhabited by workers in Ireland's cottage industries. This section is peppered with antiquated manufacturing devices, including looms, spinning wheels, a butter churn, and even a water pump. The floor becomes cobblestone and timber, and diners sit under an open loft.

The final first floor area is the Post Office/Shop Pub of the turn of the century, where villagers met to provision and gossip among the clutter of merchandise. From there it's a trip upstairs, passing under a *currach* fishing boat suspended from the ceiling to the world of St. Brendan's monks on the mezzanine, marked by a stone-carved cross and alter table and then up another flight to the "rural Country Cottage Pub."

The country pub highlights the cozy world of the small pub proprietor, with more stone and timber materials and a raised floor in one corner for entertainment. It's a contrast to the last setting of the Dublin Victorian Pub, with its velvet curtains, stained glass, beveled mirrors, and brass.

Much of the interior decorating is done with "authentic" materials, like the 100-year-old bar in the Victorian Pub that was shipped in forty pieces from Dublin and reassembled at Clark and Grand. The only incongruous note is the stools. Half the seats in Fado seem to be two-foot-high stools. That may be authentic, but I'd find it uncomfortable hanging out all night with my mates at the pub squatting, frankly, on one of those, albeit nicely padded, stools.

4

East of Eaten

A TASTE OF EASTERN EUROPE
IN THE HEART OF THE MIDWEST

> "The cliché endures: Chicago really is a city of neighborhoods—
> a vast mosaic of separate entities, each with its own history,
> personality, and particular landmarks and institutions. The
> neighborhoods originated most often as gleams in the eyes of
> ambitious land developers or as ethnic enclaves, which grew
> into towns and were in turn swallowed up by the swelling
> nineteenth-century city. The result was and continues to be
> a diverse and colorful sprawl of traditional and newly hybrid
> communities and cultures. While the idea of 'neighborhood'
> conjures up notions of time standing still in a place where
> 'everybody knows your name,' the truth is somewhere between
> that bucolic image and utter chaos. Chicago's neighborhoods
> have been most strongly characterized by two forces: people
> moving in and people moving out."
>
> —*Sweet Home Chicago*

ike the sausages that have come to symbolize this city's
contribution to our national cuisine, starting in the nineteenth century, Chicago accepted waves of Eastern European immigrants seeking the American dream and stuffed them
and their native customs and spices into a city that bulged under
the restraints of its political and big-business casings. Fleeing
repressive imperial regimes, the people of Eastern Europe poured

into Chicago and ended up supporting the local family dynasties—the hog butchers for the world, the tool makers, the stackers of wheat, the players with railroads, and the nation's freight handlers of Carl Sandburg's "Chicago."

Leaving behind the iron fist of the Austrian-Hungarian Hapsburg Empire, the Czechs, or Bohemians as they were known in Chicago (really Moravians, Slovaks, and Ruthenians, in addition to the Bohemians), were one of the first groups to migrate en masse in 1848 after the failure of a nationalistic uprising. The Czechs were some of the most literate and highly skilled Europeans to be processed through Castle Garden and Ellis Island, and they left their mark on Chicago. By the 1870s, the Czechs had established the Pilsen enclave on Blue Island Avenue between 16th and 22nd Streets and supplied workers to the McCormick Reaper Works and the Chicago, Burlington, and Quincy railroads. Anton Cermak, who was born in Prague but relocated to the Lawndale neighborhood, crushed the gangsters who were controlling local government during Prohibition and established Chicago's Democratic Machine.

> "Whatever you do, make it taste Polish. Put cabbage in."
>
> —Florence Nesbitt, *Household Management*

Other Eastern Europeans made a substantial impact on the city's development. Antanas Kaztauskis, a Lithuanian émigré, was one of the many residents of Back-of-the-Yards working in Packingtown. His 1904 article, "From Lithuania to the Chicago Stockyards—An Autobiography," inspired a young journalist named Upton Sinclair to go undercover for a year to produce *The Jungle*, an exposé of Chicago's meatpacking industry that hit the nation squarely in the stomach. Today's ultra-hip Ukrainian Village was established by a wave of Ukrainian immigrants fleeing imperial Czarist Russia prior to World War I. These Ukrainians brought with them both the Greek Catholic church and the traditional foods of Kiev.

By 1920, the Polish community had become the largest foreign-born immigrant group in Chicago, with an estimated 31 percent of all European Poles becoming American citizens in the 1920s. Originally settling in small pockets on the South Side and around the intersection of Division, Milwaukee, and Ashland, the Polish community later moved north on Milwaukee to Avondale, the 41st

Ward and home of longtime alderman Roman Pucinski.

You don't have to be the Pope to enjoy a plateful of pierogis and some of the cheapest and most extensive all-you-can-eat buffets around. A veritable Polish pig-out, a Baltic banquet, the Danubian dinner . . . there are all kinds of options around town to Serb you right if Yugo out and find them. Czech one out!

ANDRZEJ GRILL

1022 N. WESTERN AVENUE, (773) 489-3566

Found on the edge of Ukrainian Village and once cited in a now moribund former Wicker Park-based magazine as "on the verge" and "Polish with attitude," Andrzej Grill has figured out that you can successfully capitalize on a seedy location as long as you serve huge, tasty meals (only $4.50 for lunches and $6.50 for dinners). A tiny place with exactly four small tables, four chairs, and three video arcade machines, Andrzej lists a large number of selections for either "lunches" or "dinners" on handwritten cards hanging in vertical rows on the wall. Lunch selections include a dozen pierogis smothered in fried onions (optional) and sour cream. Pierogis come in cheese and potato, meat, sauerkraut, plum, or blueberry. Dinners include potato pancakes, white sausage, whitefish, chicken livers, and various chicken or pork dishes. For a light meal, try one of the many soups, including tripe stew, bean, potato, sauerkraut, and three kinds of borscht—Ukrainian, white, or red. In a hurry? Call ahead, and it'll be hot and waiting. As the grill advertises: "Be you waiting too long, call first."
Open daily. No alcohol. Street parking available.

Two other good bets for pierogis are **Caesar's Polish Deli**, 901 N. Damen Avenue, (773) 486-6190, and **Halinas European Restaurant and Deli**, 6714–6718 W. Belmont Avenue, (773) 685-8569. In business for more than half a century, Caesar's is a Polish grocery with a couple of small tables and a refrigerator case full of 12 different kinds of pierogis (along with 15 different kinds of homemade soup). Halinas serves pierogis in the standard cheese, meat, and potato versions, along with sauerkraut and plum, for $3.99 a pound.

ARGO, INC. GEORGIAN BAKERY

2812 W. DEVON AVENUE, (773) 764-6322

Opened in 1997 by a former surgeon who emigrated to the United States, the Argo is located on a stretch of Devon populated with shops serving Hasidic Jews, Russians, and other Eastern Europeans. The Argo is a small storefront that's made up of one open room dominated by a large brick kiln-like oven in the middle of the floor where two kinds of Georgian breads—long, thin shotis ($1.55) and round breads ($1.55), along with puffed round cheese-filled hachapuris, ($1.60)—are baked. Patrons, who can sit at two small tables and sip strong coffee, can watch the dough being kneaded and prepared for the depths of the beehive-shaped oven.

Closed Wednesday. Street parking available.

THE BOSNIA RESTAURANT

2122 W. LAWRENCE AVENUE, (773) 275-4100

Formerly the Bosnian Social Club, the Bosnia Restaurant caters to expats who gather to watch soccer and share their community. The cuisine is a mixture of the foods served by neighbors in Hungary, Germany, Romania, Serbia, and the Middle East without any pork or alcohol due to the influence of Islam. The national dish is cevapi lepinja, a charbroiled hamburger made from ground lamb and beef sausages served on soft, frisbee-sized, English muffin-like lepinja bread. A number of Bosnian calzone-like phyllo turnovers are also available, including burek (meat pie), sirnica (cream cheese), and zeljanica (spinach). In addition, the menu includes schnitzels, goulash, and Traunichi Sir, tart goat cheese designed to be eaten with bread or cabbages and peppers. Portions are huge, and no entrée costs more than $10.

Open daily. No alcohol. Street parking available.

HEALTHY FOOD

3236 S. HALSTED STREET, (773) 326-2724

Lithuanians first came to Chicago in the late nineteenth century and settled into the Bridgeport and Brighton Park neighborhoods located south and west of the Union Stockyards, in the area known as Back-of-the-Yards. Today, most of Chicago's Lithuanian community is centered around 69th (Lithuanian Court Plaza) and 71st between California and Western in Marquette Park, the last of the pre-World War II neighborhoods to evolve out of the Union Stockyards and Chicago's thriving meatpacking industry. Located just west of the Comiskey Park/Bridgeport neighborhood is Healthy Food, where you can get a taste of Lithuania without having to drive all the way down to the current center of Lithuanian culture. Open since 1938 and the oldest Lithuanian restaurant in the city, Healthy Food serves up bounteous, filling portions of artery-clogging Lithuanian and Eastern European specialties seven days a week at prices that haven't been adjusted for inflation. Lithuanian specials include blynai, Lithuanian pancakes with a dozen different kinds of fillings ($6), including vsysniu (sour cherry) and spanguoliu (cranberry); koldunai, boiled meat or cheese dumplings served with sour cream and bacon ($5.50); kugelis, Lithuanian potato dumplings ($6.50); and roast half duck ($13.95). Meals are accompanied by fresh-baked dark Lithuanian bread. All these Lithuanian favorites include dessert—a choice of Jell-O with a swirl of whipped cream, or kolacky, traditional fruit-filled pastries. **Open daily. No alcohol. Street parking available.**

LITTLE BUCHAREST'S EURO CAFÉ

3001 N. ASHLAND AVENUE, (773) 929-8640

Reputed to have been the home-away-from-home for the Bulgarian World Cup team during their sojourn in Chicago, Little Bucharest offers a convenient taste of Eastern Europe, whether you're coming all the way from the Balkans or just five minutes from your Lakeview abode. Although a bit on the expensive side, Little Bucharest offers a huge menu that's guaranteed to deliver both a Romanian holiday and leftovers to anyone who stops in for the huge entrées and nightly accordion music. Although chicken, veal, sausage, pork, beef, and lamb dishes, along with goose and rabbit, are available in abundance, those who want something lighter will like the stuffed vegetables—green peppers, cabbage, eggplant (all $8.95) or the Romanian stuffed red peppers ($9.95). all veggie dishes are stuffed with a ground meat combination (vegetarians need not apply here). Most entrées are served with spaetzle, those tasty little dumplings. Daily specials are a great deal; Thursday night is Mititei Night ($6.95), small Romanian sausages. Don't miss Taste of Bucharest, held every September and seemingly attended by Chicago's entire Romanian population. Take advantage of the free limo service.

Open Tuesday through Sunday. Full bar. Sidewalk seating. "Taste" festival every September. Street parking available. Call the restaurant for free limo service.

Quick Bites A FEW QUICK THOUGHTS

Some of *Cheap Chow Chicago*'s other favorite feasts from the East featured in other chapters:

OLD WARSAW
4750 N. HARLEM AVENUE, (708) 867-4500
THE RED APPLE/CZERWONE JABLUSZKO
3121–23 N. MILWAUKEE AVENUE, (708) 488-5781
Both restaurants boast huge Polish all-you-can-eat buffets. (For more details see "Chowing Down: All-You-Can-Eat Meals That Stretch Your Waistband but Not Your Wallet.") The Red Apple also features a service deli.

SIMPLON-ORIENT EXPRESS
4520 N. LINCOLN AVENUE, (773) 275-5522
From Paris to Istanbul, meals tracking the Eastern route of the fabled Orient Express. (All aboard in "Taste of Lincoln Avenue.")

Beet Generation

Loosen Up the Borscht Belt in Ukrainian Village

United by Milwaukee Avenue, the Ukrainian Village and other neighborhoods to the north have been the settling grounds for Eastern European immigrants for more than a century. At one point, the intersection of Division, Ashland, and Milwaukee was the locus of a Polish community larger than any other gathering of Poles outside of Poland. While the Poles have moved north and west, and the evidence of their old neighborhood has been practically eradicated by the current owners, the original Ukrainian community, located roughly between Hoyne and Western on Chicago Avenue, fights to retain its identity.

Churches are the enduring landmarks of the Ukrainian Village. Dedicated in 1915, St. Nicholas Ukrainian Catholic Cathedral at Oakley and Rice was modeled on the Basilica of St. Sophia in Kiev (although only 13 of the original's 32 copper-encased domes were incorporated into the Chicago version.) When St. Nicholas switched to the Gregorian calendar in 1973, a split developed between the older members of the community and newer, more conservative immigrants. Because of the split, the traditional Sts. Volodymyr and Olha Ukrainian Orthodox Cathedral (Oakley and Superior), with its gilded Byzantine domes and colorful, two-story-high mural on its facade was formed to maintain the older, Julian calendar.

An even more striking edifice is Louis Sullivan's Holy Trinity Orthodox Cathedral (Leavitt and Haddon). Built in 1901, the church was patterned loosely on wooden octagon-on-a-square churches of the old country and was designed to blend mysticism and functionalism.

The Ukraine, the region that was headed by the ancient trading capital of Kiev and that adjoins Romania and

Poland, was the breadbasket of the old Russian empire; it produced 25 percent of the staples consumed in the old Soviet Union, primarily wheat, but also corn, rice, barley, potatoes, beets, and vegetables. The regional cuisine, incorporating a crazy quilt of ethnic flavors, including Greek, Byzantine, Asiatic, Scandinavian, Turkish, and Germanic, is a substantial cuisine, a doughy, gamey, meaty, rooty, smoky menu—part comfort food, part indulgence.

Unfortunately, the area's restaurants, important gathering points themselves, have had less staying power than the houses of worship. Galans, once arguably the city's best-known Ukrainian restaurant, is closed and now in the process of going French country, leaving slim Ukrainian pickings on Chicago Avenue. **Sak's Ukrainian Village Restaurant** is one of the few remaining proprietors of Old World Ukrainian cuisine.

Sak's restaurant is accented with red—red vinyl booths, red formica tile, and red babushka-like tablecloths covered with clear plastic, which seems appropriate, since Sak's serves the best borscht in town, along with some hefty platters of other Ukrainian dishes. All dinners come with soup, salad, potato, and dessert. Entrée choices range from kapusta and kobassa (sauerkraut with ukrainian sausage), to helubtsy (cabbage rolls with meat and rice) in either a mushroom gravy or tomato sauce, to plyatsky (potato pancakes). Varenyky, Ukrainian dumplings similar to pierogis, are stuffed with meat, cheese, sauerkraut, or potatoes and smothered in either

SAK'S UKRAINIAN VILLAGE RESTAURANT, 2301 W. Chicago Ave., (773) 278-4445, and **ANN'S BAKERY,** 2158 W. Chicago Ave., (773) 384-5562, are both open daily. Meals at Sak's range from $5.95 to $16.95.
OLD LVIV UKRANIAN FOOD RESTAURANT, 2228 W. Chicago Ave., (773) 772-7250, is closed Mondays.

mushroom gravy or hot butter with bacon bits. Chicken Kiev, schnitzel, and even hamburgers are available for the less adventurous. If you can't make up your mind, have the Family Feast, which for $8.95 a person includes a taste of almost everything on the menu. Finish off your dinner with Sak's homemade apple pie, more like a square, multilayer apple torte than the American version. Cheese-filled dessert crêpes dolloped with whipped or sour cream are also a good bet if you have any room left. Rinse it all down with a cup of Ukrainian coffee, which is enhanced with something special from the bar.

If you just want to get a quick and easy intro to the Ukrainian menu, try **Old Lviv Ukrainian Food Restaurant**. A small storefront with a bar and a couple of tables, Old Lviv has a daily buffet for $5.99 that features nearly a dozen different hot dishes, three soups, and several salads. Varenyky can be ordered alone for $3. Soup is also served à la carte, and the selection will probably include borscht, cabbage, or chicken noodle.

Just a little east down the street, **Ann's Bakery** is another surviving neighborhood institution specializing in "European" rye bread, Ukrainian twist bread, fine pastries, and wedding cakes. It is also a small grocery store with an area with tables and chairs. Locals hang out in the small café area, nibbling treats and gossiping in the language of the Cossacks.

5

Curry, Be Happy

AN AFFORDABLE PASSAGE TO INDIA

The Indian subcontinent. A huge, kite-shaped peninsula stretching from the Himalayan and Hindu Kush mountains, through fertile plains and stark deserts, down to steamy coastal jungles. As early as 2,000 B.C., the Indus River valley was home to a flourishing community. Since then, waves of invaders and conquerors have moved through the land, resulting in a broad diversity of cultures, languages, religions, and food. The food of the Muslims and Hindus of Kashmir and Bengal are typified by seafood and vegetarian dishes; the Northern Tibetan Buddhists of the Darjeeling tea region specialize in stir-frys and plain and stuffed breads; the merchant Jews of Calcutta introduced Middle Eastern dishes; and the orthodox Jains, who wear face masks to prevent the accidental inhalation of tiny life forms, took vegetarianism to new heights.

> **"How I should like to visit India!"**
>
> —Becky Sharp in William Makepeace Thackeray, *Vanity Fair*

As in the United States, a wide range of climatic conditions impacted the basic development of India's various regional cuisines. Dishes from southern and eastern India are almost always supplemented by rice, which thrives in these areas of heavier rainfall. Fried and stuffed breads are staples in the drier north where wheat and barley are grown. Coastal regions serve a variety of fish, seafood, and tropical fruits; inland, fruits such as apples, peaches, apricots, and strawberries are widespread.

A common thread among these various subcontinental menus is an abundance of spices. Indian food, regardless of regional origin, is characterized by rich, complex spices, although not always hot ones. Chilies, the heat in many Indian dishes, are actually native to the Americas and were not introduced into India until the sixteenth century when they were brought in by Portuguese traders. Spices, long valued for medicinal and preservative qualities along with their role as seasonings, have played a major role in Indian and world history. In the days of King Solomon, India's Malabar Coast was a major trading center for spices and other luxuries. The Phoenicians, Greeks, Romans, and Chinese all found their way along the trade routes to India. It was the lure of the spice trade that gave rise to the Age of Exploration and Columbus and the other adventurers who braved falling off the edge of the world for the riches of India.

Similar to many other Asian groups, Indians originally came to Chicago in search of education and then stayed. Today the West Ridge neighborhood—a mile stretch along Devon Avenue—features silk and saris, 22-karat gold jewelry, and videotape copying. This is the hub of the city's Indian community of some 70,000 Indian and Pakistani residents, making Chicago one of the two biggest concentrations of Indians in the country (New York is the other). On weekends, in particular, Devon Avenue is packed with locals hungry for both shopping bargains and for traditional food. Most of the restaurants feature Northern Indian, Mughal-influenced fare (the Mongols who conquered much of the subcontinent in the sixteenth century were Moslem, and, therefore, ate meat), which many would assert is to true Indian cuisine what chop suey is to Chinese. As Chinese communities began serving Szechuan, Hunanese, and other alternatives to Cantonese once that cuisine became common and palates became educated, Indian restaurants are beginning to branch out and feature other regional specialties and many vegetarian dishes. So, start with tandoori and move on from there. Put some spice in your life.

Editors note: *Curry* is a British term derived from the Tamil term *kari,* meaning "sauce." Ethnic Indians do not use the term at all, nor do they use commercial curry powders, which are blends of several spices including coriander, cumin, red peppers, turmeric, and fenugreek. Instead, they make their own fresh blends called *masalas.*

INNOVATIVE EATERIES FOR THE FINANCIALLY FINICKY PALATE

Anchored at the intersection of Devon and Western is a nearly mile-long stretch of sari stores, jewelry shops, electronics and appliance outlets, and eateries specializing in $7.95 all-you-can-eat lunch buffets (with dinner often available for a few dollars more), featuring chicken and lamb curries, palak or mutter paneer (homemade cheese with spinach or peas), naan (tandoori oven bread made with white flour), dal (thick porridge), salads, chutneys, and sweet desserts.

Welcome to India and the numerous restaurants that will try to curry favor with you. Anchoring the strip is the elaborate **Viceroy of India Restaurant**, 2516 W. Devon Avenue, (773) 743-4100, one of the older restaurants in the area. Viceroy has an inexpensive lunch buffet, but is probably not cheap chow for dinner. Try one of the three daily chef's specials for a good intro to Indian food. Although the décor looks Italian, **Kanval Palace**, 2501 W. Devon Avenue, (773) 761-7270, specializes in both Indian and Pakistani dishes. Entrées run $5.50 and up. The charga chicken, a whole chicken cooked with mango butter and spices, is the specialty of the house. One of the best all-you-can-eat dinner buffets in town ($8) is found at **Sher-A-Punjab**, 2510 W. Devon Avenue, (773) 973-4000, and features naan along with paratha, roti (whole wheat version of naan), and other breads. **Sabrinihari**, 2511 W. Devon Avenue, (773) 465-3272, is a Pakistani restaurant that replaces Dasaprakash, which specialized in Southern India. But the street's king of Southern cooking is **Udupi Palace**, 2543 W. Devon Avenue, (773) 338-2152, which offers "pure vegetarian" South Indian dishes. Try the curry with spicy okra, Madras-style cashew pakoras (savory vegetable fritters), dosai (crêpes made from rice, wheat, or lentils), or uthappam, thicker pancakes. Entrées are garnished with sauces, chutneys, and sambar. A more recent entrant into the Devon scene, **India Garden**, 2548 W. Devon Avenue, (773) 338-2929, brings some interesting twists to the menu. "Kadhai" dishes ($6.95–$9.25) are prepared in a kadhai, an iron wok, and served in a mini copper wok. Other dishes are prepared on a tawa, an iron plate griddle. Tawa options come in lamb and various other organ meats. Try one the 20 different versions of tandoori ($4.25–

$11.25). Wash it all down with a mango shake. **Ghandi India**, 2601 W. Devon Avenue, (773) 761-8714, the first Indian restaurant opened on Devon, features both Northern and Southern dishes cooked in the tandoori (clay oven) style. Ghandi has a large menu of entrées priced $4 to $9. Desserts include payasam, thin noodles cooked in milk and honey with nuts and dried fruit. If you want to bring some of this tasty stuff home, stop in one of the **Patel Brothers Groceries**, 2600 W. Devon Avenue, (773) 764-1857; 2542 W. Devon Avenue, (773) 764-1853, after you're done eating and stock up on spices and basmati rice.

RAJ DARBER
2660 N. HALSTED STREET, (773) 348-1010

If spartan ethnic storefronts make you nervous, then Raj Darber, with its tablecloths and elegant dining room, is the place for you. Tandoori chicken ($8.95) is well-seasoned and juicy. Several biryani dishes, rice dishes made with basmati rice grown in the foothills of the Himalayas, are also a good bet. A number of vegetarian dishes, including several paneer (homemade cheese) dishes usually served with peas or spinach, are also available. All entrées are served with a side of basmati rice pilaf and a potato dish. Oven-baked breads are à la carte. Finish off your dinner with a serving of kheer ($3.95), rice pudding with pistachios.
Open daily. Full bar. Street parking difficult.

STANDARD INDIA RESTAURANT
917 W. BELMONT AVENUE, (773) 929-1123

The second of a Lakeview trio, Standard India has been around for more than 10 years. A side of naan is $0.95 here, compared to about $2 and up everywhere else. Entrées range from $9.95 for the Tandoori Mixed Grill down to $2.95 for some of the vegetarian dishes. The assorted Appetizer Platter, with samosas (triangular-stuffed pastries), pakoras, kabab, aloo-tikki (potato patties stuffed with lentils, peas, and herbs), chicken tikka papadum, and sweet and mint chutneys is a good way to start for $5.75. A buffet lunch is available on the weekends, while a vegetarian dinner buffet is spread Tuesday and Thursday evenings. Both are only $7.95.
Open daily. BYOB. Street parking available.

STAR OF INDIA

3204 N. SHEFFIELD AVENUE, (773) 525-2100

If you don't feel like hauling all the way up to Western and Devon, head for Belmont and Sheffield, which is the locus of a mini Indian restaurant community. The secret at Star of India is to go with a friend and order one of the three combination plates that will allow you a good graze through the menu. The Baadshah (king) Platter includes tandoori chicken, seekh kabab (lamb), chicken tikka, rogan josh (lamb curry), naan, rice, mixed vegetables, dalmakhni, and desserts for $12.95. The Dil Bahar Platter adds fish tikka and a couple of other dishes to the Baadshah Platter. The Begum (queen) Platter offers a taste of seven vegetarian dishes, naan, and dessert for $11.95. Once you figure out what you like, you can go back and order each entrée on its own and really dive in.

Open daily. BYOB. Street parking difficult.

SULTAN PALACE

6345 N. WESTERN AVENUE, (773) 764-8400/5588

Cab drivers tell you that Sultan Palace is the best Pakistani restaurant in Chicago. Marked by its gilded gold dome towering over Western Avenue, the family-owned Sultan Palace strives to recreate the atmosphere and the food of the Mughal emperors. One wall sports a specially commissioned mural of the Taj Mahal, which was built by the emperor Sultan Shah Jahan in 1721 when Pakistan and India were united under Muslim rule. The china, silverware, and wall rugs are all handmade in Pakistan and replicas of the Sultan Shah Jahan's own kitchenware. You can use these trappings of royalty to eat a variety of Mughlai vegetarian entrées priced $5.95 to $7.95 and tandoori, starting at $6.95. The restaurant serves only Zabiha meat, which is the equivalent of kosher meat for Muslims.

Open daily. No alcohol. Street parking available.

TIFFIN

2536 W. DEVON AVENUE, (773) 338-2143

Tiffin, which means a light midday meal, stands out on Devon with its fancy décor and its "frontier" cuisine. The restaurant, with its circular interior and hollowed out "lid," is shaped like one of the stacked metal dishes that tiffinwallahs used to carry through the streets of Bombay at noon for lunch. Tiffin serves dishes from the various borders of the subcontinent, including Afghani chole peshaware ($6.50), a chickpea and potato combination; South Indian paper masala dosai ($7.50), rice crêpes filled with spicy onions and potatoes served with sambar and coconut chutney; Northern Indian Mughal specialty murg shai korma ($8.50), chicken pieces simmered with almonds in a cream sauce; hot and sour Goan lamb vindaloo ($8.95), a west coast specialty favored in the former Portuguese territory of Goa and in Bombay; and Kashmiri rogan josh from the northwest ($8.95), lamb pieces cooked in Kashmiri masala with saffron and yogurt, among others. While standing in line for the $7.95 buffet, you can watch a chef wrapping frisbee-shaped pieces of dough around his "pillow" and dropping them on the cook fires to make naan.

Open daily. Full bar. Street parking available.

ZAIQA INDIAN RESTAURANT

858 N. ORLEANS STREET, (312) 280-6807

Zaiqa is the original eatery in the Orleans/Division area offering food from the subcontinent to legions of northern Indian and Pakistani cab drivers (a mosque is nearby). The restaurant is a spare storefront with an adjoining pool room, and half the off-duty taxis in Chicago are parked in the dirt lot next door. Zaiqa offers maybe a dozen Indian and Pakistani dishes on handwritten menus. Grab a spicy vegetarian plate and then grab a cab (if you can tear one of these guys away from the pool table).

Open daily. Street parking difficult.

GAYLORD INDIA

678 N. CLARK STREET, (773) 664-1700

If you can't make it up to Lakeview or Devon, but you're still craving tandoori and not at the downtown prices charged by Bukhara or Klay Oven, head for Gaylord India, a somewhat spiffier than usual Indian eatery reflecting the restaurant's River North location. There is attentive service, even during the lunch buffet, with nice white linens. Some good standard North India dishes are available in a daily $7.95 lunch buffet for area working professionals. Gaylord India also has tasty kulfi (Indian ice cream).

Open daily. Street parking difficult.

Quick Bites A FEW QUICK THOUGHTS

Ready for a field trip? Head to south suburban Lemont to the area's most important Hindu site, The **Hindu Temple of Greater Chicago**. This large white temple, built at a cost of $4 million and sitting on 20 acres of land, is dedicated to the Hindu deity Rama. Other Hindu deities can be worshipped in side halls.

Tibet Café

After numerous incursions, the Chinese invaded and occupied Tibet for good in 1959. The subsequent revolt of the Tibetans in the same year resulted in the Dalai Lama fleeing along with thousands of Tibetan refugees across the Himalayas to India, Nepal, and Bhutan. Since that time, Tibetans claim that over 1.2 million Tibetans have perished, more than 6,000 Buddhist monasteries have been demolished while irreplaceable ancient treasures have been pillaged, and over 110,000 have chosen to live in exile as so many Chinese have moved into Tibet that Tibetans have become a minority in their own mountains.

In spite of the country's troubles, Losar, the Tibetan New Year, is celebrated the last day of the year through the third day of the Tibetan calendar (February or March) with prayer flags flying over homes and incense wafting in the air. I decided to prep for the festivities by checking out **Tibet Café**. I thought it would be particularly appropriate to visit the restaurant with my friend Sue, a slim and fit individual who trains to climb mountains in her spare time. Leaving her clamp-ons behind, Sue and I trekked to Sheridan and Irving Park, a United Nations of the Chicago restaurant scene with Tibet Café in a storefront line-up that includes Nigerian, African, and Moroccan eateries along with numerous Hispanic establishments.

Sonam Dhargye and Kalsang Dhonoup, two former Tibetan lamas, came to the United States in 1992 and founded the Tibet Café with a partner in 1996. Kalsang, the café's chef, had sewn monks' robes back in the Gyoyo Monastery, and he used his talents to turn brightly colored, gilded sari fabrics into seat cushions and decorations that festoon the blond-wood-paneled restaurant. The walls are also decorated with butter sculptures, creamy swirls of color traditionally made with yak butter and tsampa (roasted barley flour) that depict deities, and Buddhist scenes that have been sculpted by Sonam, the host, who mastered the uniquely Tibetan art that serves as a form of prayer in the monastery. Prayer flags and, in a place of honor, a smiling picture of the Dalai Lama completes the interior.

We kicked off our meal with a pot of boe cha, traditional Tibetan tea churned with light salt, butter, and milk. I assume the natives get the real stuff with dairy products from the trusty yak, but our tea au lait, although delicately salty, seemed to be safely pasteurized and was interestingly tasty. We suffered no ill effects and later ordered another round.

Tibetan dishes borrow elements from the country's neighbors, particularly India and China, but relative to some of the other Asian palates, Tibetan seems to be a gentle cuisine served with salad, rice, or pita bread, with an abundance of vegetarian dishes. Spicy potato dishes, either shokog khatsa, served cold on greens with hot bread, or Himalaya khatsa, spicy potatoes also served cold with cauliflower, fresh peas, and tofu on greens with hot bread, are tasty vegan options. One of the menu highlights is the tsel momo, supposedly the national dish of Tibet. Momos are pot-sticker look-alikes steamed and filled with mixed vegetables or fried (tsel momo ngopa) and served on a bed of shredded salad. More momos include those made with potatoes mixed into the vegetables (Tibet Café Special).

TIBET CAFÉ,
3913 N. Sheridan Rd.,
(773) 281-6666, is
open daily, Saturdays
and Sundays only
for lunch. BYOB.
Vegetarian dishes range
from $4.95– $6.50;
non-vegetarian options
run to $8.95.

Entrées combine an extensive number of hot and cold options. Meat dishes feature beef versions of the momos, steamed beef dumplings (shaymo) or fried (shaymo ngopa). it seems like almost every culture has its own version of the hamburger, and the Tibetan burger appears in the form of sha-bhale, beef patties seasoned with shallot and herbs. Even seafood is available, a shrimp curry made with a yogurt and herbs marinade. We weren't quite sure how this could be a traditional dish of the mountains, so we said *no to-je-che*, Tibetan for "no thanks."

Our only disappointment was the Tibet Café Curry, a

chicken curry made with what we assumed was the same yogurt and herbs marinade over the shrimp. There was a lot of it, but it was relatively bland. We applied hot sauce liberally.

We finished with dysee, sweetened rice studded with raisins mounded beside a warm yogurt. Full and feeling on top of the world, we relaxed under the benign gaze of the Dalai Lama and sipped another pot of tea.

6

Out of Africa

MEATY MEALS FROM THE MOTHERLAND

Africa is a land of startling contrasts, from the Graceland of the south to the heart of darkness in the central Congo, to the savanna and sands of the north. The African continent is over three times the size of the United States and contains some 49 countries. Within its varied geography, Africa has the world's largest desert, second-largest rain forest, and second-longest river.

Africa is the birthplace of woman (and man, but the oldest skeleton discovered to date was nicknamed "Lucy" for a reason), as well as the historic birthplace of coffee.

It's a land of endlessly varied scenery, peoples, history, and, yes, even food. These days, with Chicago's increasingly international restaurant scene, you don't have to don your

> "If I know a song for Africa—of the giraffe, and the new African moon lying on her back, of the plow in the fields, and the sweaty faces of the coffee pickers, does Africa know a song for me?"
>
> —Isak Dinesen,
> *Out of Africa*

khakis and book your trip to the bush to experience the contrasts of Africa's culinary traditions. No, many of Africa's distinctive cuisines are well represented in local restaurants. A number of the city's eateries specialize in the spicy dishes of East Africa and Ethiopia, reflecting that country's position as a longtime bridge between the continent and the Mediterranean and Middle Eastern cultures to the north.

West Africa, stretching from the edge of the Congo and north to Timbuktu, was once a colonial breadbasket for Europe. The traditional bounty of Nigeria and the rest of that region, including yam porridge, fufu (cassava—also used to make tapioca), jollof rice (African rice pilaf), and goat stew, can be sampled at several Edgewater and Rogers Park neighborhood establishments. In addition, the couscous of Islamic North Africa and Morocco rock the Casbah all over town.

Over the course of a couple hundred years, West Africa, helped by a number of neighbors to the north, exported millions of its own residents. Though forcibly removed from their homes, these slaves managed to maintain aspects of their native traditions and helped shape the Afro-Caribbean cuisine of the islands and the soul food of the American South. A melding of British and African influences gave rise to the cuisine of Jamaica, while Spanish and African cooking traditions combined to produce Cuban cooking, and the whole mix—French, Spanish, African—resulted in the Creole and Cajun dishes of New Orleans and the Mississippi delta. These classic melting-pot situations are probably best illustrated by a Jamaican saying, "Out of many, one people." And one cuisine. Direct from the sands of the Caribbean and Gulf Coast to the third coast of Chicago, there's plenty of opportunity around town to indulge in these hybrid dishes.

VEE-VEE'S AFRICAN RESTAURANT
6245 N. BROADWAY STREET, (773) 465-2424

The traditional bounty of Nigeria can be sampled locally at Vee-Vee's, a restaurant in the Edgewater neighborhood that offers a fine experience in traditional West African cuisine. Dining typically consists of one-dish meals made up of a starch—usually rice, millet, maize, porridge, fufu, pounded plantains, yams, or cassava—served with a spicy "stew" or soup. The dish is often flavored with ground mango seed, melon seed, crayfish, or some tasty goat tidbits. For a number of the one-dish meals, ogbono or egusi (melon seed) soup, for example, the starches are in the form of sticky globs that the diner grabs in hunks and uses to get the soup to the mouth. Rice dishes that can be eaten with table utensils are also available. Chicken, fish, or goat can all be ordered with rice steamed in coconut milk and accented with puréed tomatoes, onions, pepper, and thyme. Our drums were really beating after tasting the coconut rice with chicken ($7.50). for those who have a hard time deciding between yam porridge (yam, meat, crayfish, tomatoes, and spinach in a sauce) and ngwo-ngwo (goat pepper soup), Vee-Vee's has an all-you-can-eat buffet ($9.99) on Sundays from noon until 6 P.M. where you can graze through the goat stew and yams prepared in various combinations in addition to jerk chicken, fried plantains, jollof rice, and more. Allow plenty of time here—service is very friendly, but excruciatingly slow. A word to the wise: Nigerian dishes, like the weather and current political situation, are hot, hot, hot. If you can't stand the heat, you'd better stay out of this West African kitchen.

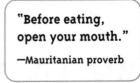

"Before eating, open your mouth."

—Mauritanian proverb

Open daily (Fridays and Saturdays till 2 A.M.). BYOB. Buffet is only served Sundays. Street parking difficult.

LINETTE'S JAMAICAN KITCHEN
7366 N. CLARK STREET, (773) 761-4823

CAFÉ PILAR
8251 S. STONY ISLAND AVENUE, (773) 375-7914

Two Jamaican restaurants fan the island breezes at the north and south poles of the city. In East Rogers Park, Linette's Jamaican Kitchen, a small storefront decorated with Jamaican seascapes and fishermen that contrast comfortably with worn wood floors, offers a cozy neighborhood atmosphere to those who want to enjoy peppered shrimp, red snapper, jerk pork and chicken, Jamaican beef, vegetable patties, or cow feet. Meals are from $8 to $8.50, and combination plates with two options are $10. Damp down the heat with a sip of sorrel (a blend of wine) or Irish moss, a seaweed health drink. Don't let the no-frills atmosphere and surly staff scare you away from the South Side's Café Pilar. Instead, allow the spicy smell of jerk chicken entice you inside. This small storefront—squeezed between a car wash and a used-car lot—uses patio furniture for dining, plays dancehall and reggae on a tiny boom box, and keeps ginger beer and Ting cold in a tiny, tiny icebox; but it also cranks out some of the best jerk chicken dinners ($8.50) in town. Feeling adventurous? Try the brown stew chicken, oxtails, curry chicken, or goat. Wash your dinner down with a nonalcoholic ginger beer or pineapple soda.

Both restaurants are open daily. No alcohol. They also serve breakfast.

MAMA DESTA'S RED SEA RESTAURANT

3216 N. CLARK STREET, (773) 935-7561

Ethiopia, where thousands of years ago *Homo erectus* first began to walk upright, has long been the conduit between Africa and the northern Mediterranean and Middle Eastern cultures. Ethiopia's food reflects these influences and can be sampled extensively through a "hands-on" experience at Mama Desta's. Here, you use strips of injera, a flat, spongy bread, to grab handfuls of doro wat, a spicy chicken in berbere sauce that is also Ethiopia's national dish; yebeg alitcha, a stew of lamb, onions, and green peppers; and yemisir wat, puréed green lentils blended with spices and herbs. a number of reasonably priced combination dishes ($7 and up) offer the adventurous eater a number of opportunities to run your hands through various vegetarian, chicken, fish, and meat dishes.

Open daily. Full bar featuring Ethiopian beer. Street parking difficult; parking lots nearby.

ETHIO VILLAGE CAFÉ & RESTAURANT

3462 N. CLARK STREET, (773) 929-8300

Those who know Ethiopian cuisine say Mama Desta's is the best, but if you're struck by Mama Desta's lack of atmosphere but are still in the mood, two other Ethiopian options can be found just up the street. Ethio Village Café & Restaurant boasts the cheapest Ethiopian on the block, including a $6.95 all-you-can-eat vegetarian buffet, live music (Fridays

and Saturdays), and honey wine served by the carafe.
Open daily. Full bar featuring Ethiopian beer. Street parking difficult; parking lots nearby.

ADDIS ABEBA

3521 N. CLARK STREET, (773) 929-9383

The other option is Addis Abeba, located just north, and offering more atmosphere than Mama Desta's but fewer amenities than Ethio Village. A good selection of sampler platters is available here, where the motto is: "We cook for you. . . . Just as we do for ourselves."

Open daily. Full bar featuring Ethiopian beer. Street parking difficult; parking lots nearby.

Talk Like an Ethiopian...

Enjera—a thin pancake-like bread prepared from fermented teff flour.

Berbere—ingredient of wat prepared from red pepper and other spices.

Wat—a spicy sauce made from berbere along with meat, fish, vegetables, or leguminous seeds.

Awaze—sauce made from red pepper and other spices.

Mitmita—powdered chili pepper seeds blended with other spices.

Alitcha—mild sauce made from turmeric and other spices, along with meat, fish, vegetables, and leguminous seeds.

CALYPSO CAFÉ

5211C S. HARPER COURT, (773) 955-0229

Day-oh. Head south for a taste of the Caribbean to Calypso in Hyde Park. Opened by the owners of Dixie Kitchen & Bait Shop right next door, Calypso serves the spices of Jamaica and its neighbors in a bright and playful water wonderland setting. Orders are generous enough to be overwhelming to anyone dining alone, but the servers, as friendly and warm as the islands, will encourage you to take home the extras. The jerk chicken wings appetizer ($8.95) is two rapier-sized skewers of jumbo wings weighing in at two pounds. Another starter, plantain strips served with chunky guacamole and a spicy Cuban black bean dip ($6.50), is a mountain of 12-inch-long crunchy strips, peeled the entire length of some very large bananas. Half orders make the menu more manageable, and the half order of curried chicken ($8.45), spicy-sweet with green apples, grapes, and raisins over white rice, is a good choice, as is the half order of house-smoked baby back ribs ($11.45), which features a barbecue sauce with just a taste of tropical fruit.
Open daily. Full bar. Parking lot.

EZULI

1415 N. MILWAUKEE AVENUE, (773) 227-8200

The sassy storefront serves up hefty portions of Caribbean cooking at prices you can't beat. Dig into the monkfish creole with black beans and rice ($11.75), fiery jerk chicken with coconut rice and peas ($9.75), or the Jamaican catfish with Ezuli sauce, sweet potato fries, and Caribbean slaw ($9.75). The sandwiches are mighty tasty, including the Ezuli burger that comes with lettuce, tomato, marinated onions, and chipotle mayonnaise ($7); veggie burger with lettuce, tomato, and spicy pineapple salsa ($6.50); and the tangy jerk chicken sandwich with lettuce, tomato, marinated onions, and cilantro mayonnaise ($8). All sandwiches come with irresistible sweet potato fries and Caribbean slaw.
Closed Monday. Full bar. Deejays spin R&B and soul music. Street parking available.

The Caribbean American Baking Company, 1539 W. Howard Street, (773) 761-0700, in Rogers Park is Chicago's only source of Jamaican beef patties ($1.05 each including tax), spicy little turnovers that are as common in Jamaica as hot dogs and burritos are here. This bakery supplies all the local restaurants in town, popping an estimated 10,000 patties a week out of the oven. Other Jamaican specialties, including Hardough bread, plantain tarts, and Bulla cake, are also available.

Slow Burn

Under the Burning African Sun, a Little Spice Is Nice

Would you savor a substance used to repel grizzly bears and muggers? Take a bite out of a bit that will trigger the effect of a blowtorch in your digestive system? Consume something so hot it can only be handled with rubber gloves? Are you addicted to the rush—the sweating, aching, burning, gasping high that comes from a bite of danger?

The proliferation of ethnic restaurants has awakened our tables and tastebuds, leading many of us in a search for a hot spot, hot stuff—and we'll do just about anything to get it while it's hot. We swirl through gallons of salsa, spritz ever-handy bottles of Tabasco over everything from fried eggs to french fries, and stand in line to raise a little hell at even chain Tex-Mex, just to get a bite of a hallowed jalapeño.

We owe all this pain and pleasure to Columbus. If you discount pepper, which grew worldwide, there were really no fire-eaters outside of tropical America until the sixteenth century, when the search for spice set the (Old) world on fire as Columbus and his crew discovered the Americas. Subsequent Spanish and Portuguese traders brought the bounty of the New to the Old, including corn, tomatoes, potatoes, sweet potatoes, and *Capsicum annuum*, otherwise known as chili peppers.

Iberian spice traders fanned the flames that heated up the world's menus, as they brought chilies from the Americas to Europe, Asia, and Africa. Chilies came to India and China through the Portuguese colonies of Goa and Macau, making possible the fiery dishes that we recognize today as the signature of Southern Indian, Szechuan Chinese, and West African cooking. Red peppers then made their way to the Balkans and into the Hungarian pepper pot via the Ottoman Turks, who were introduced to them as they laid siege and kicked the Portuguese out of their colony at Hormuz in the Persian Gulf.

Since American menus were traditionally dominated by the dishes of Northern European immigrants, it's no surprise that many of our tables were historically bland. In fact, it took a relatively recent boom in Mexican, Szechuan, and Thai restaurants for us to begin to accustom ourselves to the burn of capsaicin, the chemical component behind pepper power.

Although there's no proven physical addiction to chili's fire, some eaters revel in the exploration and accompanying pain of hot food. Dr. Paul Rozin, a psychologist at the University of Pennsylvania, labels the behavior of an eater who pushes his taste buds to the limits of pain and tolerance as "benign masochism" or "constrained risk." Rozin also notes it's common for people to enjoy the body's defensive responses to hot food, the running noses and tearing eyes that come from a bite of something red and hot.

It may not be able to hook us like nicotine, but some of us have just have got to have it. Many of our initial fire holes— Mexican, Thai, and Szechuan Chinese restaurants—have become bland, as they increasingly produce "whitened" versions, or even fusion versions, of dishes designed to meet our Midwestern American view of what a burrito or panang curry should taste like. In our quest for fire, we often find ourselves exploring where few forks have gone before, like to the menus of West Africa.

"People come in here looking both a little excited and scared," confided our waiter at **Ofie**, a Lakeview storefront specializing in West African food, much of which is meant to be eaten not with a fork but with fingers cradling an edible scoop of starchy fufu. The dishes offer incendiary heat, which can be further stoked with tabletop pepper sauces (also sold on Ofie's Web site, www.ofie.com).

OFIE,
3911 N. Sheridan Rd.,
(773) 248-6490,
www.ofie.com

Sauce #1, Mako, means "pepper" in the Ghanaian language Akan, and we're told to "add a few drops for a delicate, spicy flavor or sprinkle to your heart's desire," advice that should be taken with caution. Meanwhile, Sauce #2, Oja, which translates as "fire," lives up to its name, and back-of-the-bottle instructions are right on. "This sauce is to be used very sparingly!" Or not at all, if you've got pain receptors left in your mouth, nose, and stomach.

Our waiter informed us that Eko Okuko is one of Ofie's most popular offerings. Heat-seeking diners must also be in search of the exotic, since this is a dish of "fiery chicken gizzards cooked in ginger, garlic, and hot peppers until tender yet crunchy, then stir-fried with onions, tomatoes, peppers, and our special blend of spices." Patrons Cyd and Julius, at Ofie to celebrate Julius's birthday, further fuel this theory. "I usually celebrate my birthday with sushi," Julius explained, "But I wanted to try something different. The food here was excellent and really not too hot. In New York, an African restaurant like this would be common, but in Chicago, it's really different and a treat."

Seoul Food

BI-BIM-BOPPING THROUGH KOREAN BARBECUES

Dateline, 1988: Seoul—For perhaps the first time since the 1950s, the attention of mainstream America turns toward Korea. Amid the pomp and circumstance of the summer Olympics, Americans once again focus their attention on this elusive peninsular country.

Often called the "Irish of Asia," Koreans spent much of their history being conquered by neighbors. When not being subjugated by a country next door, Koreans were actively involved in kicking nonresidents out and keeping them out, thereby earning the nickname of "The Hermit Kingdom."

Even today, after the splash of the Seoul Olympics and countless reruns of *M*A*S*H*, not much is known in the American mainstream about Korea. Too bad, since the Koreans, like the Irish, have a fiery and colorful heritage that is expressed in every aspect of their culture, even their cuisine. Take kimchi, for example. The soul of the Korean people is pickled into kimchi, an incendiary side dish/condiment consumed at every meal and made by fermenting various vegetables in garlic and chilis. There are some two dozen different varieties of kimchi, and the average Korean family has numerous black kimchi pots perking away on the back porch. Complimentary side dishes, or panch'an, are served at every meal (a great deal—no need to order an appetizer here!), and the number

> **"A man can live without his wife, but not without his kimchi."**
>
> —Ancient Korean adage

of sides increases as the day goes on. At a typical dinner at a local restaurant, it's not uncommon to be confronted with at least nine side dishes and soup to accompany your entrée. Some typical sides include sigumchi namul, blanched spinach with sesame oil and seeds; kejang, raw crab legs marinated in red chili sauce; and tubu, marinated tofu.

Along with the abundant side dishes, Korean cuisine is also typified by "one-dish" meals, such as bi-bim-bop, a rice bowl traditionally topped with bean sprouts, bluebell root, blanched fern, spinach, a fried egg, and chili sauce on the side. Most local Korean restaurants do the "bop," although they may substitute carrots or zucchini for some of the traditional greens. Other dishes commonly found around town are galbi, beef short ribs; and bulgolgi, sliced beef; both marinated in a tangy sauce and often cooked at your table on a special grill resembling a Mongol helmet. In addition, as a country practically surrounded by water, it should be no surprise that much of Korean cuisine revolves around seafood, particularly sea skate, octopus, and squid.

Chicago has a good-sized Korean population. In 1965, immigration laws eased, allowing in a wave of Asians from politically unstable countries. Koreans settled in the old Albany Park neighborhood and established Chicago's Koreatown in the area lying between Pulaski and Foster to the north and west, Montrose to the south, and the north branch of the Chicago River to the east. Today, take a drive down Lawrence Avenue, and you may think you've suddenly crossed the international dateline. English practically disappears and is replaced with Hangul, the Korean written language. But you don't need to read about it (except in *Cheap Chow Chicago!*) to go out and eat it and enjoy it. Go for it—bop 'til you drop.

Editor's Note: The romanization of the names of Korean dishes varies all over town; some of the standards are used here.

JIM'S GRILL

1429 W. IRVING PARK ROAD, (773) 525-4050

 Also profiled in the breakfast chapter, "Early to Rise: If You've Got to Get Out of Bed . . .", Jim's Grill offers not only a great diner-style, short-order breakfast, but also a wide array of Korean options. Tiny Jim's, seating less than 20 at the counter and tables combined, is home to Chicago's cheapest bi-bim-bop, often a $3.95 special on the weekends, $4.50 regular price for chicken, pork, beef, or vegetarian (shrimp a little more), $6.50 for Dave's Deluxe, and $4.55 on Tuesdays for the hyumi, bi-bim-bop made with brown rice and oats. Bop that! Also on the menu are great deals on standbys such as bulgolgi ($5.95), mandoo with fried rice (Korean dumplings, $4.95), maki rolls (Korean vegetarian sushi, $4.95), and soy vegetarian pancakes with seaweed soup ($4.55). Wash it all down with an assortment of traditional Korean teas, including barley and ginger, very good for your yin and yang. No little side dishes here—but at these prices, you can afford to splurge on a couple of appetizers.

Open Monday through Saturday for breakfast and lunch. No alcohol. Street parking available.

CHO SUN OK STEAK HOUSE

4200 N. LINCOLN AVENUE, (773) 549-5555

Once just another neighborhood greasy spoon, the owners of Cho Sun Ok soon realized that their customers were more interested in ordering the Korean dishes relegated to the back of the hamburger menu. So they got rid of the burgers and went with the traditional. The specialties of the house—dungeness crab, pheasant, and quail—are a little pricey for us at $25, as is tabletop cooking starting at $19.95, but the rest of the menu is very reasonable, with the bi-bim-bop checking in at $6.95 and the beef dishes, gahl bee gui (charcoal broiled beef short ribs) and bul ko ki (charcoal broiled and sliced marinated beef) priced at $12.95 and $9.50, respectively. Spicy bean curd is also a good option at $6.95. Enjoy your meal with the background entertainment of KTV, Korean TV; a constant stream of soap operas and talk shows run while you eat.

Open daily. Full bar. Street parking available.

KOREAN RESTAURANT

2659 W. LAWRENCE AVENUE, (773) 878-2095

The heart of Chicago's Koreatown, Lawrence Avenue is lined with restaurant storefronts where names are displayed prominently in Hangul, the Korean written language, and English is often a second language. Korean Restaurant is one of the more established locations and is able to accommodate the language needs of "foreigners." Korean Restaurant offers more than 80 different dishes served in huge portions, 24 hours a day. Four different types of bi-bim-bop range from $6.95 to $9.95, including Chonju-style, named after the southern province where it originates and served in a heated stone bowl with a raw egg on top. Bim nengmyon, hot spicy buckwheat noodles, is a fiery specialty, and hejang kuk, chunks of beef and ox blood boiled with vegetables, at $5, is a real deal.

Open 24 hours. BYOB. Street parking available.

MANDARIN HOUSE

819 NOYES STREET, EVANSTON, (847) 869-4344

Similar to many Korean and Vietnamese restaurants that pretend to be dining establishments offering more mainstream Asian cuisines, this dumpy little storefront masquerading as Chinese is actually a good-deal Korean eatery serving a range of traditional dishes made mainly with either beef or chicken. Chicken or beef bi-bim-bop is $6.50; both the bulgogi and the galbi are comparatively good deals at $6.30. Try some tender, tasty san juk, Korean shish kebab, for only $6.75. Assorted combinations from $6.50 to $8.20 offer the adventurous diner an opportunity to graze.

Open daily. BYOB. Street parking available.

GIN GO GAE

5433 N. LINCOLN AVENUE, (773) 334-3895

Although a little pricier and more upscale, the huge selection of complimentary sides offsets the prices at Gin Go Gae, one of Chicago's best Korean establishments. Entrées are grouped into charcoal-broiled, stir-fried, and "very traditional." Try the bulgogi and the galbi, very tasty and tender Korean barbecue both priced under $11 for either beef or pork. A spicy beef soup with a red pepper base that infuses the shredded beef, clear noodles, and chopped vegetables with sinus-clearing kick, provides a sample of the heat of Korean cuisine.

Open daily. Full bar. Street parking available.

SAN SOO GAB SAN KOREAN RESTAURANT

5247 N. WESTERN AVENUE, (773) 334-1589

Out late and feeling like a Korean "hot pot" or barbecue? Try this 24/7 spot, San Soo Gab San Korean Restaurant. The restaurant's ringed with wicker-walled cubicles that create private dining rooms, allowing you to sprawl on cushions and dig in (make sure you take your shoes off before stepping on the wood steps and platform). Each table's equipped with holes into which your server drops a heavy ceramic bowl with fiery charcoal covered by a metal grill on which you can cook numerous traditional Korean dishes listed on the menu. Try the savory BulKoKii ($12.95), thinly sliced marinated beef, and the KalBi ($13.95). The tangy, spicy OjingOhGui ($10.50), broiled squid noodles, and the DukManDuGuk ($7.95), sliced rice cake soup and dumplings in beef broth, are one-dish meals. Don't overorder, since you'll get some nine side dishes with your meal and soup. Sushi is also available from the sister restaurant next door. Some language barriers.

Open daily 24 hours. Street parking available.

If you're up enjoying the sights and tastes of Korea-town, make sure you check out the **Bultasa Buddhist Temple**, 4358 W. Montrose Avenue. Chicago has five Buddhist temples, but the Bultasa is unique because of its "1,000 Buddha Temple Altar," the only one of its kind in the Midwest. Open every day from 6 A.M. to 9:30 P.M., the monks will be happy to give you a guided tour.

In the Belly of the Buddha

Awaken to Amitabul's Vegan Temptations

The corner of Southport and Roscoe saw more action one September night than the Wrigleyville area has witnessed since the Cubs last won the division. That Tuesday night, driven by the promise of free food and rumors of a spontaneous performance by the Smashing Pumpkins, 750 hungry fans stormed the doors for opening night at **Amitabul**, a new Korean Buddhist vegetarian restaurant opened by the owners of Jim's Grill.

Although just a tiny diner, Jim's itself has a huge following. At first glance, the 1429 W. Irving Park Road storefront looks like a cheap, short-order grill; a second look, however, uncovers near-overflow crowds scooping rice dishes and noodles out of shiny, deep-bottomed metal bowls, snarfing up bites of strange grain-and-vegetable pancakes, and throwing sushi-like pieces of vegetarian maki rolls into heart-healthy guts. In short, Jim's is a gustatory Asian oasis hiding behind the facade of American grease.

True believers have hoarded the knowledge to themselves, lest the word get out and the lines grow longer. Rumors had spread that a new Jim's would be opening nearby. All through that long, hot summer, one of the owners, Dave Choi, says he was peppered constantly for updates. "When, when?" pleaded the faithful, and Choi would just smile enigmatically and reply, "Soon, soon." (If you were particularly lucky, he might have shared a construction tidbit, or an anecdote about a tussle with City Hall for a license.)

Then, details about the Amitabul concept started to leak out. Not just another Jim's, Amitabul, which means "awakening", would be a forum for Choi and his family partners to let their talents with Korean Buddhist vegetarian food run wild. Devotees squirmed in anticipation. And then the big night arrived. Although music was promised, Choi discouraged speculation that the Smashing Pumpkins—big fans of the cooking at Jim's—would perform. Refusing to be discouraged, the crowds formed. Said co-owner Eric Kim, "We expected to cook for about 300. They were lined up all the way down Southport. What people will do for free food!"

AMITABUL,
6207 N. Milwaukee,
(773) 774-0276,
is open Monday through
Friday 11 A.M.–10 P.M.;
Saturday 9 A.M.–10 P.M.;
and Sunday 10 A.M.–
8:30 P.M. Dishes range
from $5.95 to $7, and
the cuisine is strictly
vegan—no dairy, not
even cream for coffee.
Beer and wine are served,
but the varietal is plum,
ginseng, nine-grain,
or rice saki.

But it was Amitabul free food—fat-free, cholesterol-free, animal by-product–free. And the faithful were rewarded for their patience. Glistening green piles of kim bop (maki rolls) in vegetable, "energy," kimchi, and jade varieties were inhaled, along with piles of vegetable pancakes—whole wheat, brown-rice, kimchi, soybean, "energy," black-bean, and whole-wheat with miso. Diners frolicked through noodle dishes, Mandoo Can Do and Kimchi Du-Bi-Du, among other creative options. They had finally found Nirvana—a salad of tofu, seaweed, vegetables, and apples designed to take taste buds to the promised land.

Long past opening night, Amitabul remains kimchi hot—most dishes are served mildly spicy to you-probably-can't-handle-it spicy. Lines continue to form for Amitabul Energy Nuts, various nuts stir-fried with honey and tangy plum sauce served over whole wheat noodles; maha pyogo, three kinds of mushrooms steamed with fresh garlic over rice; various selections of bi-bim-bop, a kind of Korean fried rice; and the ever-popular soy vegetable pancakes, which Amitabul serves with various grains and legumes. The list of daily specials is particularly popular—various menu selections are served with a choice of soup for $5.99.

For a while there, traffic at Jim's apparently began to spike on Fridays, when those who weren't able to make a complete transition to meatless bi-bim-bop got their last fix of chicken or beef. Jim's, however, is back open on Saturdays—to the great joy of unrepentant carnivores. Meanwhile at Amitabul, chef Choi continues down the true vegetarian path.

8

Oktoberfeast, Ja!

om-pah-pah, oom-pah-pah . . . Late September through October, people all over the Chicago area, most of whom do not possess even a drop of Deutsche blood, put on ridiculous Peter Pan felt hats, heft a cold plastic stein, and cavort to the big band sound of hairy-legged men encased in green shorts with leather banding. Oktoberfest season brings an opportunity every weekend to wave a brat, chug some hops while wedged between strangers at a picnic table, and let it all hang out while doing the chicken dance with 2,000 other feather-capped partiers. Ja!

Chicago, of course, has deep-rooted German traditions that have led us to today's celebrations. The city's first German settler, Heinrich Rothenfeld, relocated here in 1825. By the early 1840s, the first German settlement, New Buffalo, was formed between Chicago and North Avenue. Germans later moved north into the Old Town area and then on up Lin-

> **"Things could be wurst."**
>
> —Traditional motto of master German butchers

coln Avenue to Lincoln Square at Lincoln and Lawrence. Critical to the development of Chicago's German community and probably Chicago's persona as a whole, was the founding of the city's first brewery in 1836, bubbling out 600 foamy barrels a year. One of the original founders (sorry, not Berghoff—he didn't show up until the 1890s) then went on to expand his business in partnership with future mayor William B. Ogden. By 1856, Chicago's nine German breweries were churning out 16,270 barrels a year.

Oktoberfest evolved from a wedding reception that got out of hand—the celebration of Bavarian King Ludwig I's marriage to Therese Sachsen Hildburghause, a festive event marked by a great horse race and much partying among the residents of Munich. Today, the Munich Oktoberfest begins the next to last Saturday in September and continues until the first Sunday in October, luring tourists from all over the world to the festival on Theresienwiese (Therese's meadow).

If you can't afford the ticket on Lufthansa, there are plenty of local options you might want to check out. Although ostensibly held in October, many Oktoberfest celebrations in the Chicago area are held in September—with two of the biggest being the Berghoff Oktoberfest (second weekend in September) and the German-American Festival with its accompanying Von Steuben parade (third weekend in September).

You can also check out the four-person band playing every weekend all year at the Edelweiss Restaurant Oktoberfest on West Irving Park Road. Or, Lincoln Square anchor (see "Taste of Lincoln Avenue") the Chicago Brauhaus throws an Oktoberfest in its rear parking lot every fall, a kickoff marked by the Von Steuben parade, that continues through mid-October. If you're really desperate, check your local church—chances are, even they're probably having a little shindig where the faithful normally park. Just look around—any place you can set up a tent and tap a keg is a possibility for a little Oktoberfest *gemutlichkeit*. (That's kind of a warm *bonhomie* in German.)

THE BERGHOFF

17 W. ADAMS STREET, (312) 427-3170

Over 100 years old with its own street fair every September, The Berghoff is the best-known German establishment in the city. In spite of its downtown location, the restaurant still has reasonably priced entrées, including sauerbraten and chicken schnitzel (both $8.25). Those who want to economize can eat a hand-carved sandwich in the adjoining café while standing and draining either the Berghoff's home brew or a draft root beer.

Open daily. Full bar. Street parking difficult.

EDELWEISS RESTAURANT

7650 W. IRVING PARK ROAD, NORRIDGE, (708) 452-6040

Boasting its own Oktoberfest celebration where patrons are entertained by a four-piece band, Edelweiss is worth the drive for a truly solid meal. Complete dinners spanning the range of Deutsche offerings are priced mostly from $9.95 to $11.50. À la carte entrées, if several courses leave you numb, are $6.50 to $6.95. Hot and cold sandwiches are $4.75 to $8.25. At least three varieties of schnitzel appear daily on the menu—the one with hunter's sauce is highly recommended. Check out the interesting stuffed animals draped over the band's drumset.

Open daily. Full bar. Parking lot.

LUTZ CONTINENTAL CAFÉ & PASTRY

2458 W. MONTROSE AVENUE, (773) 478-7785

Around since 1948, Lutz boasts one of the city's ultimate "secret gardens," an astroturfed, tree-lined patio out back complete with a pool and fountain gurgling away amidst umbrella-shaded tables that may be the peaceful getaway you need after one too many steins. A sophisticated contrast to some of Chicago's other open air–celebrations taking place in beer gardens and tents, Lutz serves Viennese and southern German specialties, including homemade soups, chicken and fish, crêpes and quiche, salads, open-faced sandwiches, and some very serious tortes, all priced $3 to $12. Selections from the Fatherland include liver pâté ($5.75), herring topf (herring with sour cream, apples, and boiled potatoes, $9.40), veal served in a pastry shell ($9.95), konigsberger klopse (meatballs in wine sauce, $9.75), relished salmon ($10.95), and königens pastete (the queen's plate, $9.40). Top off your meal with a Viennese coffee and a multilayer, creme-filled, artery-clogging, eye-pleasing, tummy-busting delight— maybe a nice big baumkuchen with whipped cream?

Closed Sundays. Full bar. Street parking difficult.

RESI'S BIERSTUBE
2034 W. IRVING PARK ROAD, (773) 472-1749

German food generally is not cheap chow. Yes, you usually get a lot for your money—complete meals so weighty they knock you out for, well, in some cases, maybe 40 years (Rip Van Winkle, was he German or Dutch?). But all this bounty usually comes at a price. The true exception to this rule in town is Resi's, a snug little restaurant with an outstanding beer garden that really delivers for under $12. Complete dinners, excluding the schnitzels, with hefty main dishes and two sides hover between $7.50 and 8.95. Try the fried liver cheese and potato salad. A variety of sausages with side fixin's range from $4.75 to $8.50. Wash it all down with a choice from among 60 bottled beers and eight on tap. This place gets crowded with regulars, and you may end up sharing your picnic table in the tree-lined, lantern-lit beer garden with fellow diners who don't know your name. Service is exceptionally friendly. Ask for our waitress, Edit, a fixture at Resi's for the past 20 years. (More on Resi's in "Gardens of Eat-in.")

Open daily. Full bar—choice of more than five dozen beers. Patio dining. Street parking difficult.

MIRABELL RESTAURANT & LOUNGE
454 W. ADDISON STREET, (773) 463-1962

Out on West Addison near the highway, the Heil family, Mirabell's owners, have been serving up traditional German feasts in their lodge-like restaurant since 1977. Known for its bratwurst and other German specialties, Mirabell also serves five different versions of veal schnitzel and two of pork. Herring in wine sauce, goulash, schweinebraten (roast loin of pork)—all the foods of the Fatherland are here in a big (portion-wise) way. The large menu also includes a number of classic American options. Lots of German beers on tap at the wooden bar and an extensive list of German liquors is also available.

Closed Sunday. Parking can be tough, but check with the restaurant about using a reserved part of the Kmart's lot across the street.

Given the price of meals in some of the city's more popular German restaurants, it might be worth looking into some take-out/do-your-own spots:

LINCOLN MARKET
4661 N. LINCOLN AVENUE, (773) 561-4570
Stocking German meats and food products from Poland, Hungary, and Yugoslavia, Lincoln Market is well known for its beerwurst and sausages, which are prepared in-house by master European butchers. Lincoln Market also specializes in more unusual cuts of meats, including spring lambs and young pigs.
Open daily.

INGE'S DELICATESSEN
4724 N. LINCOLN AVENUE, (773) 561-8386
Thirty years in Lincoln Square, Inge's specializes in imported German, Austrian, Croatian, Dutch, Danish, and French gourmet foods and specialty items. A wide selection of homemade sausages, cosmetics, and beer steins is available.
Open daily.

EUROPEAN PASTRY SHOP AND CAFÉ
4701–03 N. LINCOLN AVENUE, (773) 271-7017
Bakery in the front, café in the rear. Plenty of sweet and gooey cakes, imported truffles, and tortes in both front and back.
Open daily.

Editor's Note: For more on German bakeries and delicatessens, see "Taste of Lincoln Avenue."

The Last Metro

Sampling the Specialties of Chicago's Only Austrian Restaurant

In 1882, it took a church to build a village, as the founding of St. Alphonsus on five acres of prime farmland at what would become the intersection of Wellington and Southport drew the local German community north to the village of Lakeview from its earlier home in Old Town. Lincoln Avenue was once an old Indian and fur trapper trail known as Little Fort Road that led to the Green Bay and Fox River portages. By the mid-nineteenth century it had become the main artery through Lakeview, and was soon flanked by the farms of settlers from Germany and Luxembourg.

A separate town at the time with its own liquor laws, Lakeview was particularly attractive to ethnic Germans due to village officials' tolerant attitude toward social drinking not held by the temperance-advocating bureaucrats of Chicago. The biergartens of Lakeview, also known as "Chicagoburg," flourished thanks to Lakeview's Saloon Keeper's Society, which was organized to "protect and demand their common interests by all lawful means and measures" against Nativists and teetotalers, among others.

By 1889, the village of Lakeview was annexed by the city of Chicago, and improvements in public transportation, particularly the Ravenswood El, encouraged settlement of areas to the north and west. German families moved out from Lakeview north along Lincoln to what became the posh suburb of Ravenswood and the more modest Lincoln Square area at Lincoln, Western, and Lawrence. Brauhauses, delicatessens, and pumpernickel bakeries continued to pop up further and further north to feed this movement.

In 1974, when Pepo and Ani Kostenberger opened Metro Club in the shadow of St. Alphonsus, Lakeview's traditional German neighborhood was truly in transition. The Austrian

Kostenbergers came to the United States from Europe in 1969. Pepo, a musician who spent his whole life touring bars, hotels, and restaurants, found himself as a bandleader at a nightclub on North Lincoln called Moulin Rouge. Although the stretch of Lincoln through Lakeview still had a number of German delis, restaurants, and bars servicing German residents, including the now-defunct Zum Deutschen Eck and Kuhn's Delicatessen and Liquors, "it was a bad neighborhood," remembers Pepo.

Pepo and Ani originally opened **Metro Club** as a beer hall serving just alcohol. Two years later, Ani joined the kitchen, where she still cooks up oversized platters of Austrian and German comfort food. Besides the addition of food early on, not much has changed about the restaurant except the neighborhood, which is a lot better and more expensive address these days than when Pepo and Ani moved in. In the midst of expensive town homes and condos, Metro Club remains a cozy, wood-beamed restaurant serving hot and heavy plates of pork, veal, and beef in a shadowy room that's full of traditional tchotchkes, including two wood-carved statues

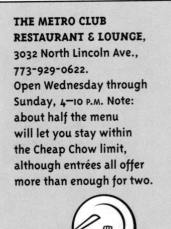

THE METRO CLUB RESTAURANT & LOUNGE, 3032 North Lincoln Ave., 773-929-0622. Open Wednesday through Sunday, 4–10 P.M. Note: about half the menu will let you stay within the Cheap Chow limit, although entrées all offer more than enough for two.

that beckon patrons in and walls and shelves crowded with dolls, antique steins, fishing pictures, musical instruments, and mounted game trophies, including a comparatively mundane deer, as well as a boar's head and rear.

"We're the only Austrian restaurant in Chicago," notes Pepo, who claims that all the other pretenders are run by Germans. "Austrian food versus German food is like comparing eating in Louisiana to Chicago. Due to the influences of neighbors like Hungary, the Czechs, and the Yugoslavs, Austrian food is prepared with more spices and uses different kinds of spices, like paprika."

Dining at Metro Club starts off with a spicy Hungarian salami and a basket of rye bread. Bowls of soup are big enough for a meal—for two. The ambitious can move on to weiner schnitzel, the restaurant's most popular dish, or one of the three other pork schnitzels that threaten to overflow 16-inch platters. Numerous other hearty and traditional menu options include a veal shank, modestly described as "for the hearty eater;" debriziner, homemade Hungarian sausage; and kässler rippchen, a hub cap–sized slab of smoked pork that tastes like a smoky honey-baked ham and is served with fried, whole new potatoes and the best sauerkraut you may ever taste. You won't possibly have room for dessert, apple strudel, or sacher torte served with real whipped cream, but you should try.

At Metro Club, where the menu bills the restaurant as "The Place Where Happiness is Homemade," everything is home-cooked by Ani, and the kitchen can be leisurely. "Our food must be cooked properly, and this cooking takes some time, but when the food comes out, it's perfect," explains Pepo. "In twenty-seven years, we haven't had one complaint about the food—except that it's too much."

Wash it all down with a hearty European beer, since Metro Club doesn't serve any domestic brews. "Goulash and Miller Lite don't fit," chuckles Pepo. "If you're going to eat German and Austrian food, you should drink German and Austrian beer."

Although their daughter now works at the restaurant, Pepo and Ani still run Metro Club, and Pepo doesn't see that changing any time soon. "We love the business and love taking care of our customers. As a small business, we have to." Depending on how the evening's going, Pepo will even entertain patrons on the accordian. "I'll occasionally play, and that has spoiled the customers. Their first question is always, 'Hey Pepo, are you going to play tonight?'"

9

Oodles of Noodles

SOUTHEAST ASIA ON A SHOESTRING

L et's dispel a few myths. They don't all look alike, and they don't all taste alike. In spite of the recent trend to combine dishes and flavors for a menu of "Asian fusion," there are a lot of distinct differences among Asian cuisines. Thai and Vietnamese dishes can be as far away from sushi and chow mein as a burrito is from a spring roll. At first glance, there may be some surface similarities, but your first bite should firmly inform you that you're not in Kansas—or Canton—anymore, Toto.

Southeast Asian cuisines, particularly the noodle dishes that are the anchor options on many of the proliferating fusion menus, can also be a bargain compared to their North Asian cousins. Frankly, it can be a lot easier to find budget pad Thai than tempura. A steady diet of Thai or Vietnamese carryout can really help save your *baht*.

Rockin' ramen . . . The Chinese and Japanese have a history of noodlemaking that goes back to 3000 B.C., which they later exported to their Asian neighbors. Once considered peasant food, noodles are now mainstream dining, and noodle vendors are as much a part of the streets of Thailand, India, China, Japan, and other Asian countries as hot dog vendors are at a baseball game. Noodles in Asia are typically long and thin because of their associations with longevity—Asians have

> "Creative cooking when you can only afford 10-for-a-dollar pasta."
>
> —Headline from Toni Patrick, *101 Ways to Make Ramen Noodles*

75

traditionally served noodles at birthday celebrations, left uncut to ensure long life.

In contrast to the West, Asian cultures commonly use flours other than wheat to make their noodles. Cellophane noodles, those noodles you often see fried into "bird's nests," are made from mung beans, which were originally grown in India. Rice noodles are the foundation of many Asian dishes, and soba noodles made from buckwheat are a staple in many Japanese dishes. In India, you can find vendors in almost every city selling spicy fried noodles made half of garbanzo flour and half of chili powder, often eaten between bites of fresh green chili peppers. Some like it hot.

Thai one on. . . . Cheap and noodles are synonymous with Thai and Vietnamese food. Chicago's first Thai restaurant opened some 20 years ago, and today, there are more than 100 in the city and more than 200 in the Chicago area—a surprising figure since Thais represent Chicago's smallest Asian group, with a population of less than 5,000 in the metro area. Chicago's Vietnamese population, one of Chicago's newest immigrant groups and more concentrated than the Thai, can be found primarily in Uptown around Argyle Street, once known as "New Chinatown" but now probably more appropriately termed "Little Saigon." Whether you run to your neighborhood corner storefront or hop the El uptown to the Lawrence stop, get out and Thai some Southeast Asian fare. You wouldn't want to miss Saigon, right?

BANANA LEAF

3811 N. SOUTHPORT AVENUE, (773) 853-8683

Where better to go if you think you live on the artistic edge than the ultrahip Music Box (3733 N. Southport Avenue, (773) 871-6604), with the most cutting-edge films in the city. Grab a bite before the flick just up the street at Banana Leaf, an Asian restaurant serving Chinese, Thai, and other Eastern-flavored noodle dishes, along with stir-fry rice dishes and soups. The Specialties of Noodles at $5.95 each are a good deal, with the peanut curry noodles being particularly tasty. Banana dishes, or the special entrées, range from $5.95 to $8.25. Nice deck here, for those few months of the year you can enjoy it.

Open daily. BYOB. Patio dining. Street parking difficult.

HI RICKY ASIAN NOODLE SHOP & SATAY BAR

1852 W. NORTH AVENUE, (773) 276-8300
3737 N. SOUTHPORT AVENUE, (773) 388-0000
941 W. RANDOLPH STREET, (312) 491-9100

Cloning that successful Penny's formula, Hi Ricky is a bright, loft-like storefront serving a variety of Asian cuisines at practically native prices, with nothing priced above $10.95 and most entrées being priced from $5.95 to $7.95. The noodles from the wok, tossed noodle, rice, soup, and curry dishes feature representatives from all of the Asian tigers—China, Thailand, Vietnam, Singapore, Malaysia, Indonesia, and even Burma. The Vietnamese bun thit or noodle grill ($7.95)—thin rice noodles, crispy spring roll, sliced grilled beef, crushed peanuts, mint, cilantro, and sprouts in a mild spicy sauce—is particularly tasty, as is the Burmese fried rice ($6.95)—spicy curry fried rice with onion, garlic, a lot of lemongrass, and a choice of meat. Thai iced coffee or tea, or soothing jasmine tea washes everything down. Free happy-hour munchies are served on Fridays and Saturdays from 5 P.M. to 7 P.M.
Open daily. Full bar. Street parking difficult at all locations.

PACIFIC CAFÉ

1619 N. DAMEN AVENUE, (773) PACIFIC

Located in a tiny converted produce market, Pacific Café opened during Around the Coyote 1995, sold out everything in the restaurant, and hasn't looked back since. Pacific Café offers Thai, Japanese, and Vietnamese dishes. There's a full sushi menu, with some innovative options, along with representative appetizers from all three cuisines. A long list of noodle dishes are priced mostly at $7.25 and under. Thai entrées, primarily curries, are $6.95 and under. There's a half-dozen Vietnamese entrées and many Japanese dishes, priced $5.95 to $10.50. The sushi and sashimi dinners are too expensive, so you have to order sushi by the piece. Service is extremely hospitable, but can be slow since the place only has one overworked sushi chef.
Open daily. Full bar. Parking lot.

PENNY'S NOODLE SHOP

3400 N. SHEFFIELD AVENUE, (773) 281-8222
950 W. DIVERSEY AVENUE, (773) 281-8448
1542 N. DAMEN AVENUE, (773) 394-0100

All three Penny's locations are small and always packed, so be prepared to wait if you want to eat on-site. Just open one of those cold beers you brought, settle in, and join the crowd. Pennies from heaven—this remains the franchise concept for the new millennium. What can you say about a place that consistently delivers a tasty meal for under $6 to packed houses and always serves with a smile? Both the wedge-shaped original location and the newer, more spacious spots are cozy and clean, appealing to scores of less adventurous eaters. Won ton soup, Thai ravioli (a personal favorite), Vietnamese spring rolls, pad Thai, udon noodles in dashi broth, all expertly tweaked for the palate of the less adventurous Chicago eater, are best enjoyed at the counter, because who wants to stand around waiting for a table?

Open daily. BYOB. Sheffield location has sidewalk seating. Street parking difficult.

SUNSHINE CAFÉ

5449 N. CLARK STREET, (773) 334-6214

Japanese noodles and homestyle cooking are featured at this one-room Andersonville storefront with an almost exclusively Japanese crowd. Noodle dishes are all priced $6 and up with Sunshine ramen-cha siu-chicken, kamaboko (Japanese fishcake), egg, shrimp, nori (seaweed), and veggies being the only $6 dish. Non-noodle dinners, priced at $8 and under, are also available and include steak teriyaki ($8), chicken teriyaki ($5.75), tempura ($7), and saba shioyaki, lightly broiled mackerel, for $7. Where else can you get Norwegian salmon, served teriyaki or shioyaki style, for $7?

Closed Tuesdays. BYOB. Street parking available.

VIETNAM LITTLE HOME RESTAURANT

4654 N. DAMEN AVENUE, (773) 275-8360

Tucked away just south of the Ravenswood neighborhood, this two-room storefront with a bright yellow facade serves a wide variety of Vietnamese food (65 dishes) almost all priced $6 and under. Dishes are delicately prepared with a homey touch, making Vietnam Little Home worth the trip off the Argyle Street beaten path. Fifteen noodle dishes are available to choose from. Seafood dishes feature stuffed squid ($5.25) and clay pot stewed fish ($6.95). Interesting starters include crabmeat soup with asparagus and Hanoi beef noodle soup.

Closed Mondays. BYOB. Street parking available.

ALWAYS THAI

1824 W. IRVING PARK ROAD, (773) 929-0100

Imagine my surprise to find one of Chicago's best new restaurants to be a small Thai storefront lurking right in the neighborhood. ("Look what some ink in *Chicago Magazine* can do for business," groused an apparent regular.) Having read that the chef spent years in the kitchen at Arun's, we were expecting big things—albeit at small prices—and we weren't disappointed in the smooth Panang curry with its rich coconutty flavor ($5.95–$6.95, depending on meat). The black fungus mushrooms in the Mixed Mushrooms were plump and tender and, combined with tofu ($5.95), an excellent veggie option. We ordered an extra bowl of rice as a plain culinary canvas to absorb the extra "special black bean sauce" from the Garlic Dish ($5.95–$6.95). Waste not, want not. Our only disappointments were the rather bland Ginger Dish ($5.95–$6.95) and the glutinous chive dumplings ($3.95) that were difficult to pry up in one piece after we'd soaked them in spicy black soy sauce. One of Chicago's best? We're thinking about going back for some moo-ping BBQ pork ($5.50) and giving it a second opinion.

Closed Sundays. Street parking available.

BIG BOWL

159½ W. ERIE STREET, (312) 787-8297
6 E. CEDAR STREET, (312) 640-8888
60 E. OHIO STREET, (312) 951-1888; (312) 951-9888
215 PARKWAY DRIVE, LINCOLNSHIRE, (847) 808-8880
1950 E. HIGGINS ROAD, SCHAUMBURG, (847) 517-8881

Another creation from Lettuce Entertain You, the Big Bowl restaurants offer fast, fresh, Americanized versions of Asian dishes in a stylishly designed Asian environment. They move 'em in and out here, so service can be a bit harried. Food is dependably tasty, prepared without MSG, and served in a smoke-free dining room. The steamed or fried dumplings with various fillings ($4.95, $6.95 combo, check the Big Bowl Web site for a free dumpling coupon, www.bigbowl.com) and kung pao chicken ($8.95) are always a good bet, as is the fresh stir-fry, in nearly 30 different combinations. Fresh ginger ale and naturally sweet red hibiscus iced tea wash everything down nicely. **Street parking difficult at most city locations.**

Noodle Feast
Argyle Street

INNOVATIVE EATERIES FOR THE FINANCIALLY FINICKY PALATE

Argyle Street, or more broadly, the area formed roughly by the square of Argyle to the north, Sheridan to the east, Lawrence to the south, and Broadway to the west, has often been called "New Chinatown," although "Little Saigon" would probably be more appropriate. Even though some Chinese and other Asian establishments do exist, the area is primarily Vietnamese with a smattering of other Southeast Asian cultures. Check out **Hoang Mai**, 5020 N. Sheridan Avenue, (773) 561-3700, a spanking-clean Vietnamese/Chinese storefront with 183 items on the menu priced from $3.95 to $8.95. Roast quail, shrimp wrapped in sugar cane with vegetables, and eel with coconut curry in a clay pot are all good bets. Traditional breakfast of steamed rice cakes with shrimp or pork fillings ($2.95) is an option if you're up early. Another storefront serving Vietnamese and Chinese, **Song Huong**, 5424 N. Broadway, (773) 271-6702, also has an extensive menu with more than 100 options, including coconut curries with frog legs or venison and stuffed Vietnamese pancakes. Finish it all off with a "sweetie," a kind of Vietnamese flurry made with mung beans, red beans, coconut milk, and crushed ice. Both Hoang Mai and Song Huong will set you back a "fork and knife."

Marked by a startling façade of turquoise and coral accompanied by two golden lions guarding the front door, **Nhu Hoa**, 1020 W. Argyle Avenue, (773) 878-0618, Chicago's Laotian option, also serves Vietnamese and a couple of Cambodian dishes and will only cost you a "fork." Laotian dishes are similar to other Southeast Asian meals but are marked by the use of sticky rice and other culinary nuances. With more than 200 options on the menu, there's a lot of opportunity to conduct your own taste test.

Enter the Dragon

Get Some Dim Sum in Chinatown

The first Chinese immigrants arrived in Chicago in the 1870s, long after other Chinese communities had been formed in California, Oregon, and Washington. The construction of the transcontinental railroad offered jobs to newly arrived Chinese, who made up nearly 80 percent of its workforce, and it wasn't until the last track was laid in 1869 and work came to an end that the Chinese population began to disperse to the Midwest and East. Driven by a lack of jobs and anti-Chinese sentiment on the West Coast, Mr. T. C. Moy, the first Chinese to move to Chicago, arrived in 1878 and was soon joined by over 80 of his friends and relatives in his first year of residence. The city's Chinese population grew steadily, and by 1890, there were 567 Chinese in the city. They took up low-profile occupations, mainly opening laundromats and restaurants. By 1900, there were 430 laundromats and 167 restaurants operated by Chinese.

The first Chinese community was built around Van Buren and Clark. In 1905, increasing hostility, rising rents, and gang infighting within the community forced half of the city's Chinese to relocate south to Cermak and Wentworth, an Italian and Croatian neighborhood. The community's move was made possible by a series of 10-year leases on buildings that were secretly contracted for by members of On Leong Tong, the Chinese Businessmen's Association, through the "H. O. Stone Company."

Chinatown experienced ongoing housing problems. Housing was cut in half by the extension of Cermak for the 1933 World's Fair and then halved again by the construction of the Dan Ryan and Stevenson Expressways in the 1950s.

The largest influx of Chinese came in 1950s and 1960s, when many Mandarin-speaking Chinese professionals took advantage of more lenient immigration laws to leave the Communist mainland and join the primarily Cantonese-speaking communities in North America. Improved Chinese-American relations also helped spur immigration. During these two decades, the Chinese population in Chicago doubled from 7,000 to 14,000. By 1970, Chicago had the fourth-largest Chinese population in America.

The influx of Chinese to Chicago in the 1960s aggravated Chinatown's space problem, which was squeezed further in 1969 by continued demolition for the city's transportation projects. In 1970, a portion of the Chinese community sought room in a new North Chinatown, which was established in the Argyle and Broadway area.

South Chinatown today has some 9,000 residents squeezed into eight blocks, bounded by Cermak Road, the railway embankment, Wentworth Avenue on the east, and 26th Street on the south. It's a one-industry town, one that is dependent on the restaurant business. Chinese restaurants have been popular since the 1920s, when eggrolls and won ton soup were introduced into Chicago's Chinese eateries. Historic **Won Kow Restaurant** was opened in 1927, reputably making it Chinatown's oldest Chinese restaurant. Located on the second floor of the building that can only be reached by climbing a set of steep stairs, Cantonese Won Kow serves dim sum every day from 9 A.M. to 3 P.M. and has catered to some of the same patrons for decades.

Some of the neighborhood's most popular destinations include **Emperor's Choice**, a small storefront with nearly 150 dishes, including excellent seafood, and **Phoenix** for dim sum. Phoenix, a relatively new and modern addition to the community for eaters who prize amenities over adventure, starts serving dim sum daily at 8 A.M. and does not knock off for the regular menu until 3 P.M.

Three Happiness Chinese Restaurant No. 3, another longtime Chinatown culinary anchor, has been serving Cantonese specialties for twenty-some years. Located just steps from the El stop, it's a local favorite for Loop workers grabbing dim sum at lunch. Other well-known options include **Sixty-Five Restaurant**, familiar to many downtowners because of its sister location on Michigan, and **Royal Pacific Restaurant**, known for its tropical drinks and great view of Wentworth Avenue and the On Leong Merchant's Building from its second-floor window seats.

Today, there are some 40 restaurants in South Chinatown, offering numerous opportunities to explore to the wee hours. Try visiting during the annual Autumn Moon Festival, held in September each year. Featuring dragon and lion dances, the annual Autumn Moon Festival is the Chinese Thanksgiving and celebrates both the beginning of the harvest season and the autumn equinox, when nights become longer and the moon, "the Queen of Heaven," waxes stronger. Celebrants enjoy moon cakes, round pastries that were used to hide messages in the fourteenth century as the Chinese strove to overthrow their Mongol conquerors, but today are stuffed with sweet mashed lotus seeds or red bean filling.

EMPEROR'S CHOICE
2238 S. WENTWORTH AVENUE, (312) 225-8800
Daily 11:45 A.M.–1 A.M. (Sunday until midnight). All major
credit cards.

PHOENIX
2131 S. ARCHER AVENUE, (312) 328-0848
Daily 8 A.M.–3 P.M. for dim sum, 3 P.M.–1 A.M. regular menu.
All major credit cards.

ROYAL PACIFIC RESTAURANT
2217 S. WENTWORTH AVENUE, (312) 842-4444
Monday–Thursday 2 P.M.–1 A.M., Friday–Saturday Noon–2 A.M.,
Sunday Noon–1 A.M. No dim sum. All major credit cards.

SIXTY-FIVE
2409 S. WENTWORTH AVENUE, (312) 842-6500
Open daily 11 A.M.–Midnight. All major credit cards.

THREE HAPPINESS CHINESE RESTAURANT NO. 3
2130 S. WENTWORTH AVENUE, (312) 791-1228
Monday through Saturday 10 A.M.–11 P.M., Sunday 10 A.M.–
10 P.M.

WON KOW RESTAURANT
2237 S. WENTWORTH AVENUE, (312) 842-7500
Sunday through Thursday 9 A.M.–11 P.M., Friday and
Saturday, 9 A.M.–Midnight. All major credit cards.

Italy on $20 a Day

TRATTORIAS WE CAN AFFORD
... LET'S GO!

Contrary to popular belief, Marco Polo did not bring spaghetti back from China and then introduce pasta to Italy and the rest of Europe. The Western world has long had its own tradition of noodlemaking. The Tomba dei Rilievi, an Etruscan tomb in Italy dating from the fourth century B.C., was found to contain the rudimentary equipment for making pasta—the wooden board, the rolling pin, and the fluted cutting wheel—still used today in Romagna, Lazio, Abbruzzo, and other regions of Italy. Dry pasta is still made from water and hard durum wheat, the same wheat that was used to make pasta in ancient Roman times.

> "Everything you see I owe to spaghetti."
>
> —Sophia Loren

The famous Romans, Horace (65–8 B.C.) and Cicero (106–43 B.C.), both were known to be fans of *lagunam*, the Latin term for lasagna. It is said that Cicero loved to eat thin strips of pasta, cooked in fat broth, and garnished with cheese, pepper, saffron, and cinnamon. Italian history and pasta have been made together. The natives of Bologna (home of the sauce) also invented tagliatelle, which was created to immortalize Lucrezia Borgia's long golden tresses. Today, pasta has become so ingrained in the Italian lifestyle that husbands phone home before they leave work and tell their wives, "Butta la pasta!" Literally, "Throw in the pasta!" In other words, "Hey, I'm on my way home, and dinner better be ready when I get there."

The wave of Southern Italians that emigrated to the United States beginning in the 1920s established spaghetti as Americans' favorite pasta. During Prohibition, the only places where a glass of wine could be drunk legally were Italian speakeasies—all of which served spaghetti.

Spaghetti was the dish Southern Italians thought of first; it was cheap, quick, and easy even for the most inexperienced cook to prepare. Pastas, spaghetti, and the some 600 other noodle shapes remain popular—in fact, Italian endures as the most popular ethnic food in the country. The average American now eats nearly 20 pounds of pasta every year. Pasta is loved not only because it's a complex carbohydrate that supplies six of the eight essential amino acids, but because eating it releases serotonin, a brain chemical that tells your body to feel relaxed and calm. Now that's what you call using your noodle.

Editor's Note: Price ratings in this chapter are typically based on the prices for pasta dishes, not for "secondi"—meat, chicken, fish, and seafood entrées.

ANNA MARIA'S PASTERIA

3953 N. BROADWAY, (773) 929-6363

If you've never heard of Anna Maria's Pasteria, that tiny jewel of Lakeview eateries, stay ignorant—we already have to wait long enough to get a table here. Since this small, unpretentious storefront opened in 1989, crowds of BYOB-toting diners have been driving the prices steadily higher. The restaurant itself reflects its success. When it first opened, Anna Maria's was a tiny, nondescript storefront with unbeatable homemade pasta and the best tiramisu in town. The restaurant then expanded south into the space next door and added another dining room and bar. Since taking over the storefront to the north formerly occupied by a pawn shop, Anna Maria's has not only added a third room, but has also totally redecorated. It now has three fancy rooms that glow with warm golden walls accented with wine-colored drapes and tablecloths. Few would expect to find this luxury at Irving Park and Broadway. Specials are always excellent, and pasta dishes ($7.95–$13.95, $16.95 with seafood) like the rotola aurora (vegetarian rolled pasta with ricotta cheese and spinach in a creamy tomato sauce, $11.95) are all great options. If you can splurge, don't miss the truly magnificent Veal marsala ($16.95), and save enough room for dessert. This is a place that pays homage to tiramisu.

Open daily. Wine and beer. Street parking difficult.

BAR LOUIE
226 W. CHICAGO AVENUE, (312) 337-3313
1704 N. DAMEN AVENUE, (773) 645-7500
3545 N. CLARK STREET, (773) 296-2500
123 N. HALSTED STREET, (312) 207-0500
1800 N. LINCOLN AVENUE, (312) 337-9800
47 W. POLK STREET, (312) 347-0000
1321 W. TAYLOR STREET, (312) 633-9393
1520 SHERMAN AVENUE, EVANSTON, (847) 733-8300
913 N. MILWAUKEE AVENUE, WHEELING, (847) 279-1199

Simply one of the best watering holes in the city (and suburbs), Bar Louie clones have popped up all over the place, including the South and West Loop, Taylor Street, Wrigleyville, and even Wheeling. And why not? Bar Louie has an abundant menu loaded with Italian pub selections, including pastas, pizzas, insalate (salads), antipasti (appetizers), and panini (sandwiches) all priced at $10.95 and under. Salads are meal-sized; the antipasto ($5.95) and the chicken and goat cheese salads ($6.50) are both highly recommended. Sandwiches should yield more than enough for now and later. Try the muffaletta—salami, smoked ham, and provolone with Sicilian olive mix ($4.95). Decorated with colorful tiles and bright murals, Bar Louie is a good place to relax in an atmosphere of soothing culture and fine Mediterranean food.

Open daily. Full bar. Difficult street parking for city locations.

CUCINA BELLA

543 W. DIVERSEY PARKWAY, (773) 868-1119
1612 N. SEDGWICK AVENUE, (312) 274-1119

Locals rave about Cucina Bella's "authentic Italian comfort foods" and reasonable prices, but beware—you can't buy a parking spot in these neighborhoods. Although some are higher priced, plenty of pastas are available for $4.95 (the spaghetti simpatico) to $10.95. Among the secondi, only the pollo romano ($10.50) and the torta rustica ($9.50), a Tuscan-style pot pie with sausage, vegetables, and tomato cream sauce, are the right price. The place has its own cookbook, and for $35, you can sit in the kitchen and sample the whole menu.
Open daily. Full bar. Street parking difficult.

BICE GRILL

158 E. ONTARIO STREET, (312) 664-1474

With prices that are more Chef-Boy-Ar-Dee than Bice, Bice Grill is the low-budget next-door neighbor to one of Michigan Avenue's longtime see-and-be-seen spots. Self-described as a "high-end cafeteria," Bice Grill offers an ever-changing selection of salads, soups, panini caldi (warm sandwiches), pizzas, pastas, and made-to-order salads. Pasta is the real deal, with a "small" serving from the daily selection of three pastas—you can mix and match—running only $4.50. On one visit, we opted for a daily double of orechiette with broccoli and sun-dried tomatoes, where the dried tomatoes were rather overwhelmed by wet tomato sauce, and paella, with big chunks of chicken but no noticeable seafood. Tasty, but remember, you typically get what you pay for. Other options are good-sized salads (grilled chicken optional) and hot sandwiches served with a cup of red sauce for dipping. A friend, a B-Grill regular, mourned the loss of the departed artiste who made the Grill's no-longer-available calzones, but found solace in a hefty slice of grilled chicken pizza. Note, dibs on that fancy tablecloth-clad spot outside the front door belong to the fancy tablecloth diners at Bice next door.
Open daily. Street parking difficult.

THE PASTA BOWL

2434 N. CLARK STREET, (773) 525-BOWL

A mini version of Pasta Palazzo, the Pasta Bowl serves fresh-made pastas, panini sandwiches, and "bona vita" ("good life" food prepared without oil, butter, or cheese), all for $3.95 to $6.50. "B.V." dishes include bow ties with chicken and grilled veggies, spaghetti primavera, and linguine with bay scallops, all of which are in a marinara sauce. The fresh-made pastas range from fettucine alfredo to ravioli, tortellini, and gnocchi in a choice of sauce, including rosemary gorgonzola for those who like it rich at a cheap price.

Open daily. No alcohol. Street parking difficult.

POMPEI LITTLE ITALY

2955 N. SHEFFIELD AVENUE, (773) 325-1900

The north branch of a Taylor Street institution established in 1909, Pompei Little Italy is a cafeteria-style Italian eatery that serves handmade pasta, handmade pizza, and Pompei "strudels." Pasta ($4.95–$7.95) is made daily and includes spaghetti with homemade meatballs and three kinds of ravioli— spicy sausage, herb chicken, and vegetarian. Eleven different versions of strudels, including the poor boy, turkey stuffing, and steak fajita, are served by the slice ($3.25–$3.50) or in small ($14–$15, serves 4–6) or large versions ($25–$29, serves 8–12). Nearly two dozen different pan or stuffed pizzas are served by the slice, half tray (serves 4–6), or full tray (serves 8–12). No surprise given the location, type of food, and prices, Pompei Little Italy attracts a young college crowd.

Open daily. No alcohol.

CLUB LAGO

331 W. SUPERIOR STREET, (312) 337-9444

Club Lago is where the Corleone family would eat if they lived in Chicago. An old-time, family-owned Italian eatery and bar opened in 1942 in the heart of chic River North, Club Lago's menu is the "full cucina Toscana."

Entrées vary depending on the day (fish is only available on the weekends), but there's always a lot of red sauce. Pastas range from $7 to $9, while veals, the most expensive entrées on the menu, are $12.75 to $13.75. The kitchen will make almost anything you want, and a half-dozen different omelets on the menu supplement the traditional Italian, for those who prefer something lighter. If you're looking for River North swank or a smoke-free environment, this is not your place.

Closed Sunday. Full bar. Street parking available.

• •

Mucho Mange   Taylor Street

INNOVATIVE EATERIES
FOR THE FINANCIALLY
FINICKY PALATE

Just south of the University of Illinois–Chicago's campus is Taylor Street, the heart of Little Italy and southern Italian–style dining. Lining Taylor from Morgan to Ashland are numerous Italian eateries, most far more expensive than the neighborhood's location and general appearance merit. There are, however, some reasonable options (made even more inexpensive if you stick with pasta or chicken). Skip the long waits at the Rosebud, skip trendy Tuscany, and try some of the lesser-known places. Anchoring the neighborhood is **Tufano's Vernon Park Tap**, (1073 W. Vernon Park Place, (312) 733-3393.) For more than 60 years, diners have been heading for the room in back of the bar where the blackboard lists the daily selections, priced $6 to $12. Pastas are served with red or white sauce, and meatballs and sausage are extra. There's a fish special on Fridays. Also, check out **RoSal's Cucina**, (1154 W. Taylor Street, (312) 243-2357.) Homemade pasta ranges from $5.95 to $9.50. Daily specials feature dishes such as spinach ravioli with Gorgonzola ($8.95). **Gennaro's**, (1352 W. Taylor Street, (312) 243-1035,) where Mama Gennaro has been making homemade pasta for more than 40 years, also has reasonable prices. If you're looking to downscale, try **Little Joe's Circle Lounge**, (1041 W. Taylor Street, (312) 829-5888,) where you can get spaghetti or mostaccioli with soup or salad for $5.75 and chase it down with a $3 pitcher of beer. Or, if you're only comfortable with the familiar, **Leona's**, (1419 W. Taylor Street, (312) 850-2222,) is a cozy addition with an outdoor patio. If you just want to grab a quick meal, head for the intersection of Taylor and Aberdeen (1100 West) where you can get a slice of pizza at **Little Gusto** or a sandwich at **Al's #1 Italian Beef**, (1079 W. Taylor Street, (312) 226-4017); open until 1 A.M., there are plenty of police cars in this parking lot. Finish off this succulent repast with a frozen lemonade across the street at **Mario's Italian Lemonade** (closed in the winter).

Penne Wise

Find a Fair Deal on Pasta

My good friend Susan once said that the one kind of food she refuses to pay a lot of money to go out for is pasta, because it's the one dish she should be able to throw in a pot and boil herself. Don't get me wrong, I love pasta, but my friend is right. Pasta should be a no-brainer. You pick plain noodles— long and skinny or short and curly or stuffed—toss them into a bubbling cauldron until pliable, and then swim them in a, preferably, cholesterol-rich cream sauce. What could be simpler? Unless you're incompetent and cook things to mush, there's no reason to pay $15.95 for a plate of farfalle pomodoro, high-priced speak for bowtie pasta with tomato sauce.

PASTA PALAZZO, 1966 N. Halsted St., (773) 248-1400, is open daily and serves beer and wine by the glass, all priced under $4. Cash only. There's an ATM across the street, but you probably won't need it with the prices here.

So, isn't it refreshing to find **Pasta Palazzo**? Finally, an Italian eatery that doesn't pretend to take us to the Tuscan countryside at downtown Rome prices. Pasta Palazzo doesn't even aspire to the pretenses that cloak the trattorias that populate our city. Billing itself as a "gourmet pasta diner," Pasta Palazzo is a change of pace that delivers hearty, tasty fare to satisfy your appetite while leaving you lire to spare.

A cozy slice of a restaurant, Pasta Palazzo skips the wine jugs and grape leaves that deck so many of the city's Italian establishments for lengthy tables that have that clean and lean look of Milan. Walls are illuminated with a bright mosaic of broken ceramic tile, and colorful pictures extend the impression of warmth where the Crayola-hued tiles leave off. The narrow interior is dominated by a counter that runs the length of the restaurant.

Now I am quite partial to counters, especially ones that have chairs with back rests. At the counter, you get to see what's going on, blend with the regulars, strike up a discussion with the stranger next to you. It's a comfort seat. At Pasta Palazzo, the counter treats you to all the usual counter benefits, along with the opportunity to observe short-order Italian. Whoever suspected chicken could be efficiently grilled up with sundried tomatoes, cream, and mushrooms like a slider waiting to be flipped on a bun? That haughty porcini mushrooms would consent to be shoved around by an industrial-strength spatula that's more often seen pushing chopped onions destined for the common Italian sausage? Or have we been fooled all along, and, in the depths of our city's most aristocratic Italian kitchens sporting pasta prices that are truly royal, is sauté really only French for grill?

Although prepared simply, Pasta Palazzo's dishes offer as much zest as any other local trattorias. Pastas include handmade options (gnocchi, tortellini, and ravioli with a choice of sauces) and "healthy" alternatives prepared without oil, butter, or cheese. The conchigliette Gorgonzola, small shells with spinach, gorgonzola cheese, tomato, and cream, is particularly good for those who don't care about their arteries. Although the various risottos served periodically as specials are tasty, they can be a little chewy, since it's tough to grill up a dish that's supposed to simmer endlessly. It's particularly refreshing to see polenta offered for a reasonable $5. A selection of panini—a.k.a. sandwiches—are also available, including "Vegetariano 1" and "Vegetariano 2."

So the next time your stomach's thinking you should treat yourself like Caesar, but your wallet's reality is Chef Boy-Ar-Dee, don't hesitate to think pasta—Pasta Palazzo.

That's Italian

The Way to the Stomach Is Through the Heart of Italy

On the South Side of Chicago is a gentrifying part of town, and if you go down there, you better just be aware of a man named Franco Gamberale.

Chef Franco is the owner of **La Fontanella**, a restaurant opened in 1971 by his Aunt Franca and Uncle Guido that he took over in 1985 when they moved back to Italy. According to Franco, people flock from all over, from the North Side, the suburbs, even Michigan and Indiana—after all, they're only an hour away, he says—to savor La Fontanella's specialties, including homemade pasta, chicken vesuvio, stuffed bragiole, a thin steak stuffed with bread crumbs, cheese, prosciutto, garlic, and spices and baked in tomato sauce, and other Northern Italian favorites that distinguish the Heart of Chicago.

Chicago has two Italys, two traditional Italian neighborhoods that welcomed immigrants in the mid- to late 1800s. Although some may know the Little Italy neighborhood better, the Tri-Taylor District centered around Taylor Street that is the home to Southern and Sicilian Italians, Heart of Italy, home to Northern Italians, was established first.

The Heart of Italy neighborhood around 24th Place and Oakley Avenue was once inhabited by thousands of Northern Italian immigrants, the first wave of which emigrated in the late nineteenth century from the Tuscany region. They were joined by a second group of immigrants after World War II, primarily from Piedmont. Originally attracted to factory jobs, like those at McCormick Reaper Works on Blue Island Avenue, many opened shops and restaurants to serve the neighborhood.

Bordered by Blue Island, Cermak, Western, and Leavitt, Heart of Italy is in the 25th Ward and, technically, in the Pilsen neighborhood. "Don't say we're part of Pilsen," requests Roger Wroblewski, who grew up in the neighborhood and, when not performing his civic duties as an aldermanic aid, runs **Ignotz Ristorante**. "We're separate from Pilsen," explains Wroblewski. "Heart of Italy is its own neighborhood between Pilsen on the east, Little Village on the west, McKinley Park to the south, and Tri-Taylor to the north."

Wroblewski was part of the ward's planning committee that oversaw a complete overhaul and streetscaping of Oakley Avenue, now renamed "Vito Marzullo Avenue" after the late 25th Ward alderman, as part of Chicago's "Neighborhoods Alive" program. Heart of Italy's newly refurbished streets and sidewalks are also celebrated at mid-June's annual Taste of the Heart of Italy, where hungry festival-goers line up at Ignotz' tent for the restaurant's specialties, including stuffed gnocchi and vodka rigatoni.

Like many of Heart of Italy's establishments, Ignotz is a family affair. Wroblewski cites another crowd favorite, Chicken à la Tippi, which was named by his cousin Frank after his father, "who liked to tiptoe around." The chicken is dipped in egg batter and cooked with parmesan, basil, lemon, and wine and served with a side of pasta. It's best finished off with apple ravioli, a dessert that's another specialty of the house.

The neighborhood's other eateries, including **Il Vicinato**, **Bacchanalia**, **Bruna's Ristorante**, and **Miceli's Deli**, also participate in the street festival and regularly play host to their own crowds. Those who graze at Il Vicinato's booth choose from meatballs, risotto, or Pasta Roger, a cream sauce–laden concoction of pasta with alfredo sauce, spinach, and peas. As owner Jim Naccarato tells it, Pasta Roger was invented over 17 years ago when "some guy named Roger walked into the restaurant and described the dish he wanted." The kitchen obligingly put it together, and it's been a specialty of the house ever since.

Naccarato takes credit for running the first Taste of the Heart of Italy in 1990. As many as 25,000 people attend the festival each year, and the crowds are typical of the area's resurgence. "The neighborhood has really started to turn around," observes Naccarato. "It's all being driven by word-of-mouth, but more and more North Siders are coming down here to eat and even moving here. It's beginning to get a little yuppie-ish, but I guess that's OK."

BACCHANALIA
2413 S. OAKLEY BOULEVARD, (773) 254-6555

BRUNA'S RISTORANTE
2424 S. OAKLEY BOULEVARD, (773) 254-5550

IGNOTZ RISTORANTE
2421 S. OAKLEY BOULEVARD, (773) 579-0300

IL VICINATO RISTORANTE
2435 S. WESTERN AVENUE, (773) 927-5406

LA FONTANELLA
2414 S. OAKLEY BOULEVARD, (773) 927-5249

MICELI'S DELI
2448 S. OAKLEY BOULEVARD, (773) 847-6873

No Raw Deal

SUSHI SAVINGS

" **I** 'd like to be . . . under the sea . . . in an octopus's garden . . . in the shade . . ." In Japan, sushi is everyday food. You can find it everywhere, even in fast-food establishments and saran-wrapped in the refrigerated section of convenience stores. In Chicago, you can find an abundance of sushi—particularly cheap sushi—in Lakeview between Belmont and Addison. Peppering Clark Street are numerous storefronts with sushi bars and sit-down tables that will satisfy your yen for bargain-priced varieties of seaweeded, rice-balled sushi delights.

Sounds kind of fishy to me. Sushi, which has more than a thousand years of history and tradition behind it, was developed by the Japanese who, using salt and rice to preserve varieties of fish, pressed the fish into thin layers until it fermented. But sushi has evolved beyond just fish to encompass a wide variety of seafood and vegetables. If the thought of raw fish doesn't float your boat, there are plenty of options available in potentially more palatable shrimp, crab, and other crustaceans. The ubiquitous California roll is, frankly, fishless. Or, you may opt to go the straight vegetarian route and order the common kappa maki (cucumber roll) or various other vegetable-only sushis.

> **"I'm interested in the sushi options for the timid."**
>
> —Sue T.,
> no friend of fish

You don't have to be a *sushi tzu* (sushi expert) to know your way around the bar. Here are some sushi sayings that'll help even a novice order from the *itamae-san* (sushi chef) with the assurance of a veteran: There are several common forms of sushi. **Nigiri** sushi are oblong bars of shari (vinegared rice) topped with a dab of wasabi (green horseradish) and a slice of fish or seafood. **Maki** are long, rolled tubes of rice and filling cut into several pieces. **Temaki** are handrolls that look like cone-shaped seaweed bouquets.

Your sushi is usually accompanied by several condiments. **Gari** is the pickled ginger that cleanses your palate between varieties. **Wasabi** is the green horseradish that masks the fishy taste by temporarily paralyzing your palate. **Murasaki** is the soy sauce you use for dipping. **Agari** is the steaming green tea that's drunk in great quantities to refresh the palate and rinse away fish fats that stay on the tongue.

Many restaurants offer a **moriawase plate**, or a mixed menu of sushi, which is a very economical way to try a number of sushi pieces. Sushi commonly found in this combination includes **kappa** and **tekka maki** (cucumber and tuna rolls), **maguro** (tuna), **sake** (salmon), **hamachi** (yellowtail), **ebi** (shrimp), **saba** (mackerel), **tako** (octopus), **tamago** (egg), and **uni** (sea urchin).

You don't have to be able to maneuver the *ohaji* (chopsticks) to eat this sometimes slippery dish. Sushi is finger food. Just pick the piece up, flip it over, dip it in the soy sauce fish side down, and put it in your mouth so that the fish hits your taste buds. *Irrasshai!* (Welcome to the sushi bar!)

Editor's Note: This chapter's price ratings were arrived at by looking at the whole menu, not just the sushi selections. We encourage you to mix and match sushi with other menu options.

SHIROI HANA
3242 N. CLARK STREET, (773) 477-1652

NOHANA
3136 N. BROADWAY, (773) 528-1902

Incredibly popular and crowded at all times, these two related restaurants set the standard for value sushi. Not only do the 'Hanas have the best sushi prices in town, but both serve very fresh fish—the proprietor was in the wholesale fish business. Both restaurants have similar menus. Both offer a Sushi Deluxe special of nine pieces and one maki roll for $7.95 (Shiroi Hana's is available daily, Nohana's only Monday through Thursday). Nohana also has a Nohana's Choice for $6.95; Shiroi Hana has a Sushi Regular, six pieces and one roll for $6.50. Both restaurants offer excellent "Dinner Box" combinations that allow you to sample tempura or teriyaki (beef, chicken, or tuna) with one California roll, three additional pieces of sushi (tuna, salmon, and shrimp), suomono (seafood and cucumber with vinegar sauce), and soup. Combinations range from $8.75 to $9.25. If you're hanging out around lunchtime, you can get a great deal on a "Lunch Box" at either restaurant—a choice of chicken or tuna teriyaki, fish cutlets, or tempura, accompanied by a California roll, tekka maki (tuna roll), soup, and salad. All lunch boxes range from $5.95 to $6.95.

Both open daily. Full bars. Street parking difficult.

WRAP 'N GO

919 W. BELMONT, (773) 929-9333

Billed as Japanese fast food and grocery, Wrap 'N Go is a tiny storefront with a handful of small tables that serves bargain basement–priced sushi in bargain basement surroundings. One wall is split between shelves offering dry goods and a cooler with prepared food; another wall is completely taken up with a self-serve counter to order freshly prepared sushi, wraps, soup, and a variety of bowls composed of chicken, beef, veggies, salmon, or eel over rice and billed as "the ultimate in healthy eating." Sushi is primarily rolls, except for the nigiri combo, which offers seven pieces, a tuna roll, and miso soup for $7.95. The raw fish roll with a nine-piece tuna roll and nine-piece salmon roll is a good deal at $5.95 ($1 extra for spicy sauce), as is the veggie roll combo, a cucumber roll, carrot roll, and shiitake mushroom roll for a total of eighteen pieces for $5.

Open daily. No alcohol.

AKAI HANA

848 N. STATE STREET, (312) 787-4881

Just west of the Magnificent Mile, casual Akai Hana offers a welcome rest stop after a grueling day of shopping, and lots of small tables and a good-sized sushi bar make it easy to get a seat and hold on to it until the feet recover. Akai Hana also provides surprisingly cheap (and fresh) sushi to a neighborhood used to paying for location. Monday through Friday, the Sushi Regular, six pieces and a roll, soup, and ice cream, is $10. There are also plenty of vegetarian options, including a succulent sweet potato tempura roll. A recent revamp of the menu to add more entrée options to sushi has left lunch a better deal than dinner, which is not as much of a bargain as it used to be. You may have to track down a server when the place gets crowded.

Open daily. Wine and beer. Street parking difficult.

TOKYO MARINA

5058–60 N. CLARK STREET, (773) 878-2900

Looking much like it spent its former life as a Roy Rogers, Tokyo Marina brings quality sushi to the Andersonville area in spite of its low-budget, fast-food decor. Tokyo Marina offers its own interesting twists on the sushi theme designed to appeal to the locals, including Windy City maki—battered nori maki deep-fried with flounder/hirame, cucumber, avocado, and Japanese mayo ($5.75), and sloppy Tokyo Marinara maki with a fried shrimp tucked inside ($5.75). All dinners start with a free appetizer, and a standard eight-piece Sushi Combo is $10. An extensive menu offers a good choice of tempura dishes, casseroles, donburi (bowl dishes), and udon (noodle dishes) generally priced between $6 and $8. Wash it all down with Japanese beer on draft or in the bottle. If you're with a partner and budget's not an issue, try the Tokyo Marinara Love Boat, at $35.50, "a dining pleasure designed for two."

Open daily. Wine and beer. Street parking available.

SANKO'S

3485 N. CLARK STREET, (773) 528-1930

If you can't stand the crowds at Matsuya a couple doors south, head up the street to Sanko. A thin series of rooms, Sanko lures in Cub fans looking for exotic adventure with its weekend karaoke in the back room. Yes, every Thursday and Friday night, you can belt out "Sanko's pop hits" from 9 P.M. to 1 A.M., Muzak at its best. If you need to build up energy for singing, you can order from a large selection of sushi that graciously categorizes offerings for the sushi novice, for example, raw, boiled, or broiled; vegetable; makimono (rolled and cut); nigiri (seafood on hand-pressed sushi roll); etc.—you won't get lost here. As with other local Japanese restaurants, Sanko has sushi specials with local appeal. Here, it's the Cub maki (broiled salmon, cream cheese, scallion, and avocado, $5.25). Sanko also serves one of the most expensive maki rolls around, the Spider, an eight-piece roll of fried soft-shell crab, cucumber, scallion, and masago, $9.75.

Open daily. Full bar. Street parking difficult.

KOTOBUKI

5547 N. CLARK STREET, (773) 275-6588

Like Akasaka, Kotobuki is pricier with more elaborate food than the standard Wrigleyville cheap sushi. This storefront located on the northern edge of Andersonville stands out with its aesthetically pleasing and innovative presentation. An excellent example is the futomaki, or big roll. Kotobuki's version of this sushi bar mainstay is an eight-piece, spinach-stuffed roll with a sweet walnut sauce ($6.95). It's more than enough for a meal. The interesting bargain here is the $17 "Temaki for 2," a platter with all the fixin's for two adventurous diners to roll their own handrolls. For dessert, in addition to the standard green tea ice cream, Kotobuki also offers ginger and red bean ice cream.

Closed Monday. Full bar. Street parking difficult.

MATSUYA

3469 N. CLARK STREET, (773) 248-2677

Matsuya has long set the standard in Lakeview for good, cheap Japanese. This popular two-room storefront almost always has a wait to sit down. A large selection of rolled makimono and molded, Osaka-style oshi-sushi is supplemented with a variety of cone-shaped temaki handrolls. Sushi combos start at $7.75 for the temaki assortment. Ginger ice cream is sometimes available.

Open daily. Full bar. Street parking difficult.

NEW TOKYO

3139 N. BROADWAY, (773) 248-1193

Three different combos are priced $9.95 and under, and all of the other entrées are $6.95 and under and served with rice and salad. This small corner Lakeview storefront is one of the city's Japanese values with its "authentic Japanese charbroiled teriyaki at fast-food prices!"

Open daily. No alcohol. Street parking difficult.

KYOTO JAPANESE RESTAURANT

2534 N. LINCOLN AVENUE, (773) 477-2788

For DePaul students and Lincoln Park yuppies who don't mind spending a lot of money on sushi, Kyoto is a convenient option just up the street from the Three Penny Theater, where you can offset what you spent on dinner with a budget movie. The cheapest combo here is $9.95 for only six pieces and one roll. If you're not going to venture north of Wrightwood for far less expensive sushi, you might want to stick with the donburi (rice bowls) or udon (noodles), all priced at $6.95 and under.

Closed Monday. Full bar. Street parking difficult.

AKASAKA JAPANESE RESTAURANT

5978 N. LINCOLN AVENUE, (773) 989-1115

No storefront here, Akasaka, located on the northern section of Lincoln Avenue in the land of small motels with neon "Sleep Cheap!" signs from the 1950s, is a full-blown restaurant with plenty of blond wood and screens to make it an appealing option to the no-frills storefronts on Clark. The sushi is excellent—large, tender slices spilling over supporting rice balls with, whoa now, noticeable amounts of wasabi to make things memorable. The cheapest sushi combo is $10.95, and lunch specials start at $6.95. Worth the drive.

Open daily. Full bar. Parking lot.

Sushi Sensations

Dive Into the Raw Fish Rolls at Jia's

Do you ever have a yen for raw fish? Weekly, if not more often, do you get the urge to swim with the sharks and gobble up salmon, mackerel, shrimp, and other chilled and sliced water creatures mounted on oblong beds of rice?

When the siren call of Charlie the Tuna becomes impossible to ignore, just head for the Coast. The Gold Coast, that is. **Jia's**, a bright, airy eatery on the corner of Delaware and State, is the scenester's sushi spot. It's a little treasure where those in the know go. Many bypass the heavy, powerbroker meals found at Gibson's and Carmine's or the frat-boy food and frolicking at Melvin B's and the Hunt Club, and head for the sleek, and inexpensive, option for sushi.

When Jia's is crowded (reservations are strongly recommended on weekends), guests can chill out in the tiny front-room bar for a cocktail. The two dining rooms, set in minimalist fashion, accommodate about 70; the sushi bar, with seating wrapped around it for ample viewing of action from the habachi bar, is ideal for those dining alone or casually. Meanwhile, the sounds of downtempo dance music and rare grooves set the mood for lounging.

Sushi, from sliced maki rolls to individual pieces, or nigiri, is bodaciously big and fresh. Slabs of glistening fish flesh nestle around plump rice balls while chunks of seafood poke out coyly from rolls of seaweed and vegetables. The standard sushi combination ($10.95) offers six individual pieces in combination with the California rolls. A good selection of other sushi combinations is available, but they're $13.95 to $17.95. So choose from the creative maki roll menu. Tasty rolls include the bagel maki (smoked salmon, cream cheese, and scallions, $3.95), dragon maki (filled with unagi, tempura crunch wrapped in avocado, $8.95) and rainbow maki (salmon skin and unagi roll wrapped in assorted fish, $12.95).

JIA'S CHINESE CUISINE & SUSHI BAR, 2 E. Delaware Pl., (312) 642-0626, fax (312) 642-4137, is open daily for lunch and dinner. Full bar, including sake selections. Street parking is difficult; valet parking on the weekends.

If you find yourself to be no fan of raw fish after all, plenty of other Asian options are available, ranging in price from $7.95 to $14.95. We like Jia's crispy chicken, breaded chicken stir-fried with vegetables in a spicy sweet glaze, the kung pao, diced vegetables and peanuts in a spicy Szechwan sauce with your choice of chicken, shrimp, or both, and the Chinese chow fun noodles, wide rice noodles hooked up with shrimp, chicken, or beef. Jia's is open for lunch and serves a Japanese lunch box priced from $7.95 to $12.95.

12

Here's a Pita Advice...

Dolmeh about it. The Middle East, that small sandy stretch on the eastern shores of the Mediterranean, gave rise to three of the world's major religions and, subsequently, a reason for endless office parties in December. Think about what civilization has gained from the Middle East: a lot of religions (Christianity, Judaism, and Islam), a lot of books (*The Source*, *Exodus*), a lot of movies (*The Ten Commandments*, *Ben-Hur*, *Lawrence of Arabia*), and a lot of food.

Oh, I'm hooked on a phyllo . . . and feta and fava and falafel. Due to close proximity and climactic similarities, Middle Eastern and Mediterranean cuisines share a variety of common flavors and ingredients, including olives, chickpeas, eggplant, spinach, bulgur, rice, feta cheese, yogurt, and lamb. Derivations of dishes that originated in the Middle East reach west all the way to the Iberian peninsula and beyond to the American heartland.

> "It is dull, Son of Adam, to drink without eating," said the Queen pleasantly. "What would you like best to eat?"
>
> "Turkish Delight, please, your Majesty," said Edmund.
>
> —C. S. Lewis, *The Lion, the Witch, and the Wardrobe*

Rock the Casbah. Whether you're up in Andersonville or in the Orthodox neighborhood at California and Devon or right down on Michigan, if shawirma is your karma, you're probably no more than a couple blocks from a fresh stuffed pita. So get out there and start sampling—there's ample opportunity to eat your fala-fil!

Hummus a Little Tune...

Cheap Chow Chicago's Guide to 1,001 Middle Eastern Delights

OVERTURE

Baba Ghanoush—classic pita spread. Flame-roasted eggplant, ground and mixed with tahini sauce and spices.

Hummus—cooked and mashed chickpeas mixed with tahini sauce and spices. A staple in coffeehouses all over Chicago.

Moroccan Eggplant—sautéed eggplant slices and chopped onions marinated in a spicy tomato sauce.

Tabouleh—"salad" of chopped parsley, bulgur, diced tomatoes, onions, lemon juice, and olive oil.

INTERMEZZO

Dolmeh—"stuffed food," usually grape leaves, eggplant, zucchini, or peppers stuffed with rice, lentils, spicy meat, etc.

Falafel—the national sandwich of Israel and New York City, ground chickpeas and spices rolled into balls and deep-fried.

Kibbeh—mixture of ground lamb, cracked wheat, and herbs.

Moussaka—casserole made with layers of potato, eggplant, zucchini, cheese, and egg custard topping. Spiced lamb or beef is optional.

Souvlaki and Gyros—Greek shish kebab and Greek cheesesteak. (How do you pronounce "gyros?")

Shawirma—Middle Eastern gyros come in lamb or chicken.

Tsaztziki—yogurt sauce to spread on everything.

FINALE

Baklava—Scheherazade's favorite, 1,001 calories worth of layers of phyllo dough, honey, and nuts.

REZA'S

5255 N. CLARK STREET, (773) 561-1898
432 W. ONTARIO STREET, (312) 664-4500

Reza's is the grande dame of Chicago's Middle Eastern restaurants. A huge, airy, multistory establishment in Andersonville, with a sister location in a former brewery in River North, Reza's has acquired a well-earned reputation for good food at a good value. As Reza's popularity has climbed, so have its prices, but it's still a great budget option. All dinners are multi-course, including a radish and feta appetizer plate, lentil soup, and an entrée. Don't order an appetizer unless you're really a pig. Regardless, you probably won't make it through dessert. Best bet is to squeeze in a sweet, sludgy Turkish coffee. Be sure to try Reza's special chicken, a marinated chicken kebab on dill rice ($7.95), and the stuffed grape leaves (with meat or vegetarian, $7.95). The Vegetarian Sampler ($8.95) is worth stopping by for weekly.

Open daily. Full bar. The River North location has sidewalk seating. Street parking difficult.

HASHALOM

2905 W. DEVON AVENUE, (773) 465-5675

Hashalom offers both price and taste to the hungry crowds that pass up the surrounding Indian restaurants to enjoy Israeli and Moroccan specialties at rock-bottom prices. You'll work hard to get the bill into double digits, and before you do, after numerous courses, you may simply run out of room. Try the Israeli Combination Plate (small, $4; large, $7.50) offering hummus, baba ghanoush, falafel, Israeli salad, warm pita, and, hands-down, the best Moroccan eggplant in the city. The specialty of the house is bourekas, triangles of phyllo dough filled with a choice of feta and onions, feta and spinach, potatoes and onions, or ground beef and pine nuts. Four bucks gets you two bourekas served with sliced tomatoes, tahini sauce, and a sliced brown egg.

Open Monday–Friday. BYOB. Street parking difficult.

COUSINS

2854 N. BROADWAY, (773) 880-0063

5203 N. CLARK STREET, (773) 334-4553

Originally just a small, sit-down storefront, Cousins has since expanded to two fancy locations decorated with rugs and pillows and featuring reliably good "Turkish dining with a vegetarian flair." Cousins offers a wide range of affordable options and a changing list of seasonal specialties. Half of the menu is vegan, except for the use of feta cheese, which can be omitted. Eight different kinds of kabobs and six types of couscous, ranging from vegetable ($7.95) and portabella à la Mediterranean ($8.95 with portabello mushrooms, banana peppers, potatoes, sundried tomatoes, and shallots sautéed in a tomato sauce) to shrimp ($10.75) are available. Try Eggplant Imam Bayeldi—in Turkish, "The Imam fainted"—roasted eggplants stuffed with tomatoes, green peppers, onions, garlic, and pine nuts ($7.95). Or, if you can't decide, try one of the many combination plates (available for appetizers) of couscous, dolmeh, kabobs, and other Mediterranean specialties. All meals are served with warm pita and chay (Turkish tea).

Open daily, BYOB. Street parking difficult.

OLD JERUSALEM

1411 N. WELLS STREET, (773) 944-0459

After being in business for 20 years, these people know what they're doing. Old Jerusalem serves some of the most reasonably priced Lebanese and Middle Eastern food in town, and always with friendly, smiling help. Sandwiches, priced $3.25 to $4.25, are big enough for a meal. Entrées ($7–$8.95) are huge, mounded platters served with salad and bread. At $8.95, Old Jerusalem's Combo Plate of shawirma, kefta kabob, shish kebab, rice pilaf, salad, and bread, is one of the best-priced grazing opportunities in town.

Open daily. BYOB. Street parking difficult.

CASBAH CAFÉ

3151 N. BROADWAY, (773) 935-3339

Casbah is a small Lakeview storefront that's more of a carryout than a sit-down restaurant. The menu is 70 percent vegetarian and offers a wide range of entrées priced mostly at $9.95 and under that include soup or salad. At $8.95, the Moroccan lamb, chicken, or Tangier (veal stew) couscous is one of the best deals in town. Lamb Marrakesh, lamb stewed with onions, raisins, almonds, and herbs, is also a great option ($7.95). The Combination Plate ($7.50) is a great opportunity to graze through yalanci sarma (vine leaves stuffed with rice, pine nuts, and currants), neevick (seasoned spinach and chickpeas), hummus, beans plaki (white beans simmered with carrots in olive oil), and falafel.

Open daily. BYOB. Street parking difficult.

ANDIE'S

5253 N. CLARK STREET, (773) 784-8616
1467 W. MONTROSE AVENUE, (773) 348-0654

The original location is next door to Reza's and has been significantly spruced up in the past couple years to compete head-to-head with its neighbor. Although Andie's is reputed to have the best falafel in the city, the rest of the menu isn't quite as tasty as Reza's. Though prices have increased with the enhancements to the décor, Andie's still remains a relative bargain and a good Middle Eastern alternative. Entrées are priced $4.95 to $6.95.

Open daily. Parking available west on Ashland Avenue.

ZOUZOU MEDITERRANEAN DELICATESSEN

1406 W. BELMONT AVENUE, (773) 755-4020

For years, one of our favorite Middle Eastern carryouts was Desert Treat on Belmont. It might have been the place's cheap prices on healthy helpings or its sassy neon sign of a palm tree waving over a dune. Well, Desert Treat and its neon oasis are gone, but a new favorite Middle Eastern carryout can still be found on Belmont, just a little ways down the street. ZouZou is a small but sparkling storefront serving fresh selections of Mediterranean dishes. Starters like tabouleh, hummus, and ful—a mixture of fava beans with tahini, garlic, lemon juice, parsley, and tomatoes—are tangy and large enough to serve as a light bite. Falafel and chicken, lamb, or beef shawirma are hearty Mideast sandwiches that come with a side of hummus and spicy harrissa for an extra 75 cents. It's nice to see a good-sized helping of vegetarian couscous priced at only $6, about the right price for a dish so simple it's usually whipped up by nomads over a campfire. Polish it all off with baklava, rich layers of phyllo, honey, and nuts.

Closed Sundays. No alcohol. Street parking available.

Quick Bites A FEW QUICK THOUGHTS

If you're looking to put your own Middle Eastern feast together, try Andersonville's **Middle East Bakery & Grocery**, where a dozen fresh-baked pitas can be had for $1.25, falafel is $1.95 a dozen or for a sandwich, and stuffed grape leaves are $4.95 per dozen. Or, make a meal out of one of the fresh-baked pies, including spinach ($0.75), spinach and cheese ($1), beef ($1), broccoli and mushroom ($1.25), chicken and mushroom ($1.55), eggplant and cheese ($1.55), artichoke and cheese ($1.55), and parsley and olives ($1.55).

A La Kazaam

Get Stuffed Like a Grape Leaf
at A La Turka

Turkey has been a global hot spot since civilization's earliest days. Much of Mesopotamia was found in what is now Turkey. Many of Homer's heroes lived on Turkey's shores in the lost city of Troy or other fabled places. Alexander the Great marched through what is now Turkey to conquer the world on a path that later became Marco Polo's Silk Road.

With one foot in Europe and the other in Asia and historically standing over all the trade between, Turkey's impact has been felt throughout the Old World since ancient times. Now that influence has reached the New World—west to the Western Hemisphere to the Midwest to a rapidly regentrifying and recivilizing strip of Lincoln Avenue.

A La Turka Turkish Kitchen is located on a stretch of Lincoln once known for hollow, abandoned department stores, now home to pricey, rehabbed lofts. A seemingly modest storefront from the street, those walking through the door enter a lush interior with a ceiling draped liked a tent and terra cotta–daubed walls. Turkish-style seating on cushions at low tables is mixed with standard Western options. Intimate conclaves of businessmen with dark hair and desert countenance huddle in conversation over steaming glass thimbles full of strong coffee or tea.

A LA TURKA
TURKISH KITCHEN,
3134 N. Lincoln Ave.,
(773) 935-6447,
is open daily. Entrées
range in price
from $8 to $15.

A La Turka's menu touts distinctive Turkish cooking as one of the world's three great cuisines. I've always thought most Mediterranean cuisine to be the same, just often spelled differently. Hummus, pita, dolmeh—it all looks the same, tastes the same, just is presented with a different combination of vowels and consonants depending on if you're eating in Greece versus Morocco versus Persia or Iran or Istanbul or Constantinople. At A La Turka, however, it's clear that a kebap is not just a kabob.

The menu is extensive and loaded with tasty, tangy options for both the carnivore and the vegetarian. The best plan that will allow you to taste with abundance without ending up stuffed liked a vegetable yourself is to order a few appetizers and then split an entrée. Good cold starters include lebni, a yogurt spread mixed with walnuts, garlic, and mint that you can spread on the homemade flat round bread served with every meal, and dolma, cold grape leaves draped in yogurt and stuffed with rice, pine nuts, onions, parsley, and currants. Imam bayildi, pan-fried eggplant stuffed with onions, tomatoes, green pepper, and onions, is also a good bet.

Hot appetizers to try include mucver, zucchini pancakes served artfully with dill and feta cheese. The adventurous should try arnavut cigeri, pan-fried calf's liver and potatoes served with onions, tomatoes, and parsley. Soups, yayla yogurt soup with rice and mint or mercimek red lentil soup with bulgur rice, parsley, onions, peppers, and mint, are filling but light with a minty flavor.

A long list of entrées is available, and if you can't make up your mind, split the Karisik Izgara with a friend. This mixed grill will give you and a companion a trip around the menu with an assortment of chicken, beef, and lamb kabobs, baby lamb chops, and doner (gyro) all arranged in a tower dedicated to the unrestrained meat eater. For a lighter option, there are a number of fish-, seafood-, and vegetable-based options, including four kinds of dolma—zucchini, tomatoes, grape leaves, or bell peppers—stuffed with ground beef, onions, parsley, and rice and dressed in yogurt and tomato sauce. There are also six kinds of karadeniz pide, a kind of Turkish pizza made from homemade bread shaped like a flat lemon and topped with a choice of ground beef, feta cheese and parsley, mixed vegetables, pastrami, beef sausage, or Turkish kashar cheese.

Desserts include the fabled Turkish Delight (that sugary, gelatinous fruity treat otherwise known as lokum), baklava, and a huge helping of sutlac, a creamy rice pudding with a sweet, cinnamony skin on top served in a small ceramic kettle. Wash it all down with sips of Turkish coffee or tea, served in tiny glasses so hot there should be a temperature warning for those who grab below the rim.

Service on a slow night is almost too attentive, like the flight attendant who wakes you on a plane to ask if you're hungry. On a busy night, the kitchen is still sometimes trying to keep up. So if you're visiting on a weekend, grab a pillow and relax.

Fast Food

Celebrating the Traditional Cuisine of Ramadan

For more than one billion Muslims worldwide, Ramadan, the ninth month of the Islamic calendar, begins every December with the sighting of the new moon. Ramadan is one of the holiest times of the year for Muslims and is marked by a month-long fast from sunrise to sunset each day.

Ramadan is believed to be the time when the Holy Quran was "sent down from heaven, a guidance unto men, a declaration of direction, and a means of Salvation."

During Ramadan, Muslims are supposed to concentrate on faith and spend less time on everyday concerns.

To facilitate concentration on the spiritual, Muslims refrain from a number of worldly distractions during the daylight hours of the month and abstain from sex, smoking, eating, and drinking.

According to the Quran, one may eat and drink at any time during the night "until you can plainly distinguish a white thread from a black thread by the daylight; then keep the fast until the night." Muslims view fasting, or *Sawm*, as delivering many benefits. The lack of preoccupation with the satisfaction of bodily appetites during the day helps the faster learn self-control. Fasting is also a way to develop sympathy for the hunger of the less fortunate and teaches thankfulness and appreciation for God's bounty. Finally, fasting is also viewed as beneficial to health and providing a break in the cycle of rigid habits or overindulgence. Notes Max Pars, proprietor of **Pars Cove**, which specializes in Persian food, "Fasting is very good. I wish I could do it one day a week all year, but my job doesn't allow it."

Muslims typically begin each day during Ramadan in the predawn with a pre-fast meal called *suhoor* and then break their fast after sunset with the post-fast meal, or *iftar*. Iftar usually commences with the nibbling of dates, following the custom of the Prophet Mohammed, and then a sunset prayer, which is followed by dinner, a social affair to which many are invited to share the meal. In the evening after *iftar*, it's then customary for Muslims to go out and visit friends.

The diligence of the observant is rewarded at the end of Ramadan with a multiday feast of the "Breaking of the Fast" called *Eid Al-Fitr*. This celebration is marked by family reunions and is a favorite holiday of children, who receive new clothing and gifts.

Sultan's Palace, an ornate northwest side restaurant boasting imported, authentic clay ovens, is cited by many local cab drivers as the best Pakistani eatery in the city. What many of us think of as "Indian" food, the tandoori chicken and the numerous beef and lamb curry dishes, are simply Northern Indian Mughul cuisine and indigenous to the region that became Pakistan in the division by the British of India's Muslim north from the Hindu south. Sultan's Palace hosts its annual Ramadan celebration with a free nightly buffet.

Over a pre-Ramadan lunch, owner Shaukat Sindhu describes his restaurant's Ramadan offerings as a "spread" and names a few of the options. "Traditionally, the *iftar* is supposed to be a lot of appetizers. We serve dates, fruit chaat, which is like a fruit cocktail, and vegetable samosas and pakoras. We also have lots of drinks, including fruit juices, Doodh Soda, a mixture of 7-Up and milk, and Rooh Afza, a traditional drink that's red and sweet and tastes like fruit punch. We offer enough for dinner, but patrons often come in and sample a couple of the free appetizers and then move on to our regular menu for more."

Although a secular country, Turkey is predominantly Muslim, and some of the best Turkish food around for breaking the Ramadan fast can be sampled at **A La Turka**. Grab one of the restaurant's ornate floor cushions and enjoy a number of traditional and special appetizers for the holiday, including the Ramadan pita.

A pillow can also be pulled up for the holiday at Andersonville's **Kan Zaman**, which is known for its Middle Eastern/Mediterranean menu. The restaurant serves special dishes like Mansef, an imported meat and yogurt dish, during Ramadan and typically features performances by belly dancers at the end of the fast period during the celebration of *Eid Al-Fitr*.

However you choose to enjoy the winter holiday season, best wishes from the lands of hot sands and the blazing sun seem appropriate: "*Kullu am wa antum bikhair*" (May you be well throughout the year).

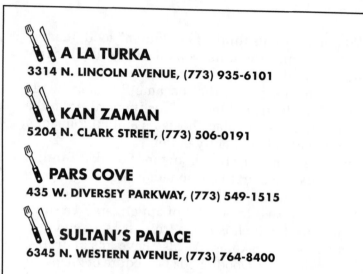

A LA TURKA
3314 N. LINCOLN AVENUE, (773) 935-6101

KAN ZAMAN
5204 N. CLARK STREET, (773) 506-0191

PARS COVE
435 W. DIVERSEY PARKWAY, (773) 549-1515

SULTAN'S PALACE
6345 N. WESTERN AVENUE, (773) 764-8400

13

Decent American Values

You say potato, I say potahto. You might question the concept of "American Food." After all, as a nation of immigrants, many of the dishes we enjoy today sailed to our shores from faraway lands. But keep in mind, when the pilgrims partied with their Native American neighbors, they feasted on indigenous food products found readily in the wilds of North America—turkeys, corn, squash, cranberries, and maple syrup. Many of these foods, including the lowly potato, were carried back to the Old Country and became staples in foreign diets.

You call it maize, we call it corn. As settlers spread in all directions to fulfill manifest destiny, distinct regional cuisines began to spring up. Some, like Southern cookin', were influenced by local conditions. In the South's temperate climate, gardens flourished and foods such as sweet potatoes, rice, okra, collards, pecans, peanuts, black-eyed peas, and watermelon became meal mainstays. The warm weather also created a taste preference for spicier and sweeter foods. In other regions, such as the Southwest, settlers borrowed from their new neighbors, synthesized flavors, and developed their own distinctive

> "Public food in America is apt to be pretentious and derivative, or vulgarized like hot dogs and hamburgers, oozing with spicy-sweet, not very interesting sauces."
>
> —Evan Jones, *American Food: The Gastronomic Story*

fare. Additional emigration to our shores continued to infuse local cooking with foreign flavors and brought new menus. Driven by economic and social change, migrations within our country's boundaries spread regional specialties to other areas—witness soul food's northward journey from the plantations of the South to the urban kitchens of the North.

So, as we contemplate our freedoms and privileges as citizens of the U. S. of A., exercise your culinary rights and sample some of the unique American dishes that truly make this the land of the beautiful. Yes, dig into that turkey and gravy, wrestle down some ribs, savor some fresh salmon, kick back, tune in da game, and enjoy a Coke, some Fritos, Twinkies, nachos with Cheese Whiz, Oreos, and other American specialties. And don't forget to vote.

WISHBONE RESTAURANT

1001 W. WASHINGTON BOULEVARD, (312) 850-BONE
3300 N. LINCOLN AVENUE, (773) 549-BONE

How many restaurants in Chicago do you know that actually serve that Southern classic, Hoppin' John? How many Chicagoans even know what Hoppin' John is? How many care? Well, Wishbone is an establishment that will give you reason to find out. Originally a single trendy bistro in an "artistic" neighborhood, Wishbone has grown into a monstrous franchise offering a variety of American regional, mainly Southern, specialties. From standard stuff served with a gourmet twist, such as baked bone-in-ham (served with a corn muffin and two sides, $6.25) and crab cakes with black beans ($7.25), to dishes not often found north of the Mason-Dixon line, such as chicken and shrimp étouffée ($8.75) and north carolina bean cakes ($7.25), Wishbone offers reasonably priced entrées that stay reasonably priced even when accompanied by a number of sides. If you're a vegetarian, be sure to try the corn cakes, served with red pepper sauce and slaw ($4.95), or one of the other numerous meatless options. (By the way, Hoppin' John is black-eyed peas served on rice with cheddar cheese, scallions, and tomato.)

Both Wishbones are open daily. Wishbone on Washington doesn't serve dinner on Sundays and Mondays. Wishbone on Lincoln doesn't

serve dinner on Sundays. Get to both before 9:30 A.M. for breakfast, unless you like long waits.

DIXIE KITCHEN & BAIT SHOP

5225 S. HARPER BOULEVARD, (773) 363-4943
825 CHURCH STREET, EVANSTON, (847) 733-9030

If it were found in Lincoln Park, it would be just another knockoff of the gone-but-not-forgotten Bub City or Stanley's, and there'd be a big sports bar up front to ruin the place. Sure, it's got that truck stop, gas station "Bubba" decor with all the kitschy memorabilia on the walls, but the menu takes you back to the real thing. Fried green tomatoes ($3.75) and oyster po' boys with rémoulade ($7.95) are tasty fixin's. The catfish fillet ($9.95) is also a good bet and a good deal. Avoid the jambalaya ($7.95), which is just not a great dish. Hot cornmeal johnnycakes start each meal instead of a basket of bread. Wash it all down with a Blackened Voodoo beer. "Do Dixie!"
Open daily. Blackened Voodoo beer. Parking lot nearby.

BROTHER JIMMY'S

2909 N. SHEFFIELD AVENUE, (773) 528-0888

Brother Jimmy's is an establishment that hasn't decided whether it's a restaurant with a hoppin' bar or a bar that just happens to serve food. That's too bad, since the cuisine here is abundant and relatively tasty. The prevailing theme is North Carolina barbecue, and if you can ignore the occasional prancing idiot standing on the bar throwing out free pig T-shirts, you'll enjoy the various sandwiches and dinners. Ribs are the larger, meatier St. Louis–style instead of baby backs, and come in Southern style (smoked 'n' spicy), Northern style (sweet 'n' tender), and "Dry Rub" (hot 'n' spicy and not very good). Barbecue side sauces come in "West Carolina–style" (thick 'n' tangy) and "East Carolina–style" (thin 'n' vinegary). Avoid the rib tips ($5.50), which are only Dry Rub. The pulled pork sandwich ($7.25) is a good bet, as are the succulent fried chicken livers (content yourself with the appetizer size for $3.95, served with a huge mound of mashed potatoes). As always, the mashed potatoes are the definitive measure of a place like this. Brother Jimmy's potatoes, although properly lumpy, are a bit too peppered. They are, however, served in massive quantities, which is always admirable. A free side of coleslaw is also served to each diner upon seating. Read the free "Bar-be-que Guide," published by the North Carolina Pork Producers Association and available at the hostess desk, while you're waiting for your order.

Open daily. Really full bar. Good happy hour. All-you-can-eat Sundays for $16.95. Kids under 12 eat free. Music on the weekends. Street parking difficult.

STANLEY'S KITCHEN & TAP

1970 N. LINCOLN AVENUE, (773) 842-0007

Situated in the old Papa Milano's "big fork" location, Stanley's has a spacious front bar packed with patrons who have shifted across the street from the excitement of Gamekeeper's and a back dining room reminiscent of a Carolina truck stop. Given the annoying sports-bar atmosphere up front and the almost too-perfect, down-home 1950s decor (complete with red-and-white checked tablecloths accented by an ant motif), you'll be tempted to give Stanley's the forks down. But then you order. Stanley's dishes up whopping portions of tasty slabs of meat loaf, tubs of Southern-style spaghetti, and creamy chicken shortcake (an updated potpie) for $8.95 and under. All "suppers" come with a choice of sides, including mashed potatoes and gravy, french fries, wet fries, coleslaw, buttered corn, mac & cheese, or Southern spaghetti. Loosen your waistband and dig in.

Open daily. Full bar. Street parking difficult.

JOHN'S PLACE

1200 W. WEBSTER AVENUE, (773) 525-6670

So popular it recently expanded next door into a second storefront, John's is a neighborhood place offering a menu of traditional American fare spiked with ethnic dishes. Barbecued chicken tacos ($10.95) mingle with soba noodles ($7.95), turkey meat loaf ($10.95), salads, and sandwiches with sweet potato fries. Add organic tofu or chemical-free chicken to your salad or sandwich if you're feeling healthy or some crispy bacon if you're craving grease. Get up early if you don't want to have a long wait in the morning for John's Crabby Eggs ($8.95, crab cakes with poached eggs and homemade salsa), chocolate-banana pancakes or pumpkin pancakes with brown sugar and cinnamon butter ($5.95, $3.95 short stack), or smoked salmon scramble ($8.50).

Open daily. Full bar. Popular sidewalk during nice weather. Street parking available.

MARGIE'S CANDIES

1960 N. WESTERN AVENUE, (773) 384-1035

What could be more American than an old-fashioned candy shop lit up by the name over the door in four-foot-high orange and pink neon script that dishes up sundaes made with homemade hot fudge and homemade 18-percent-butterfat ice cream? Margie's Candies has been serving up homemade candy and ice cream for more than 75 years and is still going strong. Margie herself sat behind the register for years, and though she passed away having lived well past 90, her legacy lives on. Wander in anytime between 9 A.M. and midnight, past the display cases of rock candy and truffles, and grab a booth ornamented with an out-of-order jukebox containing some of the 1970s greatest hits. Then, dig into one of Margie's specialties, maybe order a Turtle Tummy Buster or an Eiffel Tower. If you're extra hungry, start off with a shake ($3.25) and some solid comfort food, like a "Solid Sirloin of Beef," served with a cup of the soup of the day ($5.50).

Margie's is open daily until midnight. No alcohol. Street parking available.

THE ZEPHYR

1777 W. WILSON AVENUE, (773) 728-6070

For a North Side ice cream option, try the Zephyr, with its signature fried ice cream or, if you're with a friend, the War of the Worlds—10 scoops with four toppings. Sidewalk seating, serenaded by the click-clack of the Ravenswood el, is available in the summer.

The Zephyr is open Sunday through Thursday until midnight, Friday and Saturday until 1 A.M. Street parking difficult.

GLADYS' LUNCHEONETTE

4527 S. INDIANA AVENUE, (773) 548-4566, (773) 548-6848

The focus here is on food. Smothered or fried chicken, offered in white or dark meat. Breaded, fried catfish or perch. T-bones and pork chops. Hash and rice, corned beef and cabbage, ham hocks and northern beans, oxtails and potatoes. Meals start off with homemade biscuits and are accompanied by fresh-baked corn muffins. Sides are a highlight, and most entrées come with two, a choice of collard greens with a smoky pork flavor, squash, fried corn, or assorted other greens and roots. Save room for dessert: homemade sweet potato pie or peach or apple cobbler, syrupy sweet fruit with a rich pastry roof. Or maybe some lemon icebox pie or bread pudding. Wash it all down with iced tea, lemonade, or a strawberry pop. Most entrées range from $3.45 to $7.10.

Open daily. Street parking available.

LAKEVIEW RESTAURANT & PANCAKE HOUSE

3243 N. ASHLAND AVENUE, (773) 525-5685

One size generously fits all, whether you're a party of 1 or 10, at the Lakeview Restaurant & Pancake House. A dying breed of coffee shop, the Lakeview has a friendly staff, cushy pink booths, full-swivel counter seats, and a giant menu with a half-dozen pages of diner-priced options, ranging from hearty breakfasts, including plenty of skirt steaks, butt steaks, rib eyes, and pork chops fried up with eggs, to multi-course dinners served with soup or salad, potatoes, rolls, coffee, and dessert (top ticket, complete dinner with one of the steaks for $11.75). Drop your dining pretensions and find yourself digging into fried chicken, a hot breaded veal cutlet patty, or the pork tenderloin. For something a little lighter, opt for the julienne salad—one-third lettuce and two-thirds combo of turkey (you can have them hold the ham) and American cheese. Processed cheese, there's something very comforting about it.

Open daily early until late. Street parking available.

THE LOCAL SHACK
1056 W. WEBSTER AVENUE, (773) 435-3136

Only a shack by Lincoln Park real estate standards, this small eatery serves tasty New Orleans fare from a sparkling clean and modest storefront that's perfect for a quick bite or carryout. Housed in a former confectionery and opened by three neighbors who also own the Local Option bar, the Local Shack offers a long counter of seating in the front window and indoor and outdoor seating at tables graced by large rolls of paper towels. Jumbo lump crab cakes and heaping piles of slightly spicy Montauk Atlantic calamari curls are good starters, while the butterfly shrimp, eight good-sized Texas Gulf shrimp butterflied and served with a heap of fries, is a good follow-up. Shrimp also come in peel-and-eat and po' boy options, while blackened chicken, catfish sandwiches, and fish tacos are also good bets. Three different burgers, including the bayou option with Creole tomato salsa, feature a half-pound of certified Angus and should make the Cajun carnivore happy, while the meatless can find satisfaction in a veggie sandwich. Prices range from $7.95 to $13. Kids menu available too.

Open daily. BYOB. Street parking difficult.

Looking to get in and out? Try a pickup at the following:

BUFFALO JOE'S

812 CLARK STREET, EVANSTON, (847) 328-5525
An Evanston institution, Buffalo Joe's cranks out some of the tangiest, tastiest wings this side of Lake Erie. Prepare to drink a lot of water and use a lot of napkins.
Open daily.

HECKY'S BARBECUE

1902 GREEN BAY ROAD, EVANSTON, (847) 492-1182
Carryout only. The best ribs in the world. "It's the sauce." (For more details see "Rib Tips.")
Open daily. Street parking difficult.

HAROLD'S CHICKEN

7310 S. HALSTED STREET, (773) 723-9006
VARIOUS OTHER LOCATIONS
What Hecky's is to the North Shore and ribs, Harold's is to the South Side and chicken. Another take-out mecca that Chicagoans flock to from the far corners to carry out wings, nuggets, and fried okra.
Open daily. Street parking available.

Sweet Soul Musings

The blues, a term coined by Washington Irving in the early nineteenth century, is a form of folk music dating back to the black rural south of the post–Civil War period. A fusion of work songs, "field hollers," minstrel show tunes, ballads, church music, and rhythmic dance tunes, the blues originally evolved from Southern black men who endured field work under the grueling sun. Although some examples of very similar music have been found in Northwest Africa, particularly among the Wolof and Watusi tribes, the blues remain a singularly American art form that developed in the Mississippi delta in a triangular area defined by the cotton field work chants of Greenville, Mississippi, the King Biscuit Flour Time broadcasts of Helena, Arkansas, stretching to the gambling halls, posh theaters, and wild nightlife of Beale Street in Memphis.

> "We were always singing in the fields. Not real singing, you know, but we made up songs about things that was happening to us at the time, and I think that's where the Blues started."
>
> —Son House

In the 1920s and 1930s, although it was hard to find a blues man without Memphis roots, Chicago played a large role in the development of the "urban blues" that was first sung by Big Bill Broonzy, John Lee "Sonny Boy" Williamson, Memphis Minnie, and others. In 1947, Chess Records opened its doors at 2120 South Michigan Avenue and began to define "the Chicago Sound" with the music of Willie Dixon, Howlin' Wolf, and Muddy Waters, among others. The studio added artists like Chuck Berry and Bo Diddley, and in the 1950s, introduced new music known as "rhythm and blues" to mainstream airwaves, planting the seeds for rock 'n' roll.

Like the blues, the cooking of soul food is a uniquely American art that grew out of the plantations of the South. A relatively recent term (circa 1960), *soul food* describes the menus that developed as poor Southern blacks made do with what they were given, caught, or raised. Southern cooks learned to create flavorful dishes from chitterlings, ham hocks, hog maws, and other scraps and coarse parts that were not choice enough for the "big house," and those culinary skills remained valuable in the poverty of post–Civil War reconstruction. The meager meats that were available were then combined with local produce, like rice, black-eyed peas, collards, kale, turnip tops, and other wild greens that American pioneers had traditionally depended on.

Southern cooks drew on their heritage to make these scraps delicious. With pork lard being plentiful and flavorful, many soul food dishes were fried in a bubbling kettle of oil, a practice that harks back to an African tradition of meals made from vegetables and fruits (later pigs, once Europeans had begun their incursions) fried in palm oil. Seasonings from the West Indies—garlic, pepper, bay leaf, and hot pepper sauce—all helped turn a sow's ear into a silken meal.

As Southern blacks spread north and west from the farms of the South, they took their recipes with them, and today soul food maintains its integrity across the country. It's "honest" and easy to make, but doesn't lend itself to any shortcuts in the kitchen. And it looks and tastes much the same in Biloxi and Birmingham as it does in Harlem, Watts, Detroit, and Chicago.

Most of Chicago's soul food traditions were transported north by the Illinois Central Railroad's *Green Diamond*, which brought rural Southern blacks from the backwaters of Louisiana, Mississippi, and Arkansas directly to Illinois Station, the Ellis Island of the Midwest. Once in Chicago, these travelers gravitated to the South Side, where most of Chicago's established soul food restaurants can still be found.

Army & Lou's has been cooking up soul food on East 75th Street since 1945. Current owner Dolores Reynolds thinks good soul food is really what people are now calling comfort food. "It's not fancy or frilly. Good soul food is warm home-cooked food, like you'd expect to get at your aunt's or great grandmother's house. Even at our restaurant, everything's made from scratch—like your mom was in the kitchen." Maggie Guy, the owner of **Queen of the Sea**, agrees. "It's not out of a can or box. Good soul food is home-cooked and fresh. My greens are picked fresh every day, and our cornbread is baked fresh daily. That's what people want."

ARMY & LOU'S AWARD WINNING RESTAURANT
422 E. 75TH STREET, (773) 483-3100

QUEEN OF THE SEA RESTAURANT
212 E. 47TH STREET, (773) 624-1777

Bean Counters

Rating the Spice in the Red Beans and Rice

Woo doggy, led by James Beard–award winning Craig LaBan, distinguished restaurant critic for the *Philadelphia Inquirer* and, more important for this exercise, former restaurant reviewer for the *New Orleans Times-Picayune*, as well as a few other family members, we assembled a panel of tasters to decide who serves the best Mardi Gras traditional backwoods Cajun fare in Chicago. We skipped the jambalaya, since Chef Craig asserts, "As for real-deal New Orleans cooking, jambalaya is not a good barometer. It's not very challenging to make, and they usually come out with a reddish color for the tourists—real Cajuns make it brown. A good gumbo, on the other hand, is a real treasure to find and just as rare. Red beans and rice are also a telltale dish."

So, we carried out batches of gumbo and red beans and rice from some of the best-known Cajun contenders in the city. Then, the panel dug in to play "The Spice Is Right." Unfortunately, not much measured up to Craig's exacting standards. Only the red beans and rice from Dixie Kitchen & Bait Shop and Crawdaddy Bayou were deemed "acceptable to a native," and the gumbos, overall, were disappointing:

Dixie Kitchen & Bait Shop The clear winner, coming in first with Craig for gumbo as well as red beans and rice. Craig gave the nod to Dixie's seafood gumbo, but asked, "Was that a shrimp or a potato?" The panel was also in agreement over Dixie's red beans, which they noted as having a "complex, subtle smoke flavor."

Crawdaddy Bayou Three beans earned totally on the merit of the restaurant's red beans and rice, which were Craig's runner-up favorite and which received his approval for use of lots of celery, bell peppers, and fresh—not canned— beans, but took second place due to a distinct taste of filé powder, which Craig says doesn't belong in the dish. Unfortunately, Crawdaddy's thin gumbo didn't fare as well, coming in dead last with the entire panel. "Too soupy—like broth with meat in it."

Joe's Be-Bop Café Joe's gumbo came in second with Craig for its "good okra and nice brown roux" even thought it was "too tomatoey." The restaurant's red beans and rice didn't get quite the same praise, although one taster liked them for being "straightforward."

▌▌▖ Heaven on Seven on Rush Some might be surprised to hear Heaven on Seven ranked no higher than third and as low as fifth with the panel for both of its dishes. Craig gave the restaurant's beans and rice a bronze for their "real New Orleans look"; the other panel members thought they were "flavorless." All of the panel pronounced the restaurant's gumbo "overcooked."

▌▌ Louisiana Kitchen The panel liked Louisiana Kitchen's offerings more than Craig did, who ranked them both second to last. He noted the gumbo as having a "wussy blond roux" and commented that fish should never be served in the dish. One of the other tasters disagreed, ranking this gumbo first as "good and spicy." The restaurant's red beans and rice tasted bland to the panel and finished in the middle of the pack with the other tasters.

▌ Redfish Redfish's gumbo was only a hit with one taster, who commented, "Gluey, but nice smoky taste with some heat." The restaurant's red beans and rice were, unfortunately, "really dreadful." Craig's only comments were, "Wallpaper, anyone?"

Editor's Note: Although not part of the competition, the country gumbo from the **Maple Tree Inn**, tasted a month earlier by some of the less distinguished members of the panel, was deemed absolutely superior. No official bean rating here, but we recommend you check it out.

🍴 CRAWDADDY BAYOU
412 N. MILWAUKEE AVENUE, WHEELING, (847) 520-4800

DIXIE KITCHEN & BAIT SHOP
5225 S. HARPER BOULEVARD, (773) 363-4943
825 CHURCH STREET, EVANSTON, (847) 733-9030

HEAVEN ON SEVEN ON RUSH
600 N. MICHIGAN AVENUE, (312) 280-7774

JOE'S BE-BOP CAFÉ
600 E. GRAND AVENUE, (312) 595-5299

LOUISIANA KITCHEN
2666 N. HALSTED STREET, (773) 529-1666

MAPLE TREE INN
13301 S. OLD WESTERN AVENUE, BLUE ISLAND, (708) 388-3461

REDFISH
400 N. STATE STREET, (312) 467-1600

14

One Mag Meal
REST, RESPITE, AND REFRESHMENT
AFTER ALL THAT SHOPPING

Shop till you drop.... You've waded through the crowds at Crate & Barrel looking for that functional but fabulous gift. You've just done it with a swarm of tourists at Nike Town. You've combed through the racks at the season's last "Field Days," and you've used up all the free coupons you were sent when you signed up for a new Bloomingdale's charge card. Your personal debt level has ballooned to startling levels, you're juggling so many packages that you'll need at least two cabs to get home, and your dogs are barking. Time to take a break.

But wait—you've already made two trips to the cash station, and your wallet's empty again. Your cards are charged up to the limit. Can you even afford a cup of coffee?

You just need to know where to go. You don't have to limit yourself to McDonald's, nor do you have to settle for a cafeteria tray at the food court in the basement of Marshall Field's. Yes, a little knowledge will get you a tasty, filling meal served in a relaxing and attractive ambiance where someone else clears the dishes for less than the price of a pair of cashmere socks at J. Crew, a turtleneck at the Gap, or even a good-sized box of Frangos. My mama told me, I'd better shop around....

> "Wish I'd had *Cheap Chow Chicago* when I lived in Chicago."
>
> —R. D. Groom, former publisher of the *Cheap Chow* newsletter and former patron of Bloomingdale's lunch counter

THE IVY AT THE OAK TREE

900 N. MICHIGAN AVENUE, (312) 751-1988

Once a nondescript coffee shop on the corner of State and Oak, the new Oak Tree has spiffed up both its image and its prices since it moved into the old Carnegie Deli space on the sixth floor of 900 North Michigan. With its harvest-y decor, autumn colors, and grapevines twisted around any available post or pole, the Oak Tree supports the oh-so-chic atmosphere of the mall it calls home while still offering a large selection of tasty dishes with generous portions. Some two dozen different salads, both green and garden salads (What's the difference? Garden salads aren't necessarily green-based, ah-hah.), are priced for the most part between $7.25 and $8.25. Kind of pricey for lunch but not bad for dinner, for which they are more than ample. The Blue Plate Specials, particularly the turkey burritos ($7.50), are highly recommended. In a tribute to its predecessor, a number of sandwiches under the Carnegie Deli Favorite label are available and range from $7.75 to $8.25.

Open daily. Wine and beer. Street parking difficult; parking lot.

FOODLIFE

WATER TOWER PLACE, (312) 335-3663

Leave it to the people at Lettuce Entertain You to come up with a politically correct food court—a kinder, gentler, and definitely tastier food court. Enter and pick up your f* card, your food card. You then wander through the fantasyland of the various food stations, where you charge the items you choose to your f* card. At the end of your dining experience, you cash out all your charges and settle your "account." A wide variety of snazzy food stations are available, including pizza, pasta, Mexican, Asian, salads, desserts, rotisserie chicken, Mother Earth Grains, the Roadside Hamburger Stand, the Miracle Juice Bar (gigantic bags of carrots waiting to be puréed), and the inevitable coffee stand, the Sacred Grounds Espresso Bar. Our favorites include the chicken Cobb salad that's loaded with stuff ($5.75) and the Mondo Berry Smoothie ($3.25). The emphasis at many of the stations is on build-your-own. Food is tasty, presentation is slick, and the prices are actually right. Foodlife even has a carryout store with prepackaged options, some build-your-own "bars," a lot of samples, and prices that discount on prepared foods before closing. It's worth the trip over just to snag a few tastes of this and that. Maybe you should try opening an account here.

Open daily. Wine and beer. Street parking difficult; parking lot; valet parking at the Ritz-Carlton Hotel.

ZODIAC ROOM AT NEIMAN MARCUS

737 N. MICHIGAN AVENUE, (312) 642-5900

Does the thought of eating at Neiman Marcus conjure up images of elegantly dressed little old ladies sipping tea with lemon while they nibble on small tuna salad sandwiches? Well, that's certainly an option at the Zodiac Room, although the tuna salad can come in the form of a very tasty sandwich on a croissant with pecans and water chestnuts ($7.95). Plenty of other designer sandwiches and salads grace the menu, along with some more elaborate entrées that are almost all too expensive—try the pepper jack quesadilla ($8.95) or the orange soufflé served with the "signature" chicken salad, fresh fruit, and banana spice bread ($10). Seasonal soups come with popovers and the "signature" strawberry butter.

Open daily except Sunday. No alcohol. Street parking available; nearby parking lots.

SERVICE DELI

215 E. CHESTNUT STREET, (312) 787-4525

If you're out to shop until you drop, this is the place to stuff down a big old deli sandwich when you need sustenance. Conveniently located down the street from Water Tower and in close proximity to 900 North Michigan, the Service Deli is found by going in the back alley, past the dumpsters, and in the service entrance of one of those vintage Streeterville high-rises. Deli sandwiches the size and quality of which is rarely seen in this town run $6.95 and under. Try one of the 20 special sandwiches, one of the eight tortilla wraps, or just build your own. Three kinds of homemade soups are available daily.

Closed Sundays. Saturdays open only from 11 A.M. to 4 A.M. Street parking difficult; parking lots nearby.

CHALFINS

200 E. CHESTNUT STREET, LOWER LEVEL, (312) 943-0034

Billing itself as a "real" New York–style deli, complete with "properly insulting" waitstaff, Chalfins boasts the best pastrami and corned-beef sandwiches in the city, "flavorfully marbled with a bit of fat" and served with New York mustard. All your deli favorites are here, including smoked fish platters served with a bagel and fixings and priced $7.50 for smoked chub and up to $10.95 for baked salmon. Sandwiches run $3.25 to $6.95. Breakfast, including matzo brie and chicken liver and onion omelets, is served all day. The menu gives you a complete glossary of Yiddish terms, so you'll feel more ethnic. Wash it all down with a Dr. Brown's.

Monday 7:30 A.M. to 3 P.M., Tuesday–Sunday 7:30 A.M. to 8 P.M.. Street parking difficult; parking lots nearby.

THE SIGNATURE ROOM ON THE NINETY-FIFTH

HANCOCK BUILDING, 875 N. MICHIGAN AVENUE, (312) 787-9596

A room with a view, the $13.95 pig-out lunch buffet, loaded with hot and cold stuff, makes this one of the Mag Mile's hidden gems. All the other items on the lunch menu—sandwiches, salads, pastas—are a great deal at $9.25 and under but pretty pedestrian, so come hungry and stick with the buffet. (Hey, the waiter picked out the fettuccine with smoked chicken and broccoli florettes in a parmesan cheese sauce, $6.95, as the best pasta on the menu, and it was a huge serving, but so bland we were not inclined to take the leftovers. That never happens to the budget-minded.) You can't afford dinner here, so live it up with a nooner.

Lunch is served Monday through Saturday, 11 A.M.–2 A.M. Street parking difficult; parking lot; valet parking.

INDIA GARDEN

247 E. ONTARIO STREET, 2ND FLOOR, (312) 280-4934/4910

One of Devon Avenue's best Indian options has joined the Michigan Avenue shopping crowd. India Garden, with a $7.95 all-you-can-eat lunch buffet complete with a steaming plate of fragrant tandoori chicken delivered to your own table, offers an exotic option for those who've really worked up an appetite. Besides the extensive and fresh buffet, India Garden is known for its tawa and kadhai dishes. A tawa is an iron plate used to cook meat and bread over hot coals. The kadhai is an iron wok usually used to cook mug (chicken) and goths (meat) with chilies and tomatoes with fenugreek and coriander over hot coals. India Garden uses both pieces of cookware to prepare a variety of interesting dishes, all priced $9.25 and under.

Open daily. Full bar. Street parking difficult.

CRU CAFÉ & WINE BAR

888 N. WABASH AVENUE, (312) 337-4078

The long-standing Third Coast was reincarnated as Cru Café & Wine Bar. In its rebirth as Cru, the former coffeehouse has been sleeked up with elegant restaurant décor, and service has been vastly improved, but the menu remains essentially the same—albeit now with sleeked-up restaurant prices. We liked the idea of "flights" of regional cheeses, but for $12 a plate, we were expecting more—actually a lot more—than those tiny slivers of fromage and a couple of grapes. In contrast to the stingy cheese plates, the pasta salad is a feast, at three-quarters of the price. It's also flavorful, bursting with the tastes of the Mediterranean, a rare thing for usually bland pasta salads. Other hearty fare includes the Cru Club, that ubiquitous lobster club sandwich (layers of beef tenderloin and lobster tail for $16.50) that's become a mandatory element of menus all over town. Wash it all down with a selection from one of the 400 wines in the cellars.

Open daily. Street parking difficult.

GRILLERS CAFÉ

40 E. PEARSON STREET, (312) 274-0363
77 W. JACKSON BOULEVARD (IN THE METCALFE FEDERAL BUILDING)

A short-order grill with style, Grillers offers some of the best bargains in the One Mag Mile area—daily. With an extensive menu that ranges from hot dogs, brats, and gyros to Mexican, skirt steaks, and chicken/rib combos, Grillers has something for everyone. Daily specials, which come complete with fries, coleslaw, and garlic bread, include complete dinner deals like a full slab of BBQ ribs for $10.95, half for $6.95 (Wednesdays) and simply one of the best slabs of Cajun catfish ($6.95 on Fridays) you'll ever have the pleasure to savor north of the bayou. The half a Greek chicken is moist and flavorful, as is the BBQ version, particularly if you like tomato-ey sauce. For those who just want a burger, there are a number of options, including turkey and veggie. All dinners are priced at the "daily special price" on weekends. Desserts are comfort food, including chocolate-chip cheesecake, and chocolate and tapioca pudding. Be prepared to stand in a long line for lunch, then enjoy it outside in Grillers' pleasant sidewalk café.

Open daily. Beer only. Street parking difficult.

OAK STREET BEACHSTRO

OAK STREET BEACH AT MICHIGAN AVENUE, (312) 915-4100

Location, location, location. Not since Sesi's Seaside Café off Hollywood Beach closed has a restaurant gotten diners so close to the water. And, Oak Street Beachstro is truly a full-fledged restaurant—no short-order, trumped-up grill here. Though the Beachstro serves burgers and sandwiches (at a starting price of $9.95), the restaurant's aspirations run more toward entrées like salmon or beef filets, at $18.95 to $32.95, too expensive. Pastas, however, like rock shrimp with broccoli and tomato tossed in garlic oil and grilled chicken with spinach, sundried tomatoes, and mushrooms in a butter parmesan sauce, are good-sized and reasonable at $12.95 to $14.95. If all this sounds too fancy for the little beachcombers, they can order from a reasonably priced kids menu with hot dogs and "kid's pasta" (pasta with parmesan and butter). Chase it all down with a strawberry or piña colada frozen smoothie. Desserts include key lime pie and the World's Best Strawberry Sundae. No shirt or shoes required.

Open May through mid-October. Street parking difficult.

ZOOM KITCHEN

GOLD COAST, 932 N. RUSH STREET, (312) 440-3500

620 W. BELMONT AVENUE, (773) 325-1400

1646 N. DAMEN AVENUE, (773) 278-7000

247 S. STATE STREET, (312) 377-ZOOM (9666)

When you're thinking fast food, you're probably not picturing herb-rubbed turkey breast on fresh-baked sourdough accented with chipotle mayo, avocado spread, or caramelized onions. Or, a hand-tossed salad made with fresh toppings like off-the-cob sweet corn, roasted red peppers, jicama, pumpkin seeds, and crystallized walnuts. But at Zoom Kitchen, the concept is a cafeteria line for made-to-order comfort food with a little extra pizzazz. Take the sandwiches, for example. This is not your mother's meat loaf. Meat loaf or turkey loaf sandwiches are served on bread from nearby Red Hen Bakery and accented with tomato chutney or garlic mayo. Meanwhile, other sandwich alternatives include grilled-to-order Angus sirloin steak, yellowfin tuna, and a vegetarian with portobello mushrooms, cilantro pesto, roasted red peppers, sun-dried tomato, and caramelized onions. Never mind the temperature outside, fresh carvings and soups, like Zoom's sirloin and andouille chili, are popular in all seasons. Top it off with a slice of homemade fruit pie. Nothing on the regular menu is priced more than $6.50, and everything is prepared while you wait in line for your "custom meal." Zoom Kitchen's recipe for success carries over to weekends with an all-you-can-eat $8 brunch. Zoom's morning deal includes salads, build-your-own "Zoomwich" breakfast bagels, breakfast pizzas, the Full Montie (scrambled eggs, hash browns, and toast with a choice of ham, bacon, or homemade turkey sausage), banana pecan pancakes, corn fritters, and more. **Open daily. No street parking.**

Quick Bites A FEW QUICK THOUGHTS

Try the following if you're just looking to grab a quick bite:

CORNER BAKERY
676 N. ST. CLAIR STREET, (312) 266-2570
1211 N. STATE STREET, (312) 787-0821

Simply the fanciest cafeteria line in town, the Corner Bakery has expanded well beyond baked goods to sandwiches, crispy pizzas, soups, salads, and more, all for $8.95 and well under. The salami panini, a small baton of salami with provolone cheese and oven-dried tomatoes on country bread brushed with garlic ($2.95), gives new meaning to the term "sandwich." Check out the other locations sprinkled through the downtown area and suburbs.
Open daily. Wine and beer. Street parking difficult in the city.

BORDERS CAFÉ
830 N. MICHIGAN AVENUE, (312) 573-0564

From the dining point of view, Borders is handily winning the superstore bookstore wars. Where Barnes & Noble's most substantial offering is a scone, Borders has foccacia, chili, salads, and other light bites in addition to the obligatory coffeehouse pastries. Borders has a large dining area where you might actually get a seat (if they administer their periodic PA announcements asking those who are just camping out and not eating to vacate their seats).

Borders Café is open daily during the bookstore's regular hours. Street parking difficult; expensive parking lots nearby.

FLAPJAW'S SALOON
22 E. PEARSON STREET, (312) 642-4848

This is a rustic grill and sandwich spot for an old-fashioned sandwich or burger that doesn't strain the wallet. Fries are available in both whole and half baskets—which is great. (Don't you hate paying for what you're not going to eat?)

Open daily. Sidewalk seating in nice weather. Street parking difficult.

GHIRARDELLI CHOCOLATE SHOP & SODA FOUNTAIN
830 N. MICHIGAN AVENUE, (312) 337-9330

For those who need to tie on a sugar buzz to keep going, Ghirardelli has many options. Serving only ice cream and chocolate, not so much as a burger here, decadence doesn't come cheap. Standard, but "world famous," sundaes start at $5.95. "As famous as the Golden Gate and as thick as any San Francisco fog" is their motto.

Bread 'n' Bucks

Potbelly Updates an Old-Fashioned Sandwich Concept

For Bryant Keil, sandwiches are more than just a few slices of meat slapped between two pieces of bread. As the president of **Potbelly Sandwich Works**, an expanding empire of old-fashioned eateries that includes high-profile locations in Lincoln Park, the Loop, and the Magnificent Mile, he sees them as a way of reintroducing people to the simpler things in life.

Keil's passion for Potbelly began more than 10 years ago when he was a regular customer at the flagship store, located at 2264 N. Lincoln Avenue since 1977. In its early days, Potbelly was a charming little antique storefront owned by a husband-and-wife team. But because the antiquing business was slow, they turned on the potbelly stove in the corner and made toasty sandwiches and decadent desserts in order to bring in the cash.

Keil, who grew up in Hinsdale, Illinois, moved to Lincoln Park, discovered Potbelly sandwiches, and made them a part of his regular diet. The burgeoning businessman approached the owner, inquiring about the possibility for expansion. When the owner replied that he had not found the right person to make the appropriate steps, he knew he was on to something.

Since 1987 Keil had been investing in the hospitality industry, including Room Service Deliveries, a company that provides database marketing and online delivery services from local upscale restaurants to homes, offices, and hotels.

By 1996, Keil was the proud owner of Potbelly Sandwich Works. And by December 2000, he had opened the fifth franchise, the Magnificent Mile restaurant in the Nordstrom building.

Potbelly's menu includes classic cravers such as turkey

and smoked ham sandwiches, plus fresh new faves like the pizza sub (marinara sauce, provolone cheese, mushrooms, and Italian seasoning), A Wreck (salami, roast beef, turkey, ham, and Swiss cheese), and Big Jack's PB&J (a warm creamy peanut butter and grape jelly sandwich named after his firstborn son). They've also added sweet treats such as Sheila's Dream Bar (an oatmeal, caramel, and chocolate concoction created by his wife) and the home-made rice krispy treat covered in soft caramel and milk chocolate.

But what really makes Potbelly so popular? Keil says the fresh meat and vegetarian sandwiches and hand-dipped shakes and malts attract hungry customers, but the homey, classic atmospheres he has re-created in each store keep them coming back again and again and again.

"We've created an environment that's comfortable for people," Keil says. "Fast-food joints are impersonal and don't make people feel like lingering around. Our restaurants are warm and inviting, and encourage our

POTBELLY SANDWICH WORKS
520 N. Michigan Ave.,
(312) 644-1008
2264 N. Lincoln Ave.,
(773) 528-1405
303 W. Madison St.,
(312) 346-1234
190 N. State St.,
(312) 683-1234
1422 W. Webster Ave.,
(773) 755-1234
630 Davis St., Evanston,
(847) 328-1800
175 W. Jackson Blvd.,
(312) 957-1020

customers to stick around and soak up the atmosphere." All you have to do is look around to see what he's talking about. Somehow he's managed to duplicate and maintain that cozy, vintage vibe of the original store. Old-fashioned photos and signs dot the walls. Quirky knickknacks like odd figurines, antique bookcases, and jukeboxes add a whimsical touch. Contemporary and classic novels and board games entice folks to hang out. And eclectic selections of soul, rock, and oldies bring on nostalgia. "Sometimes when concepts expand, they lose the very essence of what made them unique in the first place," he says. "My goal is to capture the character and authenticity of the original store in each new venture. . . . It's the most important thing to me as we grow. I know I'm taking a risk every time I open a new location."

Re-creating that old-fashioned look is not easy. Keil says he has scouts antiquing nationwide for odd finds and imaginative pieces. His best coup: For the Webster Street store, he acquired several oak posts from a Civil War–era house in South Carolina that was about to be demolished.

The Webster site also happens to be his favorite because it was the most challenging to build. The triangular-shaped space was a former grocery store left in a state of dilapidation. He says that the construction team was forced to develop the restaurant from the underground up.

Though the Potbelly stores are located in trendy neighborhoods thriving on trendy and upscale dining options, Keil believes that each location can hold its own. "Sure it's just milkshakes and sandwiches and sodas," he says, "but if you look around, everybody eats those. And 25 years from now, people will still be eating them when the trend of the moment is long gone."

"It's a real good feeling when I find people who are as passionate about Potbelly as I am. It lets me know that we're doing something right and to not allow ourselves succumb to 'chainization' of our concept as we continue to grow."

15

Pass the Buck

BUCKTOWN BISTROS, WICKER PARK WATERING HOLES, AND OTHER WEST SIDE STORIES

For some of you, the ever-gentrifying Clybourn Corridor once defined your range. Yes, if you were a wildebeest and Lincoln Park a game preserve, the Webster Place Theater would have marked the edge of your territory. You roamed with the herd, and why would you venture off to some unknown watering hole westward ho?

Time passes, and things change. Now, the hippest stop on the CTA is at Damen, Milwaukee, and North. What's this city coming to when any average Lincoln Park yuppie can be found sipping a cold draft on the roof at Danny's? When J. Crew–clad hordes mob Marie's Riptide Lounge after midnight? When "Around the Coyote" can market itself like "The Taste?"

Michigan Avenue is for tourists. Lincoln Park has degenerated into post-collegiate sports bars and plastic trattorias. Today's eaters with attitude, the beautiful people and the "in" crowd, are doing Damen. Once the stomping grounds for starving artists, the area's resident tattoos and body piercings mingle increasingly with Kate Spade bags and Dockers as the cutting edge of nightlife, both for music and dining, has moved to 2000 West. From Webster south to Division, Damen Avenue is packed with culinary trendsetters feeding on Italian, Mexican, French, South American, various Asian, and solid Polish.

> **"Wanted: Urban pioneers to venture west of Western!"**
>
> —Advertisement for Rosa's Blues Club

These days, if you yearn to be a leader instead of just somewhere back in the pack, you need to venture out to neighborhoods like Wicker Park and Bucktown, the East Village and the Ukranian Village where new, trendy, and, sometimes, somewhat pricey restaurants are just busting out all over. These once fabled, once edgy West Side neighborhoods are now invaded nightly by the mainstream crowds that have discovered the abundance of eating options that can be explored at all hours in the area. Moreover, a number of these establishments also feature some of the best patio seating in the city. Others pulse with that special eclectic ambiance once found in River North before Lettuce restaurants conquered the area. So head west to find your manifest destiny or just a good meal.

BABALUCI

2152 N. DAMEN AVENUE, (773) 486-5300

Go one door north of the *trés cher* Café du Midi and its sparkly patio, and you'll find Babaluci, a dark "Italian modern" eatery at the top tip of Bucktown and another neighborhood mainstay. Babaluci is a cautious "fork & knife"—stick with one of the excellent pasta dishes, which all range from $8 to $10 (many entrées are too expensive). Try the spicy spaghetti al puntanesta with red and black olives, capers, anchovies, and eggplant ($7.75) or the tri-color rotini ($7.50). A couple of the entrées are affordable, including the chicken vesuvio ($9), sausage and chicken scarpetti ($10.50), and grilled Italian sausages with homemade polenta ($8). Don't order an appetizer; you'll be taking home extras with just a main dish. There's live music upstairs on the weekends.

Open daily. Full bar. Street parking available.

NORTHSIDE TAVERN & GRILL

1635 N. DAMEN AVENUE, (773) 384-3555

A former auto parts store, the Northside, Bucktown's established anchor, is packed all the time. The draw is the spacious patio, which is now a year-round option since the owner gave in to the allure of profit and eliminated the boccie ball court to make room for more indoor/outdoor space. Helpings are big, the waitstaff is cute, and the service is generally spotty. But hey, this is the kind of place where you want to hang out for the night anyway. You can park your motorcycle in front (squeeze it into the row of Harleys obscuring the sidewalk diners' view), and relax with a blue margarita or a large vodka and lemonade while you wait for your Pasta Special (different each night but usually includes sundried tomatoes, for around $8). In addition to the daily pastas, a full page of specials is available each day, including a soup, salad, and pizzas. Special entrées may include jerk chicken or a grilled pork chop (around $8) or broiled fish (varies, but usually around $10). Burgers are huge, and salads are big enough for two. Brunch is another good meal, with most selections running $5.95. Try to ignore the cheesy, giant neon drink sculpture that illuminates Damen Avenue and would probably be more appropriate at Dick's Last Resort in Streeterville.

Open daily. Full bar. Brunch. Patio. Late-night bar menu available to 1 A.M. Street parking difficult; valet parking.

LEO'S LUNCHROOM

1809 W. DIVISION STREET, (773) 276-6509

Leo's by day: a dingy dive with less than a half-dozen tables, a lengthy counter, and no air-conditioning offering pretty standard diner fare. Leo's by night: still rather seedy, but serving up a multiethnic array of appetizers and entrées, ranging from soba noodles ($3.75), wild mushroom risotto ($4.25), and sesame chicken wings ($3.50) to chicken tagine with couscous ($7.25), sea scallops with achiote sauce ($9), and chicken with Thai red curry and yams ($7). Dinners come with a salad. Alcohol is BYOB (no corking fee) and will be served to you in plastic teacups.

Open daily. BYOB. Patio. Street parking available.

BITE

1039 N. WESTERN AVENUE, (773) 395-BITE

So you indulged at Leo's Lunchroom on the seedy edge of Wicker Park, and you thought you just couldn't get any hipper. But if you journey around the block, just southwest to the Ukrainian Village, you can dine out at that one-word gustatory delight, Bite. Adjoining the Empty Bottle (a music locale that is, again, hipper than its near neighbor, the Double Door) and sporting bright yellow wall tiles decorated with smiling lips rolled back from clenched teeth, Bite is a storefront with character—and really good food at the right price. Sandwiches and pastas are $2.50 to $7.95, but the real draw is the nightly dinner specials. Seemingly a regular, the Indian sampler with eggplant and vegetable curry ($7) is an artistic version of what's offered up at California and Devon. Chicken with cilantro sauce, rice, and grilled potatoes ($7), leg of lamb with red pepper sauce and ratatouille ($9), and miso-marinated shark with rice, sprouts, spinach, and cucumbers ($8) all receive two forks up. Added value: Once you've snarfed down one of Bite's homemade desserts, you can roll yourself next door to the Empty Bottle for some cutting-edge music and a game of pool, saving yourself some cab fare!

Open daily. Alcohol can be purchased at the Empty Bottle. Breakfast. Street parking available.

PRIVATA CAFÉ

1938 W. CHICAGO AVENUE, (773) 394-0662

Privata Café brought inexpensive gourmet meals to the Ukrainian Village that focus on "Italian with a touch of Mexican." Privata's extensive list of creative pasta sauces includes mole verde, chipotle black bean pesto, jalapeño cream, and tomatillo alfredo, all priced $6.50 and under. The Privata burritos ($4.75–$5) are other good options and are available with grilled chicken, steak, homemade sausage, morcilla, or grilled zucchini with four cheeses. Since the entrées are so inexpensive, you may be able to splurge on one of Privata's artistic appetizers, maybe the Mexicali ravioli, two pasta pillows stuffed with chicken paté nestled on a bed of creamy red sauce, or the tangy grilled octopus with plantains, olive sauce, and couscous. **Open daily. BYOB. Street parking available.**

FLYING SAUCER
1123 N. CALIFORNIA AVENUE, (773) 342-9076

What Leo's Lunchroom was to the early, gentrifying days of Wicker Park and what Bite has been to the Ukrainian Village, Flying Saucer is to Humboldt Park—an eclectic café with a creative, well-priced menu and a tattooed waitstaff with attitude. The tattooed diners start rolling in at breakfast, where the obligatory Breakfast Burrito ($5.95) and the now ubiquitous Tofu Scramble ($5.25, $1 extra with goat cheese) are complemented by Belgian waffles ($5.25) and Huevos Volando ($5.75), eggs any style on corn tortillas swimming in ancho sauce and cuddled by Cuban black beans and pico de gallo. Lunch sandwiches, including jerk chicken ($5.75) and portobello with basil pesto and roasted red peppers ($6.25), blends into dinner with specials and regular options like meat loaf ($7.50), chicken gumbo ($3.95 small, $5.95 large), and Bob's Big Bowl, soy-basted, sesame-seed-dusted fried tofu over fresh spinach and buttered brown rice ($5.59, with fresh veggies, $7.95). Sparsely decorated walls, plenty of counter seating, unisex bathrooms.

Closed Mondays. Not open for dinner on Sundays. Street parking available.

CAFFÉ DE LUCA
1721 N. DAMEN AVENUE, (773) 342-6000

With its unfinished floors and terra-cotta half-walls studded with grills and windows, Caffé De Luca offers a romantic setting reminiscent of a crumbling Tuscan alleyway. Like most coffeehouses in the area, De Luca serves a wide assortment of beverages, light bites—the muffins and stuff—and desserts (including an assortment of gelatos). Besides its Renaissance atmosphere, what makes De Luca stand out from the average coffee bar is the abundance of more filling options, including numerous cold and grilled Italian sandwiches made with combinations of grilled eggplant, red pepper, prosciutto, capricola, mozzarella, and basil, as well as cheese plates and three kinds of pate and crostini (triangular toast points). Even your best friend can enjoy the visit, since dogs get free panini biscuits. All prices are translated into Italian lire—at a pretty good rate.

Open daily and late. Street parking available.

LA PASADITA

1140-41 N. ASHLAND AVENUE, (773) 278-2130

Run for the border for less than four bucks. The bulletin board offers two basic dishes—steak burritos ($3.24) and steak tacos ($1.46). Order with all the fixin's, and you'll get cheese, cilantro, and green salsa with an edge. If steak tacos are too tame for you, try the barbacoa (soft beef), lengua (tongue), or sesos (brains). These variations on the taco theme can also be had for $1.46.

Open daily and late. Street parking available.

Quick Bites A FEW QUICK THOUGHTS

The Map Room, 1949 N. Hoyne Avenue, (773) 252-7636, is a bar that sponsors a free "International Night" buffet every Tuesday, highlighting a different country's cuisine with food provided by a local restaurant. You can't beat that. Get there early; food goes fast. Check out the schedule for upcoming tastings at their Web site, www.maproom.com. The bar also hosts "Saturday Beer Schools" with lectures from local viewers.

Open by 7:30 A.M. Monday through Saturday with newspapers, Torrefazione coffee, and microbrewed Tazo tea.

Cloud Nine

Rediscover a Neighborhood Joint with a Silver Lining

If you typically push the culinary cutting edge by standing in line at one of the ultra-chic establishments that populate Wicker Park's six corner intersection at Damen, Milwaukee, and North, you may have overlooked the **Silver Cloud**. Although located on that hip strip of Damen Avenue, the Silver Cloud keeps to its quiet neighborhood self while establishments a few doors down attract long lines of those hoping to see and be seen.

The Silver Cloud is located in a space previously occupied by a Mexican karaoke bar. On the surface, it's a traditional Chicago bar with glass blocks in lieu of any windows to speak of, the cozy confines directly contrasted with the dark, smoky interiors of outwardly similar corner establishments. Inside is a snug albeit dimly lit room, with comfy booths, a long bar, and patrons ranging from neighborhood regulars to an occasional police officer taking a break next to a sporadic poseur who drifted a few doors too far north (more often when the sidewalk tables are out during nice weather). This is the kind of place regulars talk about with a proprietary air versus the sense of

THE SILVER CLOUD is located at 1700 N. Damen Ave., (773) 489-6212. Open daily, lunch Tuesday through Friday. Brunch served on weekends. Entrées range from $6 to $11. Sidewalk seating is available on nice days. Cigar and pipe smoking is allowed only after 10 A.M. Street parking available.

unfulfilled aspiration expressed after a visit to some of the other eateries in the area.

The restaurant debuted ahead of the recent gastronomic back-to-basics wave, and the guiding principle was to offer food like Mom would make if she was getting paid. Like its cozy, comfortable interior, the Silver Cloud serves cozy, comfort food. Small bites and sandwiches are available, along with full-blown entrées, or "good eats" that come with soup or salad, and a selection of pastas. Grandma's Meat Loaf, served with mashed potatoes, green beans, and Bell's amber ale gravy; and pot roast, "cooked till it's fallin' apart" and served with roast potatoes, carrots, and beans, are both good, traditional values.

Such standbys populate the menu but in a spiffed-up state, like the pan-fried catfish with a cornmeal crust and rémoulade sauce or the grilled chicken breast served over black beans with steamed vegetables and pico de gallo. Of the pastas, the Krazy Noodle Carbonara—thick, wavy noodles in a heavy carbonara sauce with peas and prosciutto—stands out, spreading a warm, lethargic glow as you loosen your belt and relax.

"Every day special stuff" highlights the menu. Tuesday's shepherd's pie is a deep, bubbly rendition of the original with generous layers of savory ground meat, mashed potatoes, and cheese on top. Thursday's chicken marsala with capellini is a plentiful dish of chicken breasts on a fluffy bed of pasta dressed with a tangy mushroom sauce. Friday and Saturday are the chef's choice, but don't worry, it's always good. Sunday is Jeffersons' Sunday after-church mom-style roast.

Counter Props

A Throwback to the Good Ol' Days

When I was little, I used to go visit my grandparents. Pittsburgh, where they lived, was one of those cities that still had a viable downtown. As a treat, I'd get to spend a day with my grandmother. We'd take the bus downtown. Sometimes we'd go to the beauty parlor, and she'd get her hair done. We'd go shopping—I think the local department store was called Kaufman's or something like that. And then, tired from exploring the wonders of downtown Pittsburgh, we'd go to a lunch counter for something to eat.

Good lunch counters are hard to find these days. Woolworth's used to have them. I think Chock Full O' Nuts is still around in New York City, but lunch counters are tough to find in Chicago. Many didn't even have tables. Everyone just sat at the counter, enjoyed their meal while sitting next to a stranger, and finished it off with a piece of warm fruit pie à la mode. Well, I miss my grandmother and I miss those counters. That's why I like Hilary's, a throwback to the real thing.

Located not quite far enough west to be hip Wicker Park or far enough south to be up-and-coming Noble Square, **Hilary's Urban Eatery** (HUE) reposes

HILARY'S URBAN EATERY, 1500 W. Division St., (773) 235-4327, is open daily at 7 A.M. Monday through Wednesday; closes at 9 A.M., Thursday through Saturday at 10 A.M., and Sundays at 5 A.M. Dishes are all under $16.

modestly on a stark strip of Division in the shadow of the Kennedy Expressway. In nice weather, HUE livens up its barren surroundings with impromptu sidewalk garden dining. When it's chillier, diners can enter the double wood doors with their etched decorative glass at the storefront and enjoy the cozy confines.

Two small tables sit in the windows flanking the entrance, but it's the counters that dominate the room. The main counter, with its comfy bright red upholstered seats and stone mosaic top that matches the restaurant's floor, winds around the serving area. A second counter flanks the west wall, ready to catch an overflow of eaters. Mason jars of jellybeans are spaced intermittently between sugar dispensers whose contents are speckled with colored crystals along the counter. The interior's details are completed with a tin-plate ceiling painted a plush pink. An antique baby carriage hangs from the ceiling over a TV that runs constantly with no sound. Various knickknacks and pictures, including one of a more famous Hillary, clutter the shelves over the espresso maker and throughout the interior. A back room offers more table seating in a parlor atmosphere.

Instead of the little blue-haired ladies that might have been found having a cup of coffee and a tuna sandwich at the counters of the past, many of HUE's regulars reflect the surrounding neighborhood—scruffily hip, assorted piercings in overly pale skin crowned with mops of unnaturally streaked hair. Much of the staff reflects the flavor of the patrons, but is unfailingly friendly.

Although many of the menu options have been updated from diner days, they still maintain the warmth of comfort food. Breakfast is served all day. A fluffy tower of pancakes, the Pan Special, redefines the term "stack of flapjacks" and is served in regular, blueberry, or banana oat bran. Huevos rancheros are mounded generously onto plates. The rib eye steak and eggs at $8.75 is one of the most expensive items served all day. A side of grits is optional.

Fat sandwiches, composed of chubby piles of barbecued beef and grilled chicken breasts, are served with fresh slaw and fries. Entrées range from the traditional to the healthy. A standout is the salmon cakes studded with nubbins of corn and red pepper and served with homemade Louis sauce and a side order of rice and beans or homemade macaroni and cheese. Steak fajitas are plentiful enough that you'll probably have to ask for extra tortillas. Lasagna comes in two flavors: veggie with ricotta and feta cheese, or spinach and herbed goat cheese. Other pastas and homemade pizzas with an assortment of toppings are available. The catfish, baked or fried, quesadillas, and chicken parmigiana are also good bets. Wash it all down with a cold drink served in a mason jar or a cup of coffee, steaming in a mismatched cup.

And then there's dessert: flaky homemade fruit pies (always cherry and apple), rice pudding, New York–style cheesecake and sour cream chocolate cake. These are special treats that you remember from when you were young. Go experience them again at Hilary's Urban Eatery.

16

Taste of Lincoln Avenue

With warm weather and the change of seasons comes that uniquely Chicago rite of summer, the Taste of Chicago Festival. Many city dwellers have learned to avoid the "Taste," that multiday eating orgy that long ago ceased to be cheap chow. One of the many smaller versions, however, located smack-dab on top of one of the city's worst intersections at Lincoln, Fullerton, and Halsted, offers a pleasant option to celebrate summer with the obligatory greasy assortment of entrées cradled in paper trays, washed down with numerous 16-ounce hops-based beverages.

Lincoln Avenue is steeped in the kind of tradition that entitles it to throw a "taste" type of party regularly. Once an old Indian and fur trapper trail leading to the Green Bay and Fox River portages, by the mid-nineteenth century Little Fort Road had become the main drag through the village of Lakeview and was flanked by the farms of settlers from Germany and Luxembourg. These Germanic farms made their mark early on the area's palates, feeding both nearby Chicago and the Budlong sauerkraut-pickle works.

> **"Ich bin ein Berliner."**
> **(I am a doughnut.)**
>
> —JFK's famous expression of appreciation for German pastry

The village of Lakeview was particularly attractive to ethnic Germans due to village officials' tolerant attitude toward social drinking. The biergartens of "Chicagoburg" flourished thanks to the Saloon Keeper's Society, which was organized to "protect and demand their common interests by all lawful means and measures." By 1889, the village of Lakeview had been annexed by the city of Chicago, and improvements in public transportation encouraged settlement of areas to the north and west. German families left Lakeview to settle in the posh suburb of Ravenswood and the more modest Lincoln Square area at Lincoln, Western, and Lawrence. Brauhauses, delicatessens, and pumpernickel bakeries continued to pop up farther and farther north to feed this movement.

Today, a trip up Lincoln Avenue is a study in Chicago's ever-changing demographic profile. The southern tip of Lincoln now runs through Old Town and DePaul, the city's gems of urban renewal. The former burgs of Lakeview, the historic German neighborhoods, which became increasingly Hispanic, now are under the extreme real estate pressures of regentrification. Further north, the Lincoln Square area has retained its Germanic atmosphere while acquiring various Eastern European and Greek elements. North of Lawrence, the flavor becomes distinctly Korean, with the north Lincoln Avenue stores and restaurants reflecting that trend.

Change, of course, brings opportunity—here culinary. Explore Lincoln Avenue. Just for the taste of it.

CLARKE'S PANCAKE HOUSE & RESTAURANT

2441 N. LINCOLN AVENUE, (773) 472-3525

Like its original Evanston location, Clarke's caters to students and other locals who need relatively no-frills fare 24/7 nearly 365 days a year. Burgers and shakes, salads and sandwiches, they've got it all here, but the real draw here is brunch. Clarke's serves a dozen omelets ($4.99–$5.99), including the Don Ho with pineapple, ham, and cream cheese; four kinds of waffles ($3.99–$5.99); eleven different pancakes ($2.99–$6.50), including baked German, Swedish, and chocolate chip; three different versions of the restaurant's signature dish, Northshore Potatoes ($2.99–$4.99), fresh-cut, grilled potatoes offered plain, with melted cheese, or Mexican style with hot peppers, tomatoes, cilantro, and Monterey jack cheese—a dream dish for hash brown fanatics—and ten different kinds of "skillet eggs" ($5.99), Northshore Potatoes with eggs and stuff on top.

Open daily. No alcohol. Street parking difficult.

SALT & PEPPER DINER

2575 N. LINCOLN AVENUE, (773) 525-9575

3537 N. CLARK STREET, (773) 883-9800

With its jukebox in the corner, Salt & Pepper tries very hard to be a throwback to the soda shop of "Happy Days" for the DePaul students and Lincoln Park regulars that frequent its original tiny location. Nothing on the menu is over $6.95, and greasy omelets, egg sandwiches, burgers, and real-deal, six-ounce butterfly pork chops ($5.75) are prepared in view for your enjoyment on the grill behind the counter. For those who want something more elegant, try the meat loaf on French bread or the grilled tuna steak. Veggie and black bean–veggie burgers ($4.50) are also available for those want to eat like Potsie but skip the meat.

Open daily. No alcohol. Street parking difficult.

CAFÉ ZAM ZAM

2960 N. LINCOLN AVENUE, (773) 935-0100

CAFÉ DEMIR

2964 N. LINCOLN AVENUE, (773) 755-6721

Two small storefronts, Zam Zam and Demir both specialize in Mediterranean food. Demir, which serves Turkish cuisine, has the more substantial menu and food as good or better than the fancier A La Turka, its Turkish neighbor up the street. Entrées, most of which are big enough for two and all of which are served with rice, range from $4.50 to $11.25 for the mixed grill assortment with shish kebab and doner. For something unique, try the karadeniz pade ($8.50 small, $10 large), a baked bread stuffed with a choice of ground beef, feta cheese and parsley, mixed vegetables, a Turkish beef sausage that tastes like pepperoni, and Turkish kashar cheese. It's a Turkish version of deep-dish pizza.

Just a few doors south, the brightly painted Zam Zam has a lighter menu with Mediterranean-influenced sandwiches served on either pita or French bread ($4.50–$4.95), salads, and a selection of meat, vegetarian, and sweet crêpes ($4.25–$5.50) that range from grilled salmon with corn relish and red peppers and shaved fennel, roma tomatoes, and basil to Nutella, banana, and toasted almonds. Coffee, espresso drinks, or Moroccan tea to wash it all down.

Both open daily. No alcohol. Street parking difficult.

J. T. COLLIN'S PUB

3358 N. PAULINA AVENUE, (773) 327-7467

The old Torchlight Café, a rehabbed Rexall drugstore, evolved one giant step higher into J. T.'s, almost the perfect neighborhood watering hole. A wedge-shaped, single-room bar with two sides made up of floor-to-ceiling windows, J. T.'s is a light, friendly spot where anyone can feel comfortable stopping off for a drink. Food is also lighter and a step above standard bar fare. The flat bread with Italian chicken sausage, shredded parmesan, spinach, gorgonzola, and tomatoes, served with a salad ($5.75), is more than enough for a meal. Sandwiches, at $5.75 and under, are all a good deal and served with fries. Choose from among the stuffed Gorgonzola burger, the spicy chicken burger, grilled chicken with chipotle mayo, or the Andouille sausage poor boy. If you want to get fancy, there are four entrées—a half roasted marinated chicken ($6.75), chicken with fettuccine and veggies in olive oil and garlic ($7.50), angel hair pasta with chicken sausage, goat cheese, and marinara ($6), and filet mignon kabobs served on pita ($7.25). This is the kind of place where everyone knows your name.

Open daily. Full bar. Brunch on weekends. Street parking difficult.

THE FLYING CHICKEN

3811 N. LINCOLN AVENUE, (773) 477-1090/1099

The Flying Chicken serves chicken—some of the best Mesquite roasted chicken around—supposedly produced from an old family recipe, starting at $7.99 for a whole clucker. A quarter chicken, your choice of light or dark, with rice and potatoes is only $3.99 (half a chicken is $5.49). The Chicken Platter includes a quarter chicken, chicken soup, rice, beans, salad, and potatoes for $7.99. The menu is in Spanish, and the place is always packed with patrons who speak it. You'll know the place by the humorous logo hanging over the door of a wily, skinny rooster chasing a hen.
Closed Tuesdays. BYOB. Street parking difficult.

VILLA KULA

4518 N. LINCOLN AVENUE, (773) 728-3114

Before Villa Kula, you had to get dressed up and go downtown to a fancy hotel to have a proper afternoon tea. Now you can just head for Lincoln Avenue where this intimate tea lounge offers diners an elegant wood and glass interior with tile mosaics on the wall and a stupendous tea garden next door. Tea party service includes three-tiered towers of finger sandwiches, homemade scones with champagne strawberry jam and cream, and assorted desserts with lemon curd ($15 for one, $20 for two). Individual plates of tea sandwiches, scones, or desserts can be ordered, as can a full menu of patés, salads, sandwiches, and light hot bites. An assortment of teas ranges from black and green variations to oolong and tisanes. Tea-tasting parties are held regularly, $15 per tea class; $25 for two, including tea food. Call for a spot.
Closed Tuesdays. Street parking available; nearby parking lot.

COSTELLO SANDWICH & SIDES

4647 N. LINCOLN AVENUE, (773) 989-7788

2015 W. ROSCOE AVENUE, (773) 929-2323

There are very few good delis, or even sandwich shops for that matter, in Chicago, but Costello goes a long way in filling some of the void. Entering Costello's front door is walking into a sensory adventure. Visually, the place is dominated by the Crayola-bright signature colors of Italy—birthplace of Genoa salami, capicola, provolone, and the meatball. "To bake or not to bake?" is the question here, as sandwiches come oven-baked or not. The baked, billed as "crispy on the outside, melty on the inside," include the signature Costello, a large melding of mortadella, hot capicola, provolone, marinated artichokes, tomato, black olives, and roasted peppers on an Italian sub. Unbaked include the Spicy Roscoe, hot capicola, pepper-crust turkey, pepper jack cheese with yellow peppers, lettuce, tomato, chipotle mayo, and Italian dressing on a sub. Gramma Costello's pastas, as well as a kids' menu, are also available. All sandwiches are $4.95; $1.75 for deluxe. *Buon appetito.*

Open daily. Street parking available.

CHICAGO BRAUHAUS

4732 N. LINCOLN AVENUE, (773) 784-4444

The Chicago Brauhaus, a Lincoln Square landmark, lets you celebrate Oktoberfest year-round. A traditional German oom-pah band rocks nightly, cranking out your favorite Bavarian drinking tunes and occasionally slowing it down with a little "Edelweiss." Like a Munich beer hall, this is a big place; don't let them seat you too far away from the action on the packed parquet dance floor. Dinners like koenigsberger klopse (meatballs in caper sauce) and Bavarian leberkaese à la Holstein (veal meatloaf topped by a fried egg) are both priced $9.95, while various sausages, which are all served in pairs with a choice of potatoes, sauerkraut, or red cabbage ($5.75–$5.95), will get you in the spirit. Liver dumplings and stuffed cabbage are available in bulk for carryout. Every fall, the Chicago Brauhaus throws an Oktoberfest in its rear parking lot starting the last weekend of September, a kickoff marked by the Von Steuben parade, that continues through mid-October. **Closed Tuesdays. Full bar. Nightly music. Street parking difficult; parking lot.**

....

Eatin' Large
Devon between Kedzie and Ridge

INNOVATIVE EATERIES FOR THE FINANCIALLY FINICKY PALATE

Lincoln Avenue is also known for its breakfast options and its delicatessens and bakeries. Here's a quick look at some of the best:

Breakfast Joints: The intersection of Lincoln, Wellington, and Southport is not only the home of St. Alphonsus, the church that was the center of the Lakeview German community in the late nineteenth century, but is also one of the premier 24-hour dining spots in the city. Flanked by the **Golden Apple** (2971 N. Lincoln Avenue, gigantic breakfast burritos) on one corner and the **S & G** (3000 N. Lincoln Avenue, creative assortment of egg casseroles) on the other, this intersection attracts breakfast aficionados, police officers, and sailors on leave at all hours. (For more details see "If You've Got to Get Out of Bed . . .")

Delicatessens: You can save a lot of money and still eat exotic specialties if you carry out from one of these establishments. In Roscoe Village, check out the **Paulina Market** (3501 N. Lincoln Avenue), an old-time meat market where the line is bodies deep for fresh cuts and other gourmet goodies. Heading north toward Lincoln Square, try **Delicatessen Meyer** (4750 N. Lincoln Avenue), an old-world shop stocking over 50 varieties of sausage and homemade leberkäse—a smooth veal meat loaf laced with mushrooms and bacon, and the **European Sausage House** (4361 N. Lincoln Avenue), which advertises whole pigs. (For more details see "Oktoberfeast, Ja!")

Bakeries: While **Schmeissing's Bakery** (2679 N. Lincoln Avenue) has whipped up coffee and baked goods since 1934, it's a new kid on the block in comparison to **Dinkel's** (3329 N. Lincoln Avenue), which for some 80 years has served up breads, cakes, and decorated frosted cookies commemorating holidays, seasons, the Bears, and the Cubs to the locals. Dinkel's stretch of

Lincoln was recently renamed after the bakery's founder. Take a number and get in line here.

Simplon Irresistible

Take a Culinary Ride on the Orient Express

La Belle Epoque, days of wine and roses and Art Deco, of crowned and uncrowned heads, of adventurers and femmes fatales, of "spies, murderers, and lovers" riding luxury trains that journeyed from the Mongolian steppes to London Bridge. Gleaming blue and gold "Wagons-Lits" that crossed the boundaries of Europe, the Middle East, and Asia under the names *Train Bleu*, *Golden Arrow*, *Transsiberian*, and the *Orient Express*.

Founded in 1884 and known for its gold logo of two lions holding an intertwined "WL," the Compagnie Internationale des Wagons-Lits et des Grands Express Europeans offered sophisticated travelers a luxurious environment that mixed adventure with technological performance. Wagons-Lits express sleeper trains crossed the Eastern Hemisphere carrying the brass of the continents, including Margaretha Zelle MacLeod, known better as Mata Hari, who earned frequent traveler status during World War I as she cruised the *Orient Express* in her attempts to spy for the Germans on the Allied officers aboard.

> "And now let us make the fantasy more fantastic," said Poirot cheerfully. "Last night on the train, there are two mysterious strangers . . ."
>
> —Agatha Christie, *Murder on the Orient Express*

The Wagons-Lits trains reached their sumptuous zenith in the Roaring Twenties. World War II, which wiped many of the countries from the map that once played host to the *Orient Express* and its sister trains, also marked the decline of the era's luxury rail travel.

Today, the *Orient Express* has been revived with journeys on its traditional route from Zurich to Istanbul. But you don't have to fly all the way to the Continent to experience the mystique of the legendary express train. *Non!* You can take our fair city's own less-than-sumptuous Brown Line to Lincoln Square, where you can reexperience a forgotten era at Simplon Orient Express.

Decorated like the inside of one of the luxury sleeper cars of its namesake, **Simplon Orient Express** specializes in traditional dishes from the countries the train once steamed through on its way from the capitals of Europe to the mysteries of the near East. You can eat your way through an entire continent from the comfort of one time zone.

Starting in France with veal cordon bleu, the culinary traveler can work his way—menu in hand—east through Switzerland for chicken sauté in wine sauce with a stop for Holstein schnitzel in Germany (a country a little off the train's original route unless you're counting the entire region originally encompassed by the Germanic Holy Roman Empire). Then you're off to Austria for wiener schnitzel, and you continue south to Italy for spaghetti Milanese. A zig and a zag back takes you back up through Hungary (veal goulash), Romania (meat à la Romanian), and Serbia (numerous options). A side trip to Greece for royal moussaka, and then you're back on track through Bulgaria (natur schnitzel) for your final

SIMPLON ORIENT EXPRESS, 4520 N. Lincoln Ave., (773) 275-5522/0033, is open Monday through Saturday until 2 A.M., Sunday from noon until midnight. Live music includes strolling violins and an accordion. Street parking available.

destination—Istanbul, Turkey—for a finale of sarma (rolled sour cabbage leaves filled with veal, beef, and rice—"the most popular dish").

It's clear from the menu that the real specialty at Simplon Orient Express is Serbian. We're told, "Serbian cuisine enjoys an exquisite reputation among European connoisseurs of cooking. Try it and convince yourself." We've got a number of carnivorous options to taste test, including a succulent dish of cevapcici, the ground veal and beef pieces common in a number of Eastern European cuisines, raznjici (pork tenderloin shish kebab), bele vesalice (grilled pork loin), pljeskavica (ground round steak), muckalica (a spicy gourmet dish with a pork tenderloin base), and veal shank.

For those who like to experiment, there's a combination dish of cevapcici and raznjici. And, for those who want to go over the top, there's the family-style dinner for two or more that includes the combination's two entrées in addition to royal moussaka, vegetable, potato, dessert, and coffee. All dinners include appetizers and soup. Soup is usually a choice of chicken or veal, and appetizers are a combination of chopped chicken liver, a hard-boiled egg in a tart mayo dressing, and kajmak, a fermented "milk-bread spread" garnished with an olive that originates from the Caucasus. After eating all that, you'll want to make your way to your berth to lie down.

17

Restaurants on the Edge

ROGERS PARK RESTAURANTS, EDGEWATER EATERIES, AND OTHER NORTHERN LIGHTS

Who are the people in your neighborhood? Well, if your neighborhood is on Chicago's northern border—Rogers Park, Edgewater, Albany Park, the Northwest Side—your neighbors probably reflect the mixture of ethnic groups and cultures that come together to form the mini United Nations found just south of Howard Street and the Evanston city line. Africans, Chinese, Filipinos, Germans, Greeks, Indians, Koreans, Lebanese, Native Americans, Orthodox Jews, Pakistanis, Swedes, Thais, Vietnamese, and various Hispanic groups—the list goes on and on—live in separate enclaves anchored on streets or around intersections or simply all mixed up with one other.

> "I could stroll half a block and eat in four different countries."
>
> —James L., reliving his days working at the Citibank branch at California and Devon

Chicago's North Side took off in 1907 with the extension of the El from Wilson Avenue north to Evanston on the Howard line and the opening of the Ravenswood line north from Lawrence Avenue. Edgewater, with its most recognizable landmark being the pink rococo Edgewater Beach Hotel, was a community of Prairie School–influenced mansions and luxury high-rise co-ops. Streets planned by developer John Cochran were named after stops along the Pennsylvania Railroad's main line out of Philadelphia—Bryn Mawr, Berwyn, Ardmore. Although the eastern edge of Edgewater on the lakeshore retains its exclusiveness, much of the rest of that neighborhood, along with the other northern enclaves, reflects the words of Studs Terkel, who described Uptown as the "United Nations of the have-nots." Many of the original ethnic groups, mainly European, around whom these communities developed have moved on and left these streets to those later off the boats. Some flavor of the earlier residents, however, inevitably remains, and the sights and smells of Europe mix with those of Asia, Africa, and Latin America.

From the 1960s-style high-rises on the lakeshore to the suburban-like bungalows of West Rogers Park, Chicago's northern neighborhoods offer a variety of eating options as well. Beginning in the southeast corner of this area in Uptown's Argyle Street neighborhood, diners can graze through Vietnamese and Chinese dim sum that's served daily. Head slightly northwest and find the Scandinavian and Middle Eastern options of Andersonville. Slide up the lakeshore, and you can kick back among Afro-Caribbean eateries or hang out in one of the many coffeehouses dotting the area around Loyola University. Turn west from the lake, and you'll graze through the Indian and Pakistani restaurants and Jewish delis of West Ridge and Devon. The northwest has the bar options—that would be sushi bars—along with other Japanese offerings. Moving south again, you'll end up in the Seoul of Chicago among the Korean storefronts of Albany Park. Head back to the lake, but before you finish, stop in Lincoln Square to drink at a year-round Oktoberfest. Around the world in 80 blocks. You don't need a passport, but you should be hungry when you go.

ANNA HELD FOUNTAIN CAFÉ
5557 N. SHERIDAN ROAD, (773) 561-1941

Looming over the northern stretches of Lake Shore Drive is one of the North Side's most recognizable architectural artifacts, the powder-room pink Edgewater Beach Hotel. And occupying the northwest corner of this monument to earlier times is the Anna Held Fountain Café, a combined soda fountain and flower shop that makes you believe time can stand still. Sandwiched among the flora is an old-fashioned counter where sodas, sundaes, muffins, and other desserts can be savored under black-and-white photos of old Chicago. Over-flowing cupboards and drawers offer a variety of knickknacks, children's toys, and books. Artsy T-shirts and shelf-stable gourmet food items can be found among the beribboned straw hats and stuffed animals. Anna Held is just like a visit to grandma's, when she'd let you discover the treasures of her attic and then, when you were tired, stuff you full of sweets (you were probably too young then to finish it off with a cappuccino). Coffee shop/soda fountain pricing.

Open daily. No alcohol. Street parking difficult.

TASTE OF PERU
6545 N. CLARK STREET, (773) 381-4540

This small, spartan storefront is brightened by cheery native textiles used as tablecloths and an extensive menu of Peruvian specialties. There are lots of fish and seafood options, including plenty of lobster, as well as beef and chicken. If you're with a friend and don't know where to start, try the menu for two ($29.50), which offers papa huancaina (potato with hot cream cheese), ceviche de mariscos mixtos (mixed marinated seafood), tamal (Peruvian tamale), and paella de mariscos (seafood paella). Wash it all down with an Inca Cola.

Open daily. BYOB. Parking lot.

FLOWER'S POT
7328 N. CLARK STREET, (773) 761-4388

This spare Belizean storefront is decorated primarily with pictures of various Belizean government officials. Belizean cuisine brings together the flavors of the Caribbean, Central America, Africa, Asia, and a dash of England in unusual combinations. Lunch and dinner entrées range from $5 for rice and beans to $9 for stewed pork and curried chicken, and are all served with a choice of white rice, stewed kidney beans and rice, black-eyed peas and rice, red kidney beans and rice, split peas and rice, or ducunu, which looks something like a tamale but tastes like cornbread. Special dishes, including conch soup ($10), escabeche chicken ($10, chicken cooked in spicy vinaigrette sauce and onions served with corn tortillas), and Boil Up ($12, yams, cocoa, cassava, sweet potato, and plantain cooked in tomato sauce and served with steamed fish and pig tails), are only offered on Saturdays. Lots of shrimp, red snapper, and king fish options ($12.95 or market price) are also available. Breakfast is also served. Drinks include seaweed, coconut water, ginger beer, pineapple, and kola champagne. **Open daily. BYOB. Parking lot.**

MOODY'S PUB

5910 N. BROADWAY, (773) 275-2696

Even when summer is over, it's never too late to appreciate a really good garden. And Moody's got one. Seating 150 under the shade of maples and surrounded by clinging vines and burbling fountains, Moody's is an urban oasis on North Broadway. According to management, the garden has been the scene of numerous engagements and even a few weddings. When the weather turns nasty, you can move inside to the intimate atmosphere of the pub, graced by flames from the fireplace and numerous candles. Winter, spring, summer, or fall, it's always the season for the Moodyburger ($5.25). Voted "best burger" by all three of our city's premier newspapers (*Tribune, Sun-Times,* and *Reader*), the Moodyburger is one-half pound of premium ground beef sporting an 80/20 meat-fat ratio to minimize the grease without sacrificing flavor. A platter of beer-battered onion rings are the right side ($2.75). All entrées and sandwiches run $3.25 to $6.25, and cholesterol-free cooking oil and fat-free salad dressing are used year-round. Free parking next door, large-screen TV inside, Moody Brews, Moody Moonshine, and Summer Sippers, along with sangria by the glass or pitcher, are all available. The final plus rendering Moody's unavoidably appealing is the presence of discount coupons that appear every Friday in the *Reader, Tribune,* and *Sun-Times* for half-price entrées. The kitchen's open till 1 A.M., so you've got plenty of time to get uptown to the grill.

Open daily and late. Full bar. Patio dining. Free parking.

MEI SHUNG CHINESE RESTAURANT

5511 N. BROADWAY, (773) 728-5778

Most of Chicago is sadly lacking in good Chinese food, even in Chinatown. However, there are a couple good Chinese options in New Chinatown around Argyle Street and elsewhere on the North Side. Mei Shung in Edgewater is one of those finds. The restaurant has a huge menu, but you can skip all the tasty Mandarin options and head right to the Taiwanese menu with its nearly 80 alternatives. Seafood and fish dishes, including mussels with sweet basil in a brown sauce ($8.95), silver side fish with leaf mustard ($7.95), and various types of meat in a satay sauce that doesn't taste anything like the Thai version are excellent. There are also some interesting options like two-designed sea slugs ($12.95) and hot three strips, pork, dried beancurd, bamboo, and chili strips in a special sauce ($7.95).

Open daily. Full bar. Street parking difficult.

CAPT'N NEMO'S SUBS & SOUPS

7367 N. CLARK STREET, (773) 227-6366

3650 N. ASHLAND AVENUE, (773) 929-7687

"The last good deal in great eating" and one of the city's most creative sandwich shops, Nemo's heaps meats, cheeses, eggs, and vegetables onto French bread and serves up huge, club-like meals. Free samples of Mrs. Nemo's homemade soup are offered to you before you order, and soup is sold by the cup or the gallon ($9, take-out only). Take-out sandwiches are available in lengths from two to six feet (a foot serves six to eight). Nemo's also has a branch at Ashland and Addison if it's hard for you to get up to the Evanston city line.

Open daily. No alcohol. Street parking difficult.

KOPI—TRAVELER'S CAFÉ

5317 N. CLARK STREET, (773) 989-5674

This Andersonville coffeehouse has fought off Starbucks and other more commercial chains with a unique ambiance that keeps patrons coming back. A tranquil place to relax for hours, Kopi offers numerous small tables, as well as an elevated platform in the front window, where you can relax on pillows as long as you remove your shoes. The atmosphere and food is typical coffeehouse, with a healthy and vegetarian bent. Desserts get good marks. Live music Monday and Thursday evenings. Coffee is sold in bulk, and Jalan Jalan, a boutique in the back of the café, sells travel books, ethnic clothing and jewelry, and other gifts from around the world. To add to the international atmosphere, clocks on the wall track the time across global time zones, and the restrooms are marked "water closet."

Open daily. No alcohol. Street parking easiest a block west on Ashland.

A & T RESTAURANT

7036 N. CLARK STREET, (773) 274-0036

This low-key diner in Rogers Park is breakfast heaven for the devotees who flock here for the giant omelets served all day. A fluffy cholesterol pillow built from three extra-large eggs ($3.75–$4.65, cooked in 100-percent virgin olive oil imported from Greece add $0.40), omelets come not only with veggie fillings, but also fruit options of banana, peach, or apple. Cheese blintzes with homemade fruit toppings ($3.15–$4.15) are a good bet if you're not an egg fan.

Open daily. No alcohol. Street parking difficult.

GREAT SEA CHINESE RESTAURANT

3254 W. LAWRENCE AVENUE, (773) 478-9129

A Chinese restaurant in the heart of Koreatown specializing in Mandarin, Hunanese, and Szechuan regional cuisines, the pride of Great Sea is its deep-fried barbecued chicken wings (and legs and other parts, $7.95). Coated in a spicy-sweet sauce and served heaped on platters, it's

worth the drive northwest just to gnaw on one of these.
Open daily. Full bar. Street parking difficult.

Quick Bites A FEW QUICK THOUGHTS

Affy Tapple, 7110 N. Clark Street, (773) 338-1100, Chicago's candy apple factory offers bargain prices on factory seconds—undersized apples, those that were unevenly coated, or those with broken sticks. Get up there in time for Halloween.
Closed Sundays.

Swede Emotions

In Andersonville, Scandinavia Meets the Middle East

Andersonville, the portion of Edgewater between Bryn Mawr and Foster around Clark Street that was originally settled by Swedish immigrants, has evolved into a melting pot of more recent immigrant groups and yuppies seeking to escape the high rents of Lincoln Park. Blessed with good housing stock, Andersonville has led the Edgewater community's resurgence since the neighborhood hit bottom in the 1970s.

Development of Andersonville and the surrounding Edgewater community began in the late nineteenth century by J. Lewis Cockran, who envisioned a residential enclave for Chicago's elite families, and the neighborhood still boasts numerous landmark homes that have been beautifully preserved. Not a single home facade on the north side of W. Farragut Avenue, for example, has been altered since the quiet street was developed in 1920.

Andersonville experienced its peak growth between 1890 and 1930. By 1927, more than 125,000 Swedes or individuals of Swedish descent lived in Chicago. After 1930, however, Swedish immigration slowed, and new, less prosperous immigrant groups moved into the community. Also, with the arrival of the elevated train after the turn of the century, apartments and residential hotels sprang up and attracted new residents with less money, and the neighborhood began its slow slide downhill.

Stable housing values have anchored the revival of Edgewater's retail businesses, particularly in Andersonville, where small storefronts thrive. A tolerant attitude has attracted gay professionals and has supported women-owned businesses such as feminist bookstore Women & Children First.

The neighborhood is convenient, with easy access to buses and trains, and residents like being close to the lake. All of this has helped Andersonville, and Edgewater as a whole; the residential and business base expand while the overall population in the city has been declining.

Andersonville still retains elements of its Swedish roots. The Swedish American Museum Center (5211 N. Clark Street) opened in 1976 and sees over 26,000 visitors a year. It hosts a permanent exhibit, "The Dream of America: An Immigrant's Journey," and presents a new cultural exhibit every six to eight weeks. The bellringer, who used to march up and down Clark Street at 10 A.M. every day ringing his bell to signal shopkeepers to open their doors and sweep their sidewalks, now only performs on holidays. But as a welcome from the Andersonville Chamber of Commerce, new shops on Clark Street may still receive symbolic hand-painted blue and yellow corn brooms.

Residents and visitors still line up to pay homage to the traditional Swedish table. In addition to **Svea Restaurant** and Chicago institution **Ann Sather**, both known for their

Swedish pancakes, vort limpa bread, pepperkakor, and made-to-order fancy marzipan cakes—decorated in English and Swedish as well as Spanish, Arabic, Russian, and other languages—are still hot out of the oven at the **Swedish Bakery**, the last of the Swedish bakeries in the area.

Originally opened in 1925, **Erickson's Delicatessen** is stocked with Scandinavian specialties, including salt herring, pickled herring, headcheese, potato sausage, lingonberries, and Swedish cookies and candies. Sausage, herring, and other fresh products are made exclusively for Erickson's from homemade recipes passed down for generations. **Wikstrom's Scandinavian American Gourmet Foods** further north on Clark Street also offers a diverse selection of Viking fare—and allows you to relax and enjoy it at one of the deli's small tables at the front of the store.

Though the restaurants of Andersonville serve up a United Nations smorgasbord of selections, the neighborhood's menu has increasingly reflected the flavors of the Middle East. Numerous storefronts serving hummus, moussaka, and kabobs line Clark Street. And **Reza's**, an ever-expanding Persian palace, is king of the Mediterranean restaurant scene. No small storefront, Reza's multifloor, polished wood establishment is as big as its multipage menu of Persian delights.

Reza's gets plenty of competition from numerous Middle Eastern establishments. If you're hooked on a phyllo, you can get stuffed like a grape leaf at **Andie's**, **Cousins**, **Kan Zaman**, and numerous other storefronts. Cousins and Kan Zaman, although not expensive, are swankier places, with adventurous pillow seating. Andie's is budget cuisine with some of the best falafel in town. For those who want to enjoy 1,001 nights in the comfort of their own homes, prepared foods and ingredients can be purchased at the **Middle Eastern Bakery & Grocery**.

For an easy weekend's taste of Andersonville, check out the Andersonville Midsommerfest every June. You're *vilcommin*.

ANDIE'S RESTAURANT

5253 N. CLARK STREET, (773) 784-8616

Daily 11 A.M.–11.30 A.M. Visa, MasterCard, Discover.

ANN SATHER'S

5207 N. CLARK STREET, (773) 271-6677

Monday–Friday 7 A.M.–3.30 A.M., Saturday–Sunday 7 A.M.–
5 A.M. All major credit cards.

COUSINS MIDDLE EASTERN & MEDITERRANEAN RESTAURANT

4203 N. CLARK STREET, (773) 334-4553

Sunday–Thursday 11.30 A.M.–10.30 A.M., Friday–Saturday
11.30 A.M.–11A.M. Visa, MasterCard.

ERICKSON'S DELICATESSEN

5250 N. CLARK STREET, (773) 561-5634

Monday 9 A.M.–5 A.M., Tuesday–Friday 9 A.M.–6 A.M., Saturday
9 A.M.–5 A.M. Sunday 11 A.M.–4 A.M. Check or cash only.

KAN ZAMAN

5204 N. CLARK STREET, (773) 506-0191

Monday–Thursday 11 A.M.–11 A.M., Friday–Saturday 11 A.M.–
Midnight, Sunday 11 A.M.–10 A.M. Visa, MasterCard, Amex.

MIDDLE EASTERN BAKERY & GROCERY

1512 W. FOSTER AVENUE, (773) 561-2224

Monday–Saturday 9 A.M. –9 A.M., Sunday 9 A.M.–7 A.M. All
major credit cards.

REZA'S

5255 N. CLARK STREET, (773) 561-1898

Daily 11 A.M.–Midnight. All major credit cards.

SVEA RESTAURANT
5236 N. CLARK STREET, (773) 275-7738
Daily 7 A.M.–4 A.M. Cash only.

THE SWEDISH BAKERY
5348 N. CLARK STREET, (773) 561-8919
Tuesday–Friday 7 A.M.– 6 A.M., Saturday 7 A.M.–5.30 A.M.
Closed Sunday, Monday.

WIKSTROM'S SCANDINAVIAN AMERICAN GOURMET FOODS
5247 N. CLARK STREET, (773) 878-0601
Monday–Saturday 9 A.M.–6 A.M., Sunday 11 A.M.–3 A.M. Visa,
MasterCard.

18

Northern Exposure

EVANSTON AND BEYOND

Do you need to make a quick getaway? Can't afford that rejuvenating jaunt to Mexico? Feeling stuck with no way out? Well, it doesn't have to be that way. In fact, just a hop, skip, and a jump away is a beautiful lakefront community offering spectacular views of the water, abundant trails and paths to hike or cross-country ski, tobogganing, downhill skiing, exclusive shopping, and numerous cozy establishments where a comforting hot meal can be savored with a refreshing drink. One catch—don't count on that drink being fermentation-based, because the bucolic community we're talking

> **"This place is worthless."**
>
> —Père Marquette steps ashore at Grosse Pointe bluff and discovers Evanston, 1674

about is Evanston, the North Shore's outer frontier, the academic jewel of the North Side, 847 heaven for real estate investors, and the historic home of the Women's Christian Temperance Union.

History aside, things have loosened up a lot in Evanston. Although still influenced by Evanston's patron and the founder and first president of Northwestern University, John Evans, who established a four-mile alcohol-free corridor around the University, absolute temperance is now a thing of the past. There now exists a selection of restaurants besides the dining room at the Orrington Hotel serving alcohol as an accompaniment to their menus. In addition, Evanston and its North Shore neighbors now sustain a number of restaurants that bridge the culinary and monetary gap between McDonald's and the four-star Trio. From rib joints and cushy coffee shops to perky bistros and casual sit-downs, Evanston and its North Shore neighbors offer a variety of eating opportunities that won't tax the wallet.

CHEF'S STATION

915 DAVIS STREET (BOTTOM LEVEL OF METRA STATION), (847) 570-9821, WWW.CHEFS-STATION.COM

Found on the lower level of the Davis Street Metra stop, Chef's Station is a relative newcomer to the Evanston dining scene in a part of town that was truly "the other side of the tracks." Opened in 1998 after a year of rehab, the outside of the restaurant resembles a European bistro, while the interior looks like a ship's galley. Chef's Station's menu is as varied as its appearance and features a changing selection of eclectic, ethnically influenced dishes, about half of which will allow you to stay on budget. Try the cornmeal-encrusted catfish with spicy tomato-jalapeño chutney, Taos tartar sauce, and creamy grits; the Caribbean marinated chicken breast with plantain rounds, brie, and apple salsa; or the butterfly pork chop with bulgar and mustard piquant sauce (all $13). Two different homemade soups are offered daily from a menu that includes options like curried orange, Thai coconut-shrimp, Cuban black bean, potato peanut, and squash bisque, among others, and on cold days, diners are greeted at the door with a cup of hot apple cider. Chef's Station also boasts the North Shore's largest alfresco dining area for nice days.
Open daily. Street and paid lot parking available.

LUCKY PLATTER

514 MAIN STREET, (847) 869-4064

Lucky Platter bills itself as "funkalicious superfood," and it's Evanston's resident shabby-chic diner. A changing monthly menu offers an array of global eats ranging from Thai grilled catfish and tandoori grilled salmon (both $13.95) to tofu fajitas ($10.95) and spicy turkey meatballs over linguini ($6.95). Pizza, with a choice of four ingredients for $6.50, and sandwiches served with a choice of a side and cornbread and including options like open-faced Mexican polenta served with black beans, guacamole, tomatoes, and mozzarella ($7) or a classic Philly cheese steak ($7.50), are also good options. Wash it all down with a homemade cream soda.

Open daily. Street parking available.

KABUL HOUSE

3320 W. DEMPSTER AVENUE, SKOKIE, (847) 763-9930

Years ago, the Helmand stood guard at the intersection of Belmont and Halsted, bringing delicious and inexpensive Afghan cuisine to the adventurous eaters of Chicago. Long gone, there are no more Afghan restaurants in the city, but there is one in Skokie—Kabul House, which lives up to the legacy of the Helmand. Having moved from its original storefront in Evanston, that also served pizza, Kabul House serves an assortment of broiled kabobs and rice for $7.95 and under, as well as tasty national dishes like quabili palau, chunks of lamb with rice, fried sweet carrot strips, raisins, and meat sauce, and kadu chalau, sautéed pumpkin topped with homemade yogurt and sprinkled with mint over rice, both for $7.95. The most expensive options on the menu, two combos, one vegetarian ($8.95 and $10.95), offer the option to graze and sample if you've got a big stomach. Save room for Persian ice cream for dessert.

Open daily. Street parking available.

WALKER BROTHERS

153 GREEN BAY ROAD, WILMETTE, (847) 251-6000

825 DUNDEE ROAD, ARLINGTON HEIGHTS, (847) 392-6600

1615 WAUKEGAN ROAD, GLENVIEW, (847) 724-0220

620 CENTRAL AVENUE, HIGHLAND PARK, (847) 432-0660

200 MARRIOTT DRIVE, LINCOLNSHIRE, (847) 634-2220

A spiffed-up IHOP, for some 40 years the Walker Brothers on Green Bay Road has been serving breakfast selections all day to the patient crowds of patrons who park it in the front lobby for up to two hours on weekend mornings for the pleasure of digging into some hefty stacks of batter-based, syrup-laden, whipped cream–garnished pancake, waffle, and

French toast tasties. Most of the pancakes run $2.95 to $5. Classic pancake dishes include Swedish, chocolate chippies, and Georgia pecan. There are six different "crêpe pancakes" and five types of Belgian waffles. Specialties include apple pancakes ($6.25) and German pancakes ($6.75). While you're waiting for your order, take time to admire the stained glass windows surrounding the dining areas, which, along with the food, truly distinguish Walker Brothers from the run-of-the-mill pancake house. In case you've run dry on things to do while waiting to eat, the history of the stained glass is detailed on the back of the menu.

Note that the Glenview and Arlington Heights locations carry through on the oak, brass, and stained glass look, while the Lincolnshire restaurant maintains "the oak appearance but added an English country theme." Both Lincolnshire and Highland Park have expanded menus with salads and sandwiches.
Open daily. No alcohol. Parking lots.

BLIND FAITH CAFÉ
525 DEMPSTER AVENUE, EVANSTON, (847) 328-6876

Staid Evanston's answer to the "granola" element every college town claims, the Blind Faith Café is one of the few restaurants in Evanston that manages to stay in business as well as span the gap between McDonald's and the former multistar Café Provençal. Now a big enterprise, the Blind Faith Café's concept of a healthy lifestyle encompasses sit-down restaurants, a self-service café, and a catering service. "Favorites" are $6.95 to $9.50 and range from the barbecue seitan sandwich to the macrobiotic plate, which is supposed to resemble the traditional Japanese diet by combining whole grains with land and sea vegetables and eliminating fat, meaning you can actually enjoy a plate of brown rice topped with shiitake mushroom sauce, vegetable and bean of the day, steamed kale vinaigrette, sea vegetable, cup of miso soup, and a pickle (probably not dill). Light entrées, including pastas, healthy Mexican (such as bean tostadas and chili enchiladas) and various combinations of seitan, tofu, and tempeh, range from $8.50 to $10.50. Breakfast is served every day until 2 P.M. Scads of North Shorers are keeping the faith. Maybe you should check it out.
Open daily. Wine and beer.

LULU'S

626 DAVIS STREET, EVANSTON (847) 869-4343

With its bright decor and no-frills style, the original Lulu's is the Penny's of the North Shore. Lulu's takes Penny's a step further in creativity, however, and serves a selection of "fusion Asian," including dumplings and other "small eats," soups, salads, and stir-fries. Dim sum is a big hit, especially on Mondays from 5:30 to 9 P.M. and Sundays when it's $10.95 all-you-can-eat between 11:30 A.M. and 3 P.M. Try the blue mussels steamed in an iron pot in broth flavored with chilis, ginger, garlic, and cilantro ($5.95). Or spear a dumpling filled with pork and scallions ($4.75). Entrées are priced $6.50 to $7.25 and play on a range of Japanese, Chinese, Thai, and Vietnamese themes. Noodles are big and can be found in both soups and salads. The Vietnamese rice noodle salad topped with grilled beef and a spring roll is a big hit ($7.75), as are other entrées such as jumbo shrimp and mixed veggies with Thai panang coconut curry and rice ($7.25). In white bread Evanston, Lulu's is the place that has "dim sum and then sum." **Open daily. Beer, wine, and sake.**

BUFFALO JOE'S ORIGINAL RESTAURANT

812 CLARK STREET, EVANSTON, (847) 328-5525

BUFFALO JOE'S SEAFOOD

2000 GREEN BAY ROAD, EVANSTON, (847) 868-5400

Listen to a story about a man named Joe. . . . Buffalo Joe's is one of the North Shore's most successful franchises. Founded by former Buffalo resident Joe Prudden, who created his own sauce recipe and pioneered wings in the Chicago area, Buffalo Joe's has gone on to expand into three sauces (tasty mild, powerful spicy, and suicide) and multiple locations. Buffalo Joe's Original Restaurant is a cafeteria-style spot that still hums daily with students and other wing devotees from near and far. The second location, Buffalo Joe's Seafood, is almost exclusively carryout, with a couple of stools at the counter if you want to munch on-site. The seafood place has some excellent hot and spicy homemade gumbo, starting at $1.59 for a bowl, ranging up to $12 for a gallon. The full pound of jumbo shrimp for $7.99, though not spicy, is a great deal. **Both of the Joe's are open daily. No alcohol.**

ROXY CAFÉ

626 CHURCH STREET, EVANSTON, (847) 864-6540

The Roxy Café has replaced the old J. B. Winberie's and its cheese fondue with a very reasonably priced and attractive Italian-American bistro serving a variety of thin-crust pizzas, salads, and entrées, most of which are too expensive for *Cheap Chow* purposes. The Roxy also recently brought in a new chef from the Culinary School of Kendall College. Pizzas and the calzone of the day are priced $5.95 to $6.95. Meal-sized salads range from $5.50 to $10 for the shrimp caesar. Pastas are $5.95 to $8.95 and include a tasty seafood linguine and an Italian sausage lasagna.
Open daily. Full bar.

NOYES STREET CAFÉ

828 NOYES STREET, EVANSTON, (847) 475-8683

Located up the street from the Noyes El stop, the Noyes Street Café, along with the Roxy Café, have managed to fill a gaping hole in Evanston's eating options by providing creative dining at prices reasonable even for students. There's nothing like savoring linguine with garlic, olive oil, sundried tomatoes, and roasted pine nuts—or a pesto fettuccini—with garlic bread and a salad for $10.05 (most places force you to order the extras separately, setting you back again the price of an entrée). A number of chicken dishes are also priced at $10.05. A large variety of sandwiches, burgers, and meal-sized salads range from $3.60 to $8.05.
Open daily. Wine and beer.

CROSS RHODES

913 CHICAGO AVENUE, EVANSTON, (847) 475-4475

Forget the Athenian Room. Forget Greek Town. If you're looking for tasty, cheap Greek food, this is the place to go. The Greek salad ($3.50) and a full meal are simply the best—millions have been consumed by legions of Northwestern students. The vegetarian salad ($4.60) dressed with copious amounts of large, greasy Greek fries, is also great. The half a Greek chicken, with white wine sauce or barbecue sauce (both $7.35), is another good option.

Open daily. Wine and beer.

CAFÉ EXPRESS

615 DEMPSTER AVENUE, EVANSTON, (847) 864-1868

Evanston's enduring coffee house, a bustling hot spot when a Chicago-based Starbucks was just a twinkle in the eye of a savvy investor, Café Express and its spartan menu and interior steams ahead, ignoring growing competition. You can get a croissant or bagel sandwich while you read your subversive Northwestern student literature. Desserts are under $2.50, a deal for this kind of place.

Open daily. No alcohol. Sidewalk seating. Live jazz Sunday afternoons.

DAVE'S ITALIAN KITCHEN

1635 CHICAGO AVENUE, EVANSTON, (847) 864-6000

The traditional bastion of cheap chow on the North Shore since 1972, Dave's packs in hordes of devotees and students who are out for something "nice." Long one of the only places in town where you could get a decent homemade meal for under $6, Dave's and its adequate Italian food remain a fixture for cheap eating. Start with one of the homemade pasta dishes and finish with a slice of homemade tiramisu.

Open daily. Full bar.

MERLE'S #1 BARBECUE

1727 BENSON AVENUE, EVANSTON, (847) 475-7766

Nothing personal to Merle's, but if you're in Evanston and craving some baby backs, I can't believe you wouldn't be up the street at Hecky's, unless you need a sit-down place. If you need it "for here," Merle's will do the trick, especially the half slab of St. Louis ribs ($7.95). Merle's serves carryout by the pound or slab, but for that, you should definitely be at Hecky's.

Open daily. Full bar.

Quick Bites A FEW QUICK THOUGHTS

Other North Shore establishments, some of which we may have written about in other chapters, that you may want to check out include Hecky's (the best ribs in town) and the Flat Top Grill.

19

Gardens of Eat-In

SIDEWALK CAFÉS, GARDEN PATIOS, AND OTHER SPOTS TO INDULGE AU NATUREL

We have a long history of communing with nature, from the founding of our country and the subsequent push westward through the wilderness to fulfill manifest destiny, to the nineteenth century when Thoreau shucked the shackles of civilized constraints to retreat to the pond, to this century's periodic resurrections of Woodstock. Today, those of us who cannot satisfy our latent primal urges to chuck it all and go back to the bush have to find substitutes in the urban jungle that release the tensions built up driving the information highway into cyberspace.

Come pleasant weather—in Chicago, defined as any moderately sunny day when there's no snow on the ground, generally found only between the months of May and October—a primitive drum starts to beat in the blood of

> **Tran·scen·den·tal·ism (tran-sen-den-t'l-izm)** *n.*: a nineteenth-century intellectual movement that assumed the immanent presence of God within both man and nature and elevated the powers of intuition over logic and reasoning. Characterized by the writings of many American authors of the era celebrating nature and a raw, open new continent.

our urban fellow residents, driving them to fulfill their basic instincts to strip down and bare pasty, winterized bodies to the elements to absorb the life-renewing rays and balmy breezes. As spring moves into summer, the denizens of our city are driven by an increasingly frantic need to just be outdoors, with each day passing meaning one more day of fair weather over, one day closer to the inevitable cold, one less day to just do it.

Coupled with this need to heed nature's call comes the urge to fulfill the most basic impulses, including eating, of course. To the average citizen of Chicago, there's nothing grander than a picnic by the lake, a dog in the bleachers, or a leisurely afternoon in a beer garden quaffing some cold ones while nibbling on some wings. Yes, Adam and Eve may have lost out on Eden, but at least their descendants discovered patio dining.

> "Give me books, fruit, French wine and fine weather, and a little music out of doors, played by someone I do not know."
>
> —Letter to Fanny Keats, John Keats, August 29, 1819

At the first sign of warm weather, savvy restaurants and bars all over Chicago liberate their plastic furniture from storage. Many commandeer an adjacent piece of public walkway and, violà, instant sidewalk café. But, if you're interested in a real place to dine, you're searching for one of those rarer establishments that offer an authentic patio or porch—some separate dining area that no one is going to walk his dog through as you dabble in your calamari and an iced latte.

Since the summer's too short to waste time debating patio vs. sidewalk vs. possibly your own backyard, here's a range of outdoor eateries to satisfy your needs, from simple to formal. And, being very sun sensitive, they're ranked by that all-important exposure factor:

SPF 2: A sidewalk café or other open place that's going to leave you vulnerable not only to the dangerous rays of the sun, but also to the potential mishaps of bikers, in-line skaters, and other passing bodies that may hurtle through your dining space without regard to your delicate digestive requirements.

SPF 8: A separate deck or patio space that's been built to detach the diner from the hurly-burly of the sidewalk, but does not necessarily provide the patron with any more serenity or view than that found at the makeshift sidewalk SPF 2 café.

SPF 15: A separate, enclosed patio often found at the back of the restaurant that graciously shields the patron from the potentially grim realities of the city seen from the front of the restaurant. The ultimate SPF 15 includes trees, well-groomed gardens to perfume the air, and a bubbling fountain, preferably with tasteful statuary.

Whatever your idea of the perfect outdoor dining experience, you can find it in Chicago. They're all open for business—whether it's lunch at high noon or dinner during some enchanted evening. So get out of here.

LE COLONIAL

937 N. RUSH STREET, (312) 255-0088

The Après Déjeuner Menu is as seasonal as Le Colonial's sidewalk café, which is set in a semi-enclosed area off bustling Rush Street. Available May through September only, the inexpensive exotic eats are a way to soak in the scene at one of the city's most sophisticated—and expensive—restaurants that delightfully fuses French and Vietnamese cuisine. Light bites include the cha gio, Vietnamese spring rolls with shrimp, pork, and mushrooms ($6.50); chao tom, grilled shrimp wrapped around sugar cane with angel-hair noodles, lettuce, mint, and a peanut sauce ($7.50); and banh uot, grilled sesame beef over flat rice noodles, cucumber, and fresh herbs ($7.50). And for those who want to graze like a rabbit, try the goi atiso, a filling salad of artichoke, crabmeat, sesame, tomato, and tamarind dressing ($8.50); goi ga, a salad of cabbage, chicken, roasted peanuts, and herbs in lime dressing, served with shrimp chips ($7); and the irresistable goi bun so, grilled sea bass, garlic noodle salad, roasted peanuts, fresh herbs, and chili lime dressing ($8.50).

SPF 2. The Après Déjeuner menu is served Monday through Saturday, from 2:30 P.M. to 4 P.M. Street parking difficult; parking lot nearby.

TILLI'S

1952 N. HALSTED STREET, (773) 325-0044

Opened in the summer of 1997 by three siblings who grew up in their father's suburban Italian restaurant, Tilli's is a year-round garden in a former garden center. One of the sisters was the head chef at Tucci Milan, so the menu has a good number of Italian options, but is really global with Asian soups and salads, Middle Eastern appetizers, and good old American entrées joining the pastas and pizzas ($3.25–$8). Entrées are served with a side and include "top secret" barbecue chicken ($7.95), many-herbed chicken breast ($8.95), and the Gorgonzola pork chop ($10.95). For those of you who get tired of wandering the world gastronomically, there's the big @#!!! Burger for $6.95.

SPF 8. Open daily, full bar. Street parking difficult; valet.

ATHENA RESTAURANT

212 S. HALSTED STREET, (312) 655-0000

We don't usually frequent restaurants so big and busy they need to call parties for seating over a PA system, but we made an exception to the rule for the patio at Athena Restaurant. Truly one of the classic outdoor dining spaces in the city, Athena offers a full city lot worth of patio with a fountain and a spectacular view of the southwest Loop in all its glory. Food is acceptable to pretty good, and as with most Greek restaurants, you get a lot for your dollar. For grazers, the Combination Plate with moussaka, pastitsio, dolmades, roast leg of lamb, rice, potato, and vegetables is an excellent option. Those who prefer a lighter sampling can have the Cold Appetizer Combination, but should be warned that everything is very salty. The two "giant broiled" pork chops are accurately described.

SPF 8. Open daily and serving late. Street parking difficult; parking lot nearby.

PONTIAC CAFÉ

1531 N. DAMEN AVENUE, (773) 252-7767

A converted fruit stand, this Wicker Park sandwich place comes into its own every summer as it flings open the doors to the elements. A spacious patio fronting the café allows diners to relax on Damen Avenue and sip fruit smoothies and slushes, which are served by the glass or by the pitcher ($7.50 for slushes and $9.50 for smoothies). Dining options are primarily sandwiches, with a couple salads thrown in. Ten kinds of subs—from old standards to New Age cool breezes (smoked turkey, mozzarella, alfalfa sprouts, cucumber, oil, and balsamic vinegar)—are served in eight-inch ($4.50) and twelve-inch ($6.50) versions. Add one dollar for "double stuff" combos of two meats. Similarly, nine kinds of panino are served in the same sizes for the same prices. Try the olive panini with calamata olives, artichokes, orange zest, and olive oil. Seven different combinations of stuffed tomato foccacia, including one with artichokes, red pepper, and provolone, are $4.75 each.
SPF 8. No alcohol. Open daily. Street parking difficult.

RESI'S BIERSTUBE

2034 W. IRVING PARK ROAD, (773) 472-1749

Resi's Bierstube, a cozy year-round Oktoberfest celebration tucked away in an old North Side neighborhood, nudges out Moody's Pub (see "Restaurants on the Edge.") for best beer garden. Moody's has an expansive, tree-studded patio graced with two fountains that seats 150, and the half-pound Moodyburger, but Resi's urban oasis wins on breadth of menu, both for food and drink. Hefty entrées usually served with two sides can be enjoyed for around $7.50 to $8.95 (except for the five types of schnitzels, which are slightly more pricey). Various sausages, no less than six kinds of wursts—bratwurst (both regular and Sheboygan-style), smoked thuringer, knackwurst, wieners, and liver and blood sausage—range from $4.75 à la carte to $8.50 with sauerkraut and other fixin's. Hackepeter, a German steak tartare ($6.50), is available on the weekends. There are over 130 beers to choose from, including over two dozen weissbiers and 70 bottled imports—all of which can be enjoyed within the snug confines of its tree-shaded, flower-studded back patio. Lift a stein served to you by your Frau waitress, who has probably been with the establishment for about 20 years, and to share your good cheer with a stranger with whom you may also have to share your picnic table if the place gets packed. (For more details on Resi's see "Oktoberfeast, Ja!")

SPF 15. Open daily. Full bar. Street parking available.

TWISTED SPOKE

501 N. OGDEN AVENUE, (312) 666-1500

 Once a hardcore biker's bar, Twisted Spoke is now a hangout for the khakis crowd. But it still pipes out edgy rock music, and the outdoor rooftop patio is still a great place to take in a burger and a beer. For balanced meals, check out the daily $7.95 specials, including "Monday Meatloaf Night," all-you-can-eat meat loaf, accompanied by a mound of garlic and blue cheese smashed potatoes topped with mushroom gravy, and crispy green beans; "Thursday Beef Stew," steak, potatoes, celery, and carrots, slowly simmered until tender, and served with a crispy salad and warm, crusty bread; and the "Friday Po' Boy Special," tasty shrimp piled high on top of tomatoes, romaine lettuce, and Cajun mayo nestled in a garlicky toasted french bread, and served with a side of slaw, fries, and a pickle. Come back for brunch on Saturdays and Sundays, but leave room for the 16-ounce bloody Road Rash Mary & Beer Back, garnished with cheese, salami, pearl onions, green chili, and green olives. It's a meal in a glass for $5.

SPF 15. Open daily. Full bar. Street parking available.

DAO THAI RESTAURANT AND NOODLE PALACE

230 E. OHIO STREET, (312) 337-0000

Outside of its loft space, Dao Thai is the proud owner of one of the finest dining patios in the 312 area code. A second-floor wood platform that's sheltered from the traffic on Ohio, the Dao's deck transports diners from the hustle and bustle of Streeterville to a tranquil dining experience punctuated by excellent spring rolls and pretty good ginger chicken ($5.75). The menu is fairly standard Thai, with standouts being beef with basil leaves ($4.95) and bamee and barbecued pork soup ($5.50). Specials include lots of currys. It's a treat just to come here to get out of your office and hang out on the patio, sipping an iced coffee. **SPF 15. Open daily. Full bar. Street parking difficult; parking lot nearby.**

COROSH

1072 N. MILWAUKEE AVENUE, (773) 235-0600

A surprisingly attractive restaurant and bar with an emphasis on Italian, this East Village establishment is worth the trip just for the atmosphere. The loft-like feel is reinforced by brick walls, handcrafted hardwood floors, and a polished wood bar. A tree-lined outdoor brick patio, complete with pink marble–topped tables and bullet-proof glass camouflaged by trees, sits calmly outside. Salads, including the Caesar Combo ($8.50), are extremely well endowed. Secondi entrées are really too expensive, but almost all of the pastas are good options. The fettuccini alfredo comes with a choice of vegetables, chicken, shrimp, or straight-up cheese ($8.50–$11.95). The fusili corosh, spiral pasta with sausage, peppers, escarole, and cannelini beans in a light tomato touch, is also a good choice. **SPF 15. Open daily. Kitchen open until midnight. Patio. Street parking available.**

BAR SAN MIGUEL

3313 N. CLARK STREET, (773) 871-0896

An attractive bar specializing in "traditional border food," Bar San Miguel is inevitably overshadowed by its trendy next-door neighbor, Mia Francesca. No problem, the hordes can wait in line next door while you sip sangria in the shady arbor of Bar San Miguel's back patio. Enjoy a balmy summer evening by munching a molieta, a Mexican pizza ($5.75–$6.50, try the four cheese with toasted almonds and capers), under the trailing grapevine. Other light meals include enchiladas ($6.50–$7.75) and sandwiches ($6.50–$7.50). If you need something more substantial, there are a number of Platos de Casa, including roasted pork with black bean sherry sauce ($9.75), chicken breasts stuffed with three cheeses, poblano peppers, and garlic in a caper cilantro sauce ($10.50), and fajitas ($9.95–$11.95).

SPF 15. Open daily, full bar. Street parking difficult.

SOUTHPORT CITY SALOON

2548 N. SOUTHPORT STREET, (773) 975-6110

The Southport City Saloon is a gem of a watering hole with one of the most picturesque patios in the city. The broad limbs of a tree shooting up through the bar shade diners lazing at finished wood tables. On brisk days, the outdoor fireplace throws off warmth to the more determined outdoor eaters. Although most entrées, except the half slab of ribs ($10.50) and the barbecue chicken ($11.25), will put you over the "fork & knife" limit, a large selection of sandwiches, salads, and burgers is available, most for between $6.95 and $10.25. Among the entrées, the daily Blue Plate Special is a deal. Different every night, the Blue Plate is a full-course meal priced at $8.95 before 7 P.M. and $10.95 after 7 P.M.

SPF 15. Open daily. Full bar.

Some of the city's bars offer some of the best inexpensive outdoor dining options in the city:

404 WINE BAR

2852 N. SOUTHPORT AVENUE, (773) 404-5886

Ah, there's nothing like sipping wine in the summertime! 404, a European-inspired lounge, features quality inexpensive wine and light bites to relax with on the spacious outdoor patio. Guests can choose wines by the flight, by the glass, or by the bottle. And pair it with a selection of pizzas, cheeses, or sandwiches. Candlelit tables add a romantic touch to the backyard garden.

SPF 15. Open daily. Street parking available.

VILLAGE TAP

2055 W. ROSCOE AVENUE, (773) 883-0817

The Village Tap is, hands down, the best garden/food value for the money in town. A classic neighborhood bar with a lot of gleaming dark wood and an extensive drink list, the Village Tap also has the kind of cozy garden you can hang out in all night, year-round, as long as you respect the sensibilities of the neighbors. The food is highlighted by entrées that are mainly $7.95 and under and served quickly with minimum fuss. The vegetarian burrito ($5), a weighty tortilla cylinder stuffed with beans, cheese, sprouts, broccoli, and other healthy stuff, is served with a side of chips and salsa and is highly recommended. The falafel and hummus plate ($5.50) is also a good choice and usually yields another meal for later. Burgers, salads, and a couple of different grilled chicken breast sandwiches are also a good bet.

SPF 15. Open daily. Full bar. Street parking available.

JUSTINS

3358 N. SOUTHPORT AVENUE, (773) 929-4844

Justins is more than just a neighborhood sports bar with a dozen TVs and three satellite dishes that can hone in on "a field hockey game in Morocco at the drop of a hat." Justins's spacious, tree-studded beer garden, ornamented by a table and chairs on the roof, serves good-sized portions of standard bar food for very reasonable prices, along with 13 "pretty decent" beers on tap.

SPF 15. Open daily. Full bar. Street parking available.

SHEFFIELD'S WINE AND BEER GARDEN

3258 N. SHEFFIELD AVENUE, (773) 281-4989

It doesn't get much cheaper than this! Sheffield's defines the meaning of BYOB—bring your own beef. Tucked off Sheffield behind a picket fence is one of Lakeview's best-liked bars and beer gardens, complete with grills so that you can do your own. What you save on dinner, you'll probably drink away here, so don't feel too fiscally smug.

SPF 15. Open daily. Open late. Street parking difficult.

Quick Bites A FEW QUICK THOUGHTS

Some great outdoor dining options are covered elsewhere in this book:

MOODY'S PUB
5910 N. BROADWAY, (773) 275-2696

Moody's, one of this town's classic pubs, has a tree-shaded patio seating 150. Diners are serenaded by two fountains underneath a canopy of leafy branches. Moody's flash is in the flora, not the food, which is hearty pub fare. (More on Moody's in "Restaurants on the Edge: Rogers Park Restaurants, Edgewater Eateries, and Other Northern Lights.")

SPF 15. Open daily serving until 1 A.M., full bar.

LUTZ CONTINENTAL CAFÉ & PASTRY
2458 W. MONTROSE AVENUE, (773) 478-7785

Around since 1948, Lutz boasts a tiny walled garden out back, complete with greenery and a small fountain, bubbling away among the umbrella-shaded tables. The menu has some heavy, traditional Austrian selections, light meals, including crêpes and sandwiches, along with some very serious tortes. (For more details see "Oktoberfeast, Ja!")

SPF 15. Closed Sundays.

Street Fare

The Evolution of Street Festivals

The traditions of street food go back thousands of years. In ancient Greece, vendors pushed carts of freshly roasted nuts and seeds while making the rounds at local tavernas. In Medieval Europe, crowds congregated at crossroads where street vendors with large baskets gathered to sell bread, local produce, and savory pies. After a time, full-fledged markets developed and became the center of social life, where locals could get medical care, watch a performance, or stock their kitchens with street vendors' wares. "Shouting like a fishwife" advertised mussels and whelks for sale, while "a deafening noise close to the ear" was thought to stimulate salivary glands.

Gastronomic delicacies can be bought on street corners around the world. Whole lambs can be seen on the spit in Istanbul, while in Lima, Peru outside the Plaza de Toros, the second-oldest bull ring in the world, there're almost always vendors selling grilled kabobs called "anticuchos" (beef hearts marinated with 15 cloves of garlic, hot peppers, and cumin—they used to be made with llama hearts until those became scarce).

In Japan, street vendors specialize in the artful presentation of yakitori, teriyaki, tempura, or noodles. Thai vendors have worn yokes with two hanging baskets for hundreds of years. Food and condiments are carried in one basket, while a smoldering charcoal grill for on-the-spot cooking is carried in the other.

Here in Chicago, we've blended ancient traditions and ethnic tastes to evolve street fairs and the fare that accompanies them into an art form. Nowhere else have town dwellers and visitors from the countryside, appropriately dressed in Bulls championship T-shirts and athletic stretch shorts, so mastered the fine art of juggling a barbecued turkey leg with egg rolls, slippery pad Thai, or skewered jerk chicken on a bed of rice and beans, and several plastic 16-ounce vessels of frosty festive beverages.

According to ancient city lore and the Illinois Restaurant Association, the **Taste of Chicago**, the big daddy of all al fresco pig-outs, was founded over 20 years ago by Arnie Morton with 30-some restaurants. In recent years, over 60 different restaurants have participated. In addition to those manning booths, 11 different "fine-dining establishments," one each day, hold court in the gourmet dining pavilion. Fine-dining establishments highlighted have included Prairie, Printers Row, La Strada, Hotel Inter-Continental, Italian Village, Magnum's, Palette's, Nix (The Knickerbocker Hotel), Fado, and Hacienda Tecalitlan—a group some might view as a mixed bag as far as Michelin stars seem to go.

Food vendors for the Taste are chosen by the Illinois Restaurant Association. According to executive director Colleen McShane, there's no truth to the persistent rumors that regular participants have a "grandfathered" lock on the event. "We send out applications to everyone—close to 4,000 (every) year. We get about 100 applications back, and we typically have 25-percent to 30-percent turnover in the restaurants participating." All successful applicants must be year-round restaurants. They must pass an inspection that checks for sanitation and determines the restaurant's ability to satisfy the high volume demanded by their 10- by

20-foot booth while not adversely impacting their regular operations. Restaurants fill spots in multiple food categories, including pizza, ribs, seafood, dessert, corn, ethnic, and general.

In addition to the nine blockbuster lake front festivals scheduled through September, some 70 (at last count) neighborhood festivals citywide are scheduled to deliver entertainment and food, glorious food, throughout the summer. Many of the neighborhood festivals are run by outside event managers. While all of these events give first choice on space to local restaurants, many rely on "outsiders" to man the extra grills.

"We try to highlight the locals, but many of them find it difficult to staff and equip a booth unless it's right outside their door. They also see a certain amount of financial risk in participating. If the weather doesn't cooperate, the festival will be a bust for them," says John Barry of Barry Events, which manages numerous nonprofit events, including the Lakeview Mayfest, Andersonville Midsommerfest, Rock Around the Block, Retro on Roscoe, and Oktober Fest.

When they can't get enough locals, Barry Entertainment turns to a huge database of outside cooks. "Some of these vendors make a business of traveling from festival to festival across the country doing street fairs," adds Barry. With these hired guns (and spatulas), the show goes on—from May through September.

It's time to go out and play in the streets now. Just save a turkey drumstick for me.

For more information, contact the Mayor's Office of Special Events: (312) 744-3315, or visit the City of Chicago's Web site at www.ci.chi.il.us/Tourism/.

Solstice Searching

Uncovering Chicago's Summer Solstice Celebrations

Summer Solstice, also known as Midsummer, Litha, or St. John's Day, marks the longest day of the year and the beginning of summer. Celebrated in some form since the Stone Age, solstice is derived from the Latin word *solstitium* for "that the sun stood still."

Solstice was celebrated in ancient Celtic Europe with night-long bonfires blazing in places like Stonehenge, the Plain of Salisbury, and numerous wooded groves. Druids led the ceremonies that celebrated the fertility of the earth. Sexual unions during these festivities were an essential part of the rites, since the Celts believed trees and plants could not be fertile without the complementary union of human beings.

City dwellers today continue to celebrate summer by flocking to our own modern-day sacred groves, sidewalk cafés, and beer gardens. And, like the festivities of old, these gatherings are overseen and behavior is mandated by our society's current supervisory body.

Chicago's latter-day druids are to be found in the Department of Revenue in Room 107 at City Hall. Here work the wise ones who publish the 12 pages of rules and regulations (complete with dos and don'ts graphics) on the city's Sidewalk Café Program.

Some things have changed since ancient times. No more all-night rituals that celebrate the rising sun. Sidewalk cafés are licensed to operate only between the hours of 8 A.M. and midnight. Gatherings now have more structure. Sidewalk cafés must leave "six feet of clear space for pedestrian movement between the outer edge of the sidewalk café and the curb line, and no sidewalk café can be located within 15 feet of a bus stop, bus shelter, or rapid transit station entrance." No rules, however, about bon-fires or public acts of romance.

Like the ancient Celts, City Hall reveres nature and publishes some very specific points (complete with illustrations) entitled "Guidelines for Landscaping Out-door Cafés." Under "Provision of Greenery," the "Quan-tity of Green Area" is clearly defined. "The railing, fencing, or other such method to enclose a space for the use of a café in a public right-of-way shall have no less than 50 percent of its railing, top of fence, etc. covered with planter boxes . . . In addition, for every 100 addi-tional square feet of area beyond a 300-square-foot café, the applicant shall provide one, 24-inch shrub in a suit-able planter which will allow the shrub 100 percent vis-ibility above the rail, fence, etc. . . . . For example, a café with a 630-square-foot area would provide two shrubs, and a café with 660-square-feet would provide three shrubs . . . A small tree may substitute for a 24" shrub."

Shady and secluded beer gardens have to fulfill such strict protocols that the rules can't even be published. Instead, a prospective beer garden host needs to head down to Room 107 with a liquor license and meet with a case manager to see if, first, his neighborhood is zoned for beer-garden revelry.

In spite of the structure imposed today, denizens of the city seem to be able to find nearly as much pleasure in our outdoor gathering places as the pagans of the past did in theirs. Take the patrons of the **Zephyr**, who sit under the shade of an expansive awning complete with ceiling fans on an astro-turfed stretch of Wilson Avenue in Ravenswood. Summer decadence knows no bounds here where diners gather from 8 A.M. until 1 A.M. on the weekends (midnight during the week) imbibing festive beverages and frolicking through all manner of frozen, buttery creations with names like War of the Worlds, the Titanic, and the Grand Hotel.

Urban warriors looking for a sidewalk sanctuary off

Michigan Avenue can commune at **Bella Luna Café**, a neighborly Italian restaurant at Dearborn and Superior. The twinkling white lights hanging over the sidewalk seating reflect the soft jewel tones of the restaurant's interior. Surrounded by an uncanny silence, diners can enjoy a selection of pizzas, generous pastas, and entrées, including cappellini canne strelli, thready pasta with pillow-sized scallops and spinach in a marinara sauce, and bistecca al pizzaolla, grilled NY strip sautéed with tomatoes, black olives, garlic, and white wine, topped with fresh mozzarella.

For those who want to let it all hang out that one special night, the **Museum of Contemporary Art** hosts an annual 24-hour Summer Solstice Celebration starting on the Friday in mid-June closest to the solstice at 5 P.M. and running through 5 P.M. the next Saturday. Billed as "an exuberant festival of contemporary art, dance, music, and activities for audiences of all ages, packed into 24 exhilarating hours," the party usually features artfully prepared sustenance from **Puck's**, as well as other edibles like a couple thousand slices of Bailey's Millennium Cheesecake from Eli's to kick things off and a free breakfast with Krispy Kreme donuts the next morning.

BELLA LUNA CAFÉ
731 N. DEARBORN STREET, (312) 751-2552

PUCK'S AT THE MCA
220 E. CHICAGO AVENUE, (312) 307-4034

THE ZEPHYR
1777 W. WILSON AVENUE, (773) 728-6070

20

Diversionary Dining

EAT NOW, HANG OUT LATER! A WHOLE EVENING OF DISTRACTION FOR $20 OR LESS

"**W**hat good is sitting alone in your room? Come hear the music play. . . . " So, what do you want to do tonight? These days, is your definition of "dinner and a show" take-out and a rental from Blockbuster? Was your cousin's wedding the last time you dined and danced—or was it your high school prom? Do the words "On Broadway" conjure up images of a big-ticket production at the Auditorium Theater or just that classic George Benson album stuffed into the back of your closet? Can you spell p-o-t-a-t-o, as in couch?

Sociologists have declared the two biggest issues negatively affecting relationships to be (1) not enough quality time together and (2) channel surfing.

> "3. B & V beats sittin' on your butt gettin' fat at home."
>
> —Chicago *Reader* advertisement, describing "3 things you might not have known about the Brew & View."

Both of these evils can be drastically alleviated by just getting out and having a good time. So, what's stopping you? Are you simply lacking in the "I"s—imagination and income?

Imagination, creativity, spontaneity—some of us are more bodaciously gifted than others. For those of you who are sadly lacking in those areas, you can shore up your deficiencies, make friends, and influence people. Yes, with a little direction, you may not become the life of the party, but at least you'll know where it is. And, even better, you'll be able to afford to go to it.

Acquire some cultural enrichment in your life (or at the very least, a T-shirt from the show—overpriced event T-shirts are not included in *Cheap Chow Chicago* pricing.) And, making it even better, you're going to do it all, and you're not going to be hungry! So, read on and get out. Just do it. Be young. No more excuses—save those for your boss.

MUD BUG

901 W. WEED STREET, (312) 787-9600

Open 8 A.M. until 2 A.M. with over 100 televisions, most of which are focused on live thoroughbred and harness racing from tracks across the country, a tele-theatre, sports bar, and access to the Illinois Lottery, Mud Bug is your conveniently located off-track betting resource. The place has two eating options, a cafeteria line and a sit-down restaurant, both of which have the same pub grub with some emphasis on the Cajun. (Mud Bug is a legend about a Louisiana thoroughbred who was slower than a "mud bug" until a miracle happened, and the horse became faster than any other four-legged critter around.) Ordering in the restaurant will cost you $1 per item more than the cafeteria line (plus tip, of course). Nightly specials include:

Sunday: Italian combo ($5.95) or BBQ roast beef ($4.95)
Monday: Meat loaf ($5.95) or chili dogs ($4.95)
Tuesday: Chicken stir-fry ($6.95)
Wednesday: Teriyaki chicken ($6.95) or meatball sandwich ($4.95)
Thursday: Beef shish kebab ($6.95) or chili dog ($4.95)
Friday: Fish & chips ($6.95) or macaroni & cheese ($4.95)
Saturday: Roast beef with mashed potatoes ($6.95) or the tuna melt ($5.95)

Races run after 2 A.M. and can be pre-wagered with results and cashing available the following day.
Open daily. Full bar.

ISAAC HAYES/FAMOUS DAVE'S RIBS 'N' BLUES

739 N. CLARK STREET, (312) 266-2400

It's tough to resist a lure that reads, "Get ready to have your mouth smacked and your butt rocked, as Famous Dave's, which has teamed up with Isaac Hayes for music, brings his pit-smoked ribs, fire-roasted chickens and live blues back to the streets where he grew up." Founded by Dave Anderson, a native of Humboldt Park, Famous Dave's Ribs 'N' Blues brings Dave's reverence for the holy trinity of "Smoke, Meat, and Sauce" back home. Portions at Dave's are as big as the live music blasting out nightly from the main stage and are slathered with Dave's "butt rockin" special sauce, a tangy topping with kick. For those who can't make up their minds, go with the All-American Feast—a full slab, whole chicken, half-pound beef brisket or chopped pork, coleslaw, fries, and some of the tastiest roadhouse beans around—so big it's served on a garbage can lid. Word of caution, while the pit-smoked ribs are tender enough to be eaten off the bone with a fork, the tips have more fat than a beached whale, which is what you'll feel like after you eat a plate of these.

Open daily. Street parking difficult; valet; lot nearby.

Boogie Bites

CHICAGO BRAUHAUS

4732 N. LINCOLN AVENUE, (773) 784-4444

Are you ever in the mood to just dance, dance, dance? Well, if you want to get out and try some dancing that's not, say, strictly ballroom, check out either the Chicago Brauhaus or Lalo's.

The Chicago Brauhaus (for more details see "Taste of Lincoln Avenue"), the established German restaurant and nightclub anchor in Lincoln Square, offers a reasonably priced menu of assorted wursts, schnitzels, and other German delicacies that can be danced off six nights a week to the energetic strains of the Chicago Brauhaus Band. Patrons are not shy here. Requests and singing along are encouraged in addition to dancing.

Open daily. Full bar.

LALO'S

1960 N. CLYBOURN AVENUE, (773) 880-5256

If you feel like rhumba-ing late into the night to the strains of salsa and merengue, try the lower-level dance club at Lalo's. The Mexican restaurant specializes in hearty, south-of-the-border bites such as enchiladas de mole poblano, three rolled-up corn tortillas stuffed with shredded chicken and topped with mole sauce ($11.95), bistec con rajas y queso, marinated portions of ribeye steak, grilled with onions, tomatoes, and green peppers ($12.95) or the camarones empanizados, butterfly shrimp breaded with Lalo's secret spices, served with spanish rice and salad ($13.95). The kitchen is open until 2 A.M. There is a dress code—no jeans or sneakers; shiny suits or tight skirts and high heels preferred.

Open daily. Full bar. Street parking available; valet.

Cultural Cuisine

BIG SHOULDERS CAFÉ
(CHICAGO HISTORICAL SOCIETY)

1601 N. CLARK STREET, (312) 587-7766

If you've been absorbing enough culture to work up an appetite, you don't have to settle for the museum cafeteria (depending on the museum you're visiting). The Big Shoulders Café at the Chicago Historical Society, named in tribute to Carl Sandburg, is a greenhouse-y café serving healthy American fare, including Sheboygan bratwursts, wild rice cakes with wild mushroom sauce, and jalapeño cornbread, all for under $10. In nice weather, the outdoor café encourages dogs, and profits from the "bowser bistro biscuit menu" go to the Anti-Cruelty Society.

The Big Shoulders Café is open daily for lunch from 11:30 A.M. to 3 P.M. and Sundays for brunch. Full bar.

PUCK'S AT THE MCA
(MUSEUM OF COMTEMPORARY ART)
220 E. CHICAGO AVENUE, (312) 307-4034

Puck's is both a sit-down restaurant and a carry-out counter featuring "a menu influenced by Mediterranean and Asian cuisine" created by Spago Executive Chef François Kwaku-Dongo. Actually, except for the entrées, most of the sandwiches and salads, including the classic Spago Chinois Chicken Salad, are available at the carry-out counter. The sit-down option adds Wolfgang Puck's well-known pizzas, as well as a number of more filling entrées, including meat loaf wrapped in pancetta and served with roasted garlic potato purée, a mountain of grilled onions, and port wine sauce; roasted rosemary chicken with mashed potatoes and red wine sauce; and grilled salmon paillard with braised autumn vegetable provençal.

Tuesday 11 A.M. to 3 P.M., 4:30 P.M. to 7 P.M. (cocktails and hors d'oeurvres); Wednesday–Friday 11 A.M. to 3 P.M.; Saturday–Sunday 10 A.M. to 3 P.M. (brunch).

McKLINTOCK COURT GARDEN RESTAURANT (THE ART INSTITUTE)
110 S. MICHIGAN AVENUE, (312) 443-3508 SUMMER,
(312) 443-3530 OTHER SEASONS

McKlintock Court Garden Restaurant at the Art Institute offers outdoor dining by the courtyard fountain during nice weather, along with After Hours Jazz on Tuesday evenings from 4:30 to 7 P.M. ($7 minimum). Sandwiches and salads are all under $10, with the most expensive being the lamb niçoise salad at $9.95. All the entrées, however, will put you over the limit.

McKlintock Court Garden Restaurant is open daily, Memorial Day through September, from 11 A.M. to 3:30 P.M. (seating only until 2:30 P.M. on Tuesdays). Full bar.

THE PARK PLACE CAFÉ

2200 N. CANNON DRIVE, BEHIND THE LION HOUSE, (312) 742-2000

If you find yourself ready for your own feeding time during a visit to the wild kingdom, try the Park Place Café inside the Park Pavilion, which was originally the city's first aquarium and later served as the Zoo's Reptile House before being renovated. The bright and shiny Park Place Café offers seven theme food stops to hungry visitors, including the Gorilla Grill with four kinds of reptile-shaped french fries, pretzel bread, baguette-like "walking sticks" and other deli sandwiches from Safari Sandwiches; Festa Italian; the Mexican Market; salads; and to-go items from the Zoo Express; ice cream and yogurt at the Polar Cap; and beverages at the Watering Hole. The Café is designed to be family-friendly, and prices are reasonable. Proceeds from the Park Place Café help the Zoo retain its status as one of the last free zoos in the country and one of the only cultural attractions in Chicago that doesn't charge admission.

Open weekdays 10 A.M.–5 P.M., weekends 10 A.M.–7 P.M. (Memorial Day through Labor Day). Indoor and outdoor seating.

BOCADITOS

8400 W. 31ST STREET, (708) 485-0263

Bocaditos is Brookfield Zoo's first full-service restaurant. Meaning "little bites," Bocaditos, which is found in the South American exhibit, serves sandwiches, salads, and a variety of hot and cold tapas, most of which are priced under $5. Options include the ubiquitous baked goat cheese in tomato sauce; shrimp fritters; a "sandwich" of fried Chilean sea bass with red peppers sprinkled with lime juice; and cold plates like alcachofas, a blend of artichoke hearts, black olives, and roasted peppers; black bean and corn salad; and three kinds of traditional Peruvian potato dishes.

Bocaditos is open daily for lunch. The restaurant has a children's menu and serves South American beers and Chilean wines.

SOUNDINGS RESTAURANT
(SHEDD AQUARIUM)
1200 S. LAKE SHORE DRIVE, (312) 986-2286

The Shedd lets you check out the marine life and then continue to admire the marina and the city's skyline from its Soundings Restaurant. An assortment of entrées, including pastas, seafood, and grill, are priced $4.95 to $11.95.

Lunch is served from Noon to 2:30 P.M. daily.

Eats 'n' Beats

ABBEY PUB
3420 W. GRACE STREET, (773) 463-5808

Chicago offers a number of options where you can absorb food for the soul and music for the ears. The Abbey Pub serves shepherd's pie, lamb stew, and Irish soda bread to the tunes of Irish bands on Wednesdays and Thursdays, folk, blues, or rock on Fridays and Saturdays, and a weekly Irish jam session on Sundays. Monday is the weekly barn dance, and Tuesday is an acoustic open stage.

Open daily. Full bar. Live music. Street parking difficult.

BUDDY GUY'S LEGENDS
654 S. WABASH AVENUE, (312) 427-0333

SCHUBAS TAVERN
3159 N. SOUTHPORT AVENUE, (773) 525-2508

THE BEAT KITCHEN
2100 W. BELMONT AVENUE, (773) 281-4444

Buddy Guy's Legends offers the best in blues along with Cajun specialties, prepared by Chef Jason Girard, author of *The Blues Highway Cookbook*, every night until midnight. If you're less concerned about the food than the music, other good options for grabbing a burger and a band are Schubas Tavern and the Beat Kitchen. Schubas is Chicago's spot for rockabilly and country music. The Beat Kitchen has actually enhanced its bar grub menu with a selection of 16 individual designer pizzas (priced $7.95 and under), soups, salads, and Bayou-style meat loaf.

All are open daily. Schubas serves brunch. Full bars.

RAVINIA FESTIVAL

1575 OAKWOOD AVENUE, HIGHLAND PARK, (773) RAVINIA

The Ravinia Festival, of course, is one of the ultimate summer dining and culture experiences, whether you BYOB and graze on the lawn or cough up some bucks to eat at one of the ever-increasing numbers of on-site dining establishments and later plant yourself in the pavilion. The music starts in June and continues through August. Lawn seats are $10; pavilion seats start at $20.

Wine and beer. Parking lot.

You may not always be able to think of your stomach first, but if you're stuck spending your time taking care of business, why not give yourself the option to grab a bite to eat at the same time.

SAGA'S LAUNDER-BAR AND CAFÉ/ THE NEWPORT BAR & GRILL
3435 N. SOUTHPORT AVENUE, (773) 929-9274

Throw in a couple loads and come back around for a burger, sandwich, or plate of pasta. Sip some suds while you run through the rinse cycle.
Open daily. Full bar. Street parking difficult.

NIKKI & PETE'S FABULOUS DELI/ WE'LL CLEAN
1520 N. HALSTED STREET, (312) 943-6100

If you're spending $150 to have your car detailed, you may as well toss in another $5.75 for a sandwich at Nikki & Pete's Fabulous Deli. Test drive the Porsche 911 (tuna sandwich), a Lamborghini (chicken breast), or a Classic '59 'Vette (veggie)?
Open daily. Full bar. Street parking available.

Lucky Bars

Uncovering the Secrets of Successful Irish Pubs

I visited Cuzco, Peru, the oldest continuously inhabited city in the Western Hemisphere. There, smack dab in the middle of the ancient capital of the Inca empire, was Paddy Flaherty's, an Irish pub. Where once the fermented beverage of choice was *chicha de jora*, or maize beer, you can now just as easily get a Guinness.

Irish pubs have spread all over the world, and the big barking dog of worldwide Irish pub design is, appropriately named, the Irish Pub Company. Headquartered in Dublin with a U.S. office in Atlanta, the Irish Pub Company has built over 300 pubs since 1991 in 38 countries throughout Europe, from Spain to Russia, as well as in the cities of Hong Kong, Tokyo, Bangkok, Singapore, Kuala Lumpur, and Dubai. Affiliated with Guinness Brewing Worldwide, the Irish Pub Company will not only design and build your pub with materials imported completely from the Emerald Isle, but will also recruit real Irish staff, set up and train your kitchen to prepare nearly 100 Irish recipes and identify quality suppliers for those dishes, help you pick out playlists of Irish music or even steer you to a Dublin-based booking service for the live stuff, supply you with "bric-a-brac and tailored merchandise," and last but not least, stock your pub with a complete Irish drinks portfolio. Truly, it's a bar-in-a-box for

> "There's nothing in the world quite like an Irish pub. It's a rare mix of music and conversation. Of good food and drink. Of hospitality and humor. And an exceptional investment opportunity."
>
> —The Irish Pub Company, Corporate Literature

only an estimated $140–$180 per square foot of public space, after acquiring the real estate.

The Irish Pub Company offers several designs, each highlighting a different period feel. There's the Gaelic Pub with its prehistoric and medieval Celtic touches, the rough and cozy Irish Country Cottage Pub, the Traditional Irish Pub Shop, the ornate Victorian Dublin Pub, and the Irish Brewery Pub, "reminiscent of St. James Gate Brewery in Dublin," home of—you guessed it—Guinness, the "world's most famous stout."

Can't decide what pub scene works for you? No worries, you can also order *fado*. Meaning "long ago" in Gaelic, the fado concept was first introduced in the United States in Atlanta. For $1.5 million, five different pub designs were blended into a multistory environment to create "a walk through Irish pub history." A huge success, the Irish Pub Company notes the original investment was paid off in under three years due to annual sales of "$700–$800 per square feet" and margins "further enhanced by an 80/20 beverage to food mix."

Chicago is no second city to anyone when it comes to a love for anything Irish, especially anything Irish related to drinking, and we got our own **Fado** in River North's Touristaville area in September 1997. Notes Manager Chris Robinson, "By virtue of our location, patrons tend to be a combination of tourists, businesspeople, and regulars. I'd say, of the regulars, 50 percent to 75 percent are Irish."

Like the template in Atlanta, Chicago's version is a sprawling history lesson of multiple scenic rooms tracing the cultural development of Ireland. "Everything in the pub décor-wise, including the wood and stone, was imported from Ireland and then reassembled in Chicago," says Robinson. The bar upstairs in the Victorian Pub room, for example, is over 100 years old and came from a Dublin bar formerly known as the Pretty Kitchen.

In spite of what some would consider overdone kitsch, Chicago revels in anything Irish, and the place is frequently packed. Fado lures in the crowds with live music and a full menu of Irish specialties, including boxtys, or Irish pancakes. The fish and chips and the shepherd's pie, both of which wash down well with a pint of Guinness, are by far the most popular. Live music, ranging from traditional Irish to alternative, also brings in patrons on Sundays, Tuesdays, and Saturdays.

But you don't have to be backed by a big corporate organization to open a cozy, traditional pub serving an authentic, all-day Irish breakfast. Billy Lawless opened the Irish Oak in the heart of Wrigleyville in June 1998, after selling his previous hotel and bar in Galway and moving to Chicago. He worked with the same independent designer in Belfast to create the **Irish Oak** who had designed his former property. "Every piece of the bar— from the wood to the wallpaper—was designed and built in Ireland and then shipped overseas in two 40-foot containers," Lawless explained. "The focus on design has made a huge difference. We're one of the most authentic Irish bars in the city. Most of the Irish that come in can't believe how much it feels like a pub at home. That was our goal."

FADO
100 W. GRAND AVENUE, (312) 836-0066

THE IRISH OAK
3511 N. CLARK STREET, (773) 935-6669

21

Rib Tips

RACK 'EM UP!

Love me tenderloin, love me sweet. . . . For years, Chicagoans have had a love affair with ribs. Yes, there's nothing like a slab in the winter for that warm, contented feeling or a rack right off the grill in the summer heat at the "Taste" dribbling down your Bulls T-shirt and Lycra stretch shorts. The debate, however, rages on as to who has the tastiest, the tenderest, the spiciest ribs around. Even after "Rib Tips," the controversy may still exist, except on one point where we should all be absolutely clear—where to pig out for less.

Some history to spare . . . Up to the end of World War II, pork was the principal meat in this country. GIs returning from service, however, had developed a taste for beef in the military messes, and pork was eventually nudged out of its top spot. Pork, though, remains the only meat considered suitable for barbecuing in the Carolinas, Georgia, Alabama, and most of the Deep South. Barbecue traditions vary immensely between regions. For example, in eastern North Carolina, the whole hog is cooked and garnished with a vinegary pepper sauce; in western North Carolina, the ribs are cooked, the shoulder is sliced, and all is

> **"The word 'barbecue' may stem from the French** *barbe à queue*, **meaning 'from whiskers to tail.' The expression indicates that the whole animal has been cooked. (And every part is eaten except the piggy's squeak.)"**
>
> —Irena Chalmers,
> *The Great Food Almanac*

coated in a tangy red sauce. In contrast, throughout Texas and much of the rest of the Southwest cattle country, beef ribs are cooked and served in a spicy red sauce. Many of Chicago's old-time rib joints reflect the influences of the Deep South, as much of Chicago's rib traditions were transported north by the Illinois Central Railroad's *Green Diamond*, which brought African Americans from the rural backwaters of Louisiana, Mississippi, and Arkansas directly to Illinois Station, the Ellis Island of the Midwest.

Where's the beef? Here are some tips if you're going to try it at home or you just don't know what to order. There are three different kinds of pork ribs; spareribs, cut from just behind the pork shoulder; the shorter back ribs; and country-style ribs, cut from the pork loin. Beef ribs, which come from a totally different animal, look much like pork back ribs. The Department of Agriculture defines barbecue as "cooked by the direct action of dry heat resulting from burning hardwood or coal therefrom for a sufficient period of time to assume the usual characteristics . . . which include the formation of a brown crust." So, if the fat is in the fire, you're broiling; you've got to be smoking to be really barbecuing—the only good argument for smoking we support.

Editor's Note: Price ratings for this chapter are based on an order of tips, not necessarily on the whole menu.

BONE DADDY

551 N. OGDEN AVENUE, (312) 226-6666

Not to be confused with Smoke Daddy, Bone Daddy, which is under the same ownership as Twisted Spoke, specializes in free-range pigs that are butchered fresh and shipped to the restaurant the same day. Marinated in their house sauce for a day or two, then slow smoked with a mix of sweet and savory hard woods, the pork is so tender on these ribs that it almost melts in your mouth. You can get a half slab of baby back ribs for $11 (or 11 bones as the menu says), which includes sweet potato chips and an "accessory" like the black beans, mac & cheese, or homemade tater tots; the full slab is $18. Also good are the thick pork chops for $14. For $7, you can get one of the juicy sandwiches, including the jerk chicken, jerk portabello, or pulled pork. Finish the meal off with a slice of homemade pie, made daily, which varies from blueberry to banana cream. Live blues and rock nightly.

Open seven days a week; brunch on Saturday, Sunday. Full bar. Street parking available.

THE SMOKE DADDY

1804 W. DIVISION STREET, (773) 772-6656

Barbecue and blues are combined seven days a week at Smoke Daddy, where the "WOW" is flashing over the door in neon and in the flavor of the food. The Smoke Daddy cooks up peppery "Memphis-Texarkana" pig parts, spareribs, tips, turkey, beef brisket, and veggie burgers in the Little Red Smokehouse, a barbecue pit made in Texas that cost $15,000 and weighs 1,900 pounds. A combination of burning wood, fans, and a stone embedded in the door of the pit helps duplicate the flavor of an old-fashioned brick barbecue pit. A half slab of spareribs is $7.95, and rib tips run $4.95 for a half plate, $7.95 for a full; sandwiches—pork shoulder, brisket, chicken, turkey, or combo—are $4.95 to $5.95. Vegetarian specialties include the vegetarian barbecue sandwich ($5.45). Sandwiches are served with the house Mo-Jo sauce and chow-chow relish. Hot music is available some nights to go with the hot sauce.

Open until 2 A.M. Monday–Saturday; Sunday until 1 A.M.

ARMY & LOU'S

422 E. 75TH STREET, (773) 483-6550

At $16.95, Army & Lou's full slab of meaty baby back ribs is one of the only selections on the menu that, technically, isn't cheap chow. To bring this tangy treat, with meat so tender it falls off the bone, in under the "fork & knife" limit, share a slab with a friend and then supplement your order with one of Army & Lou's Southern specialties, most of which run under $12. Maybe some fried chicken with two sides ($9.75) or the catfish filet ($11.95). Or, the fresh mixed greens steamed with smoked bacon and accompanied by either smoked turkey or ham hock ($8.95). All dinners come with corn muffins and a waitperson with personality.

Here are some other South Side soul food restaurants you might want to check out:

Barbara's Restaurant, 353 ½ E. 51st Street, (773) 624-0087. Monday–Saturday, opens at 5 A.M.

Jackie's II, 425 E. 71st Street, (773) 483-4095. Specializing in beef short ribs. Open 24 hours.

ROBINSON'S NO. 1 RIBS

655 W. ARMITAGE AVENUE, (312) 337-1399

Located in Lincoln Park across from Lincoln Park High School, Robinson's is remodeled, offering a bright new dining area and an outdoor café. In spite of its yuppie location, Robinson's serves up ribs that rival the best of what the South Side offers. Using the No. 1 sauce recipe that has supposedly been in the Robinson family for more than 200 years and 14 generations, Robinson's cranks out tender tips with a noticeable hickory-smoked tang. A tip appetizer, enough for a meal in itself, can be had for as little as $3.75. There're also good rib tip combos, including the tips and links ($6.45) and the chicken wing combo ($7.50). Both baby backs and beef ribs are available in both full slabs ($14.35) and half slabs ($9.95), a nice option for those of us who would like to pay less in lieu of hauling home a huge doggie bag. For those who aren't feeling partial to pork, there are seafood and fish options, including the grilled Cajun catfish fillets ($7.25) and the half pound of batter-dipped fried shrimp. ($9.45). There's even a veggie burger.

Open daily. Street parking difficult.

Quick Bites **A FEW QUICK THOUGHTS**

Hate to keep going back to the same places, but more good rib tips can be found in "Diversionary Dining" and in "Decent American Values."

RIBS 'N BIBS

5300 S. DORCHESTER AVENUE, (773) 493-0400

THE ORIGINAL LEON'S BAR-B-Q

8251 S. COTTAGE GROVE AVENUE, (773) 488-4556

1640 E. 79TH STREET, (773) 731-1454

1158 W. 59TH STREET, (773) 778-7828

Two South Side originals, and you can smell the hickory smoke practically to Lake Shore Drive and in the ivy-covered halls of the University of Chicago. Ribs 'N Bibs is where Hyde Park rib die-hards go for carryout. Maverick Munchies (tips and fries) are $6.90. Chix 'n Tips are $7, and the Tips 'n Link combo is $6.90. Leon's is a South Side mainstay where the ribs are rumored to be rubbed down and marinated as much as two days ahead of cooking to lock in the flavor. The aroma is the best advertisement money can't buy. Tips come in three price sizes—$2.82, $5.87, and $7.23.
Both open daily.

ISSAC HAYES/FAMOUS DAVE'S

739 N. CLARK STREET, (312) 266-2400

Get your fill of live, hot-buttered soul—and barbecue—at this celebrity-driven club teaming up with Famous Dave's Ribs 'N' Blues, which was founded by Dave Anderson, a native of Humboldt Park. In addition to regular performances by the Grammy Award–winning star, expect some of his famous friends to hit the stage. Portions are as big as the live music blasting out nightly and are slathered with Dave's "butt rockin" special sauce, a tangy topping with kick.
Open daily until 2 A.M. Live blues nightly. Sunday brunch. Street parking difficult; nearby lot; valet.

BROTHER JIMMY'S

2909 N. SHEFFIELD AVENUE, (773) 528-0888

Take time out for a treatise on North Carolina barbecue. Bring your whole fraternity to feel right at home.
Open daily. Full bar. Music. Street parking difficult.

Hot Secrets

A Saucy Look at Barbecue

Labor Day Weekend. Summer's last hurrah, and what more fitting way to celebrate than with a blowout barbecue? And, as Sherman Kaplan of WBBM Newsradio 78 once said in a review of the now, sadly, defunct Hoxie's, "The key to great barbecue lies with the sauces."

The right sauce is actually a finishing touch. Most barbecue sauces will burn on the grill if brushed on too soon, so meat is typically basted with tomato-based sauces and other sauces containing sugar only during the last 30 minutes of grilling. As we all know, liberal amounts should then be set aside to serve at the table. Last-step sauces are enhanced by seasonings applied in advance of grilling.

HECKY'S BARBECUE,
1902 Green Bay Road, Evanston, (847) 492-1182. Open daily. Carry-out only.

According to the National Pork Producers Council (NPPC), "The first step to grilling is selecting flavorful seasonings. And since pork marries well with a variety of flavor profiles, the options are endless." The NPPC recommends marinades, rubs, and brine. Marinades are created by mixing oil and an acid component, such as fruit juice or vinegar, with herbs and spices; rubs are mixtures of spices and herbs that add unique flavors when rubbed onto the surface of meat and, when combined with the meat juices, work as dry marinade, while brine contains either salt or sugar and additional flavors from spices, seeds, herbs, and other aromatics such as citrus peel that drive extra moisture into meat.

Hecky Powell has been serving his spicy red sauce from his self-named Evanston storefront for nearly 20 years. The place is take-out only and usually has a line of cars with blinking lights parked in front and a line of hungry customers parked inside.

Hecky's motto is, "It's the Sauce," and, when pressed for details on his secrets, he explains, "It's an old family recipe. My mother was a Creole from New Orleans, so it's a Louisiana-style sauce. It's got some garlic in it, which gives it a unique taste." Hecky's sauce can be purchased on the meat or off in an 18-ounce jar. It comes in original or hot and is noted as the "Official Barbecue Sauce of the Chicago Bears."

Unfortunately, summer isn't endless. Make sure you get it while it's hot.

22

Love Bites

ROMANTIC EATERIES OFFERING CHEAP THRILLS

Food and love have had associations since our earliest days. The word *aphrodisiac* has its roots in the name "Aphrodite," the ancient Greek goddess of love, and even in the most primitive of times, many foods have been given credit for mood or performance-enhancing attributes. Mandrake root, tiger's milk, and oysters may all come to mind, but some research will show that almost every plant, herb, leaf, or fruit has, at some time, been known for its aphrodisiacal powers.

> **"Love and scandal are the best sweeteners of tea."**
>
> **—Henry Fielding**

Certain vegetables were imbued with sexual powers because of their shapes. The ancient Greeks believed the carrot excited passion and facilitated conception. Both Pliny and Athenaus mention the carrot and its romantic qualities, and one ancient thinker once wrote, "the root winneth love." The Kama Sutra advised boiling treacle and asparagus, another phallic vegetable, in cow's milk and glue and adding spices and licorice. The mixture was then eaten once a day to increase sexual power and prolong life.

Fruits also had their place in the bedroom. Introduced to Europeans in the sixteenth century by the Spaniards (by way of the Mexicans), the tomato was known to the English as "the love apple," to the French as *pomme d'amour*, and to the Germans as *liebesapfel*. Thinking that it encouraged immortality, the Puritans spread the rumor that the tomato was poisonous to discourage them from being eaten. Grapes may owe their place in the history of the boudoir to the Duc de Richelieu who, in the seventeenth century, used to serve bunches at his parties—which everyone had to attend completely in the buff.

In fact, it seems as though everyone had his own approach to gastronomic seduction. The Moors of Morocco believed honey was a love stimulant and used large quantities in marriage ceremonies, which often became sexual orgies. The bride and groom ate honey, and the wine and food were made with it. The Romans, who were always adventurous when it came to food, imported all kinds of delicacies from their conquered territories. Game was considered an aphrodisiac, as was the womb of a sow and the flesh of the skink, a long, thin lizard.

Shellfish and fish have long been given credit for stimulating flagging sexual appetites. The Greeks associated the fruits of the sea with Aphrodite, who was born in the water and who first reached the shores of Greece riding, as portrayed by Botticelli, on a scallop shell. The Elizabethans had great respect for the crab as an aphrodisiac and found it far cheaper than caviar. The ancient Egyptian priests forbade the eating of fish, which they credited with increasing sexual activity.

These days we know the ancients were on to something. Fish is loaded with phosphorus, and a half-dozen oysters contain five times the recommended daily allowance of zinc, an important mineral to male testosterone. Those who didn't like oysters could have tried a turkey leg. The dark meat is also rich in zinc, which may account for how Henry the Eighth was able to make it through six wives.

A recent survey found that modern Americans' idea of a romantic dinner is based on their paycheck; a lobster dinner in a candlelit restaurant is the answer for loving couples—the ones who make more than $30,000 a year. Those who are less flush settle for pizza. Whatever your means, take your cookie, your dumpling, your honey, lamb chop, little cabbage, peaches, pumpkin, sugar, or sweetie-pie out for something special. Whether it's the general sense of relaxation and well-being good food induces or some real magic, you won't know until you go. Just go easy with the skink.

JANE'S

1655 W. CORTLAND AVENUE, (773) 862-JANE

A tiny, renovated Bucktown bungalow with exposed brick walls and a vaulted wood beam ceiling with skylights, Jane's intimate space is always packed with some 38 beautiful people sardined together so closely at tables that, if you're intent on whispering sweet nothings to your dining companion, you'd better plan on sharing them with everyone seated around you. In spite of its lack of elbow space, Jane's, particularly the tiny tables of two in the front windows, is charming. Food is of a healthy bent—"vegetarian and clean cuisine." In the past few years, prices have gone up, and now only the lighter meals qualify for cheap chow. Pastas include homemade paperdelle tossed with port, marsala, and wild mushrooms with fresh herbs and truffle oil ($11.95). The baked stuffed tofu burrito with roasted vegetables ($9.95) is very tasty, as are the garden burgers and the grilled chicken breast with molinari toscano salami, arugula, and jack cheese on French bread (both $7.95). A full brunch menu is served with most dishes priced at $10 and under. Brunch entrées are served with turkey sausage and dill potatoes.

Open daily serving till midnight. Full bar. Sidewalk dining. Brunch. Street parking available.

CAFÉ SELMARIE

2327 W. GIDDINGS AVENUE, (773) 989-5595

Tucked away on the plaza off Lincoln Avenue, this eclectic, quiet spot also offers a full-service bakery and has expanded into a third storefront. The bakery does a brisk business in wedding cakes, and in January and February, the cake tasting events are very popular. Entrées in the cozy dining room vary with the seasons. Entrées range from $8.75 to $13.95 and include pork chops, roast chicken, and various pastas. Chicken pot pies and whole-wheat calzones are $8.95.

Open daily. BYOB. Sunday brunch. Street parking available.

JOHNNY ROCKETS

910 N. RUSH STREET, (312) 337-3900

In spite of being in the center of touristville, Johnny Rockets is an enjoyable flashback to those innocent happy days when a big date was a trip to the soda shop for a burger and a shake. The name of the game here is a burger ($3.70 for the original) and fries washed down by a shake or a malt ($3.15). For those who need something healthier, egg salad sandwiches and garden burgers are available. Seating is primarily at one of the counters that runs the length of the restaurant. Your server will give you free nickels to feed the juke box for classic hits like "Midnight Train to Georgia" and "My Boyfriend's Back."

If you're with someone special and in the mood for something hot (and fudge-y), but find yourself a little farther north, try Margie's Candies or the Zephyr (see "Decent American Values") for sundaes you can both dive into.

Open daily. Milkshakes, no alcohol. Street parking difficult; parking lot nearby.

CAFÉ ZINC

3443 N. SOUTHPORT AVENUE, (773) 281-3443

With its crêpe warmers, rattan chairs, and the gleaming wood namesake "zinc" bar with brass accents, Café Zinc, the front section of Bistro Zinc, transports you to romance in Paris for just a few francs. Café Zinc serves quiche, crêpes, croques (sandwiches), and salads—all for under $12— allowing you to get a taste of trendy Bistro Zinc without paying its trendy prices. The Café also usually affords you the opportunity to get served an hour sooner than if you wait for a seat in the back. As you might expect in a French café, an extensive dessert menu can make up for all the light bites you ate first. In nice weather, service is "à la fenêtre" as diners spill out onto the sidewalk patio.

Open daily. Full bar. Patio. Street parking difficult.

GRECIAN TAVERNA RESTAURANT & LOUNGE

4535 N. LINCOLN AVENUE, (773) 728-1600

With its airy, whitewashed walls enclosing sun-bronzed tiles to create the illusion of a Mediterranean villa, Grecian Taverna is a pleasant alternative to the raucous eateries in Greek Town. Imagine the sea breezes caressing you while you select from a huge menu, with an extensive number of well-priced seafood options, offering you and your dining companion the opportunity to savor the flavors of the Greek Islands. Various combination plates—the Cold Appetizer Combination ($6.25 per person), Hot Combo Plate ($10.95), Special Combo ($10.50), and Family-Style Plate ($12.95)—are a good way to explore. In nice weather, you can take it outside to a tree-shaded patio protected from the surroundings by high, white walls.

Open daily. Full bar. Patio. Street parking available; valet parking.

BITTERSWEET

1114 W. BELMONT AVENUE, (773) 929-1000

Pastry chef Judy Cotino opened this spun-sugar-pink eatery to serve breakfast and light lunches. Windows allow diners at the few tables to watch the pastry chefs work on wedding cakes and other decadent sweets. Soup and either a half a sandwich or the quiche of the day is a good deal for $5.95. The fully stocked pastry case at the counter, the fruits of the labors in the back room, will tempt you to splurge on treats like raspberry brown butter custard tarts or espresso ganache tarts.

Open daily for breakfast and lunch. No alcohol. Street parking difficult.

ALBERT'S CAFÉ

52 W. ELM STREET, (312) 751-0666

If the last stop on your shopping agenda is the Treasure Island on Elm to pick up those special ingredients not found at the Jewel or Dominick's, pop into Albert's across the street for a little relaxation and ambiance. Albert's, a European-style patisserie, serves light entrées, sandwiches, and salads to be washed down with steaming cups of tea or espresso. It's an oasis of serenity in the shopping frenzy.

Open daily. Wine and beer. Street parking difficult.

Quick Bites A FEW QUICK THOUGHTS

Since **Pop's For Champagne**, 2934 N. Sheffield Avenue, (773) 472-1000, discontinued its Sunday brunch, it's now a club with hors d'oeuvres and desserts instead of a real restaurant. The Fruit and Cheese or the Charcouterie Platter (both $9.50) are good options to nibble while you and that special someone sip champagne to the club's ever-present background jazz. Don't miss Pop's Bastille Day celebration, held every year in July.

Greener Pasteur

Savor a Vietnamese Institution's Fresh Start

Oh what a difference a fire can make. By 1995, **Pasteur**, the best-known Vietnamese restaurant in the city, had expanded to two locations. There was Pasteur Café, a small storefront on Chicago Avenue known for its cheap lunch buffet, and the original location at Lawrence and Sheridan, which although larger, was still not much more than a storefront itself.

Then fire swept through and destroyed the original location. The Chicago Avenue effort also closed. But in mid-1997, Pasteur rebounded with the opening of a brand-new restaurant in Edgewater north of Argyle Street.

Not surprising from a proprietor who once collected business cards from patrons and followed up with a Christmas card at the end of the year, the new Pasteur is as different from its former storefront as an Oak Street retailer is from a thrift shop. It's sleek and elegant while retaining the quality of food found at the former location—practically the Arun's of Chicago's Vietnamese restaurants.

And, it's lushly romantic. Entering the new Pasteur is like stepping back into the post–World War I era into a scene from Duras's *The Lover*, a shimmering trip back to the waning colonial days of Indochina and the declining sophisticated decadence that marked the French occupation in its latter days.

PASTEUR,
5525 N. Broadway,
(773) 878-1061,
is open daily and
has a full bar. Meals,
for Vietnamese, are
on the expensive
side, and main
courses range from
$8.50 to $13.50.

Pasteur's atmosphere is reminiscent of a former colonial mansion's rooms. A cozy bar off the entranceway encourages visitors to enjoy a drink in snug, rattan comfort. Up several teak steps, a more intimate dining room opens off to the side of the main room. The restaurant's main dining room resembles a large, airy courtyard. Warm, peach-colored walls enclose a patio with drop ceiling fans that create lazy breezes. Palms wave over deep-seated wicker armchairs pulled up to tables with snowy white tablecloths. Colorful floor-to-ceiling paintings portraying traditional scenes grace the walls. The front window panels swivel out to patio dining in the summer. You can almost feel the sultry tropical heat year-round.

Designed for a sultry climate, Pasteur's menu includes many dishes that involve crisp, uncooked vegetables and light sauces, many of which are founded on nuoc mam, a fermented sauce made from small fish and salt that many of the Southeast Asian cultures employ in cooking as the Chinese use soy sauce. Other accents include lime, lemongrass, chilies, purple basil, banana blossoms, shallots, and several varieties of mint. Dishes may start with cuons, rice paper rolls filled with rice noodles, mint, and poached shimp, pork, or other meats. Meals can continue with cold rice noodles that serve as a base for nuong, barbecued meats or prawns. Where some Asian cuisines, Thai, for example, emphasize flavors, and others, like Japanese, stress simplicity and purity, Vietnamese dishes concentrate on texture, mixing cooked ingredients with raw, spicy or sour ingredients with mild, and cold foods with hot.

Food experts have said that Vietnamese cuisine, with its exotic flavors combined with French influences, tends to be milder but more complex than other Southeast Asian foods. That's a matter of a personal taste, but the cooking Pasteur offers stands up to some of the best Vietnamese around.

The helpful picture books that guided patrons at the old Pasteur in their dining decisions are gone as are, in keeping with the restaurant's new upscale theme, the abundant editorial on the menu—the many "specialty of the house," the claims of authenticity—but all of the old standout dishes are still there. Fragrant chicken sautéed with ginger in a sturdy brown clay pot (ga kho gung) or filets of catfish baked in the same clay pot and simmered with a concentrated sweet-tart glaze made from fish sauce, soy, and caramelized sugar lead the list of old favorites, along with bo cuon la lot, delicate rolls of grilled beef wrapped in grape leaves and stuffed with minced chicken and shrimp, grilled scallops with sesame seeds and lemongrass sauce, and an East-meets-West combination of a seafood noodle bouillabaisse soup. As with most Asian restaurants, there's also a good selection of vegetarian dishes, including a combination of vegetables, tofu, and coconut milk.

Starters include full-length pieces of grilled eggplant studded with garlic and peppers, rice paper spring rolls filled with shrimp, vegetables, rice noodles, and mint, and chao tom, Vietnamese wraps made from charbroiled shrimp paste wrapped around daggers of sugar cane that can then be enfolded in rice paper with vegetables and a savory sauce.

Meals can be washed down with strong French coffee, a memento from the colonial days, iced and sweetened with condensed milk. That's just one of the old traditions you can revisit in this newer location.

23

Chowing Down

ALL-YOU-CAN-EAT MEALS
THAT WILL STRETCH YOUR WAISTBAND
BUT NOT YOUR WALLET

Gluttony, one of the seven deadly sins. The repercussions of overindulging have been chronicled through the ages. Think of Alice. She could have avoided nearly getting her head chopped off if she had kept her mouth shut and her hands to herself, instead of grabbing drinks and eats off any available table. Augustus Gloop. Augustus, not Charlie, might have inherited the Chocolate Factory if he had restrained himself from diving into Willy Wonka's chocolate river in an attempt to suck the whole thing down. And then there was Pooh, who got himself into a really tight place after not knowing when to say no. The list of unfortunate examples goes on and on.

Historically, the Romans are credited for establishing the art of pigging out. Romans prided themselves on and derived an obscene sense of power from hosting gargantuan, expensive banquets made up of endless dishes of delicacies, including eels and other elusive sea animals, indigenous species from numerous subjugated countries, and various fried reproductive parts from common herd animals, served to large crowds of politicians and business associates reclining on couches and sofa beds. Things got so bad that the Romans finally passed the sumptuary laws, which restricted how much could be spent on a feast. In addition to honing the exercise of binge and purge, the Romans

> "Better a burst stomach than wasted food."
>
> —Old Pennsylvania Dutch saying

also invented the napkin, or serviette, which was originally used to carry home leftovers to the wives and families who were never invited to the party.

Although there aren't too many food orgies (at least reasonably priced ones) available today in Chicago, there are still a select number of places where you can really shovel it in. The numerous $7.95 (or under!) Polish, Thai, and Indian all-you-can-eat lunch buffets, weekend brunch buffets, and the Friday night fish fries (no surprise in a town both adjacent to Wisconsin and full of Irish sports bars) seem to be the most common opportunities to eat till you're beat. In addition, happy hours—true all-you-can-eat specials where you get endless new plates of piping hot food versus endless chafing dishes of Sterno-ed delights can still be found. Take your pick, take your time, take your Alka Seltzer, and try them all. But take it easy—remember, Rome wasn't built in a day.

OLD WARSAW RESTAURANT & LOUNGE

4750 N. HARLEM AVENUE, (708) 867-4500

CZERWONE JABLUSZKO
(THE RED APPLE)

3121–23 N. MILWAUKEE AVENUE, (773) 588-5781

No argument, the daily buffet tables at these two Polish restaurants provide the best pig-out for the dollar in town. Both provide hot and cold buffets on room-length tables groaning under the weight of salads, assorted traditional Polish dishes and sides, including sauerkraut, stuffed cabbage, dumplings, roasts, sausages, goulash, blintzes, potato pancakes, fritters, and more. Old Warsaw, where blue hair is the predominant but not mandatory attire, has the better dessert offerings with a huge number of kolacky (fruit-filled traditional Eastern European cookies) pastries, cakes, puddings, and, of course, Jell-O. Old Warsaw charges $5.95 for lunch, $7.95 for weekday dinners, and $9.50 on weekends in the evening. The Red Apple counters with lower prices ($6.95 for dinner), baked apples, and a greater number of authentic dishes, including assorted pork parts (hocks and snouts), and a fully stocked grocery store next door, just in case you didn't get enough and need to take some home. The Red Apple's buffet also includes a beverage, soup, and ice cream, which you have to ask your waitperson for.

Old Warsaw is closed Mondays, while the Red Apple is open daily. Full bar.

CLARK STREET BISTRO

2600 N. CLARK STREET, (773) 525-9992

Do you ever get up on a Sunday morning knowing that when you're done doing your damage, the only thing you'll be fit for is to go back to bed? Clark Street Bistro has the kind of all-you-can-eat Sunday brunch that leaves you fit for little more than occupying couch space in a vertical position while bleerily focusing on TV. For $10.95, you get the obligatory juice, coffee, eggs, fresh fruit, and other standbys. But, as you graze through the chafing dishes and Sterno cans, you'll also be able to treat yourself to heaps of Italian tasties—assorted hot pastas, cold pasta salads, tangy chicken breasts, Italian sausages, baked artichokes, cold marinated vegetables—dishes that have no business being consumed by anyone who has not been awake for at least four hours. A pleasant and perky little eating option in Lincoln Park, Clark Street Bistro's atmosphere still isn't going to be nearly bright enough if you're really intent on doing some damage in the brunch buffet line. If you need to be lean and mobile later, stick to the individual servings on the menu, but you'll still probably be walking out with a doggy bag. FYI, free parking is available during brunch hours at Columbus Hospital, two blocks west of Clark Street Bistro on Deming.

Open daily. Full bar. Buffet only served Sundays until 3 P.M.

THE RIVERSIDE DELI

1656 W. CORTLAND AVENUE, (773) 278-DELI

The Riverside Deli is a hidden Bucktown gem, probably discovered only if you take the Armitage bus or you live down there (in which case, you've probably kept it a secret). Old-time décor with old-time prices, the Riverside has a menu of items all under $5, with deluxe sandwiches running under $4. All of these delicacies can be savored on a shady, elevated wood deck tucked away on the north side of the restaurant. Here, an all-you-can-eat $8.95 Sunday brunch is a winner with sideboards groaning under the weight of cereals, breads, fruit, cold salads, and hot entrées ranging from pancakes and eggs Benedict to cheese blintzes with fruit to fried tamales. To do this brunch justice, you should plan to relax a good part of your early Sunday here.

Open daily. Street parking available.

MONGOLIAN BARBEQUE
3330 N. CLARK STREET, (773) 325-2300

THE FLAT TOP GRILL
319 W. NORTH AVENUE, (773) 787-7676
3200 N. SOUTHPORT AVENUE, (773) 665-8100
1000 W. WASHINGTON BOULEVARD, (312) 829-4810
707 CHURCH STREET, EVANSTON, (847) 570-0100

Both of these stir-fry grills make hibachi participatory and hip. Straight from those cutting-edge cities of Royal Oak and Ann Arbor, Michigan, the Mongolian Barbeque offers a "raw" bar of meats and vegetables for you to mix and match and then stir-fry. Chicken, beef, pork, calamari, and tofu are available to combine with various vegetables and sauces to make sweet 'n' sour, curry, garlic, and other combinations (suggested recipes are listed on the wall). A salad bar is also available. An all-you-Khan-eat dinner is $11.95 (one bowl at lunch is $9.95).

The Flat Top Grill offers much of the same in a slightly more upscale atmosphere at a cheaper price. Dinner at the Flat Top is $9.95, and lunch is $6.95. Expect long lines at North Avenue.

Both are open daily. Full bar.

FOUR FARTHINGS TAVERN & GRILL

2060 N. CLEVELAND AVENUE, (773) 935-2060

Four Farthings is one of the best all-you-can-eat options in town, an option made even more attractive by the price: $0. In the comfy atmosphere of its 100-year-old location, Four Farthings offers a complimentary weeknight hors d'oeuvres buffet, along with a free hot dog/chili bar on Saturdays and a free taco bar on Sundays, both served after 3 P.M. Weather permitting, you can make as many trips down the buffet line as your stomach can handle from a breezy seat ensconced within Four Farthing's sidewalk café.

Open daily. Full bar. Sidewalk seating. Street parking available.

Happy Gorge · Spirits with Delectable Delights

INNOVATIVE EATERIES FOR THE FINANCIALLY FINICKY PALATE

Happy-hour spreads are a great source for cheap gluttony. Other good ones include:

Trattoria No. 10, 10 N. Dearborn Street, (312) 984-1718: This elegant underground wine cellar offers a taste of Italy weekdays from 5 to 8 P.M. for $10 with a $5 drink minimum. Shrimp, made-to-order pasta, beef tenderloin, pasta salads, antipasto—you name it. This is the Charlie Trotter's of after-work indulgences.

Brother Jimmy's, 2909 N. Sheffield Avenue, (773) 528-0888: Brother Jimmy's lures the crowds nightly from 4 to 8:30 P.M. with free "pig pickin's." Rib tips, wings, endless towelettes, and cheap drinks—what some might define as hog heaven. Sundays, Brother Jimmy's hosts all-you-can-eat, all-the-draft-you-can-drink rib tips for $12.95, and whole hog ribs for $18.95 for those not restricted by price.

JOHN BARLEYCORN
MEMORIAL PUB

658 W. BELDEN AVENUE, (773) 348-8899

Just up Lincoln from Four Farthings is another tavern that's been around (the Barleycorn building was built in 1890 and was operated by an Irish immigrant who moonlighted as a Chicago policeman), John Barleycorn serves a different $4 pasta platter four days a week: Mondays (spaghetti), Tuesdays (ravioli), Wednesdays (spaghetti), and Thursdays (fettuccine alfredo). Although not technically all-you-can-eat, the price does include two servings, which, according to the staff, is about all most people can handle. Barleycorn also has a great patio if you can stand the Lincoln Park crowds.

Open daily. Full bar. Patio dining. Street parking difficult.

Basement Taste

Gorge on Buca di Beppo's
Old Country Cuisine

My friend Tina grew up Italian in Boston. Her whole family lived in a brownstone—grandma and grandpa on the ground floor, aunt, uncle, and cousins in the middle, and Tina's branch of the family on the top. Tina goes back to visit occasionally for weddings and family affairs, and we're always eager to hear her updates. There are the bridal showers, so big they're held in a hall with a deejay announcing the gifts, "We've got another toaster oven here, folks." And the weddings with the white tuxes and black shirts and the groom's sister who nearly lost her spangled tube top as she lunged for the tossed bouquet.

Buca di Beppo might make Tina do a double take and ask herself if she'd gone back in time to the old neighborhood. The restaurant pays tribute to the gusto and spice, the bodacious warmth, the stereotypical over-the-top exuberance of southern Italy. Designed as a series of connecting wine cellars, oversized colored Christmas lights rim the ceiling of each room. Every inch of wall space is covered with postcards, black velvet paintings, decorated plates that Tina assures me are still all the rage in her former stomping grounds, and framed pictures—religious imagery, Sophia Loren, relatives, memories from the old neighborhood. Gilded statues sprout from corners, and bathrooms are stocked with creams, curlers, and the assorted other retro paraphernalia that used to make a working girl squirm with excitement to powder her nose. Enough visual noise to leave you moonstruck.

On our first visit, we were graciously given a tour through the kitsch by the friendly waiter Jerry. Besides the main dining rooms and bar, the restaurant has the wine room with a roof of latticed bottles, the Pope's room, which accommodates at least three generations in an intimate setting around a huge, round table with a lazy Susan that spins the food around to everyone, and a table that seats eight in the kitchen à la Charlie Trotter.

If the decor is Ed Debevic's gone Old World, then the food is Leona's on steroids. Meaning "Big Joe's Basement," Buca di Beppo harks back to the restaurants opened by Italian immigrants in their base-

**BUCA DI BEPPO,
(773) 348-POPE,
is located at 2941
N. Clark St. Entrées
are priced $14.95 and
up and meant to be
shared. It's best to go
with a large party—
and a hungry one.**

ments that served huge portions, enough for the entire family's Sunday dinner and the rest of the week as well. At Buca di Beppo, towering salads lead into basins of pasta and platters of veal and chicken, matched with signature sides of green beans and garlic mashed potatoes, that should be shared among, at minimum, with your immediate family—and mine and all of our first cousins.

The restaurant's business card pictures a map of Italy that portrays the country as the area between the triangle formed by three cities—Napoli, Calabria, and Palermo—and the flavor focus is the garlic and tomato sauces of southern Italy, where every day is Prince Spaghetti day.

Some of the spaghettis and fettuccinis can be ordered in two sizes—large and larger—but the rest of the pastas and entrées need to be shared and shared and shared. Meatballs are large enough to be mistaken for 16-inch softballs, and thin-crust pizzas are big enough to serve as a welcome mat for your front door. Some nice touches like fennel sausage and olives in the red pomodoro sauce baked over home-made gnocchi and linguine with enough fresh seafood to leave a barrier reef picked clean help elevate the food well above Chef Boy-Ar-Dee status. Appetizers are enough to sidetrack even the most determined diner. Garlicky mussels marina are piled high in a deep ewer, and the monumental Beppo 1893 Salad is a king-size bed of greens with olives, two kinds of cheese, mortadellla, pepperoni, peperoncini, onions, cucumbers, and tomatoes. Baskets filled with wedges of foccacia bread induce the diner to sponge up anything on the plate that may have gotten left behind.

Wash down all the fine fare with a fine vintage beverage—poured right from the keg into a bottle for your table. Dessert includes slabs of bread pudding big enough to feed my entire village, and if it's your special day, a birthday cake as big as an ottoman decorated with pastel sprinkles and topped by the green and red boot of Italy in frosting.

Buca di Beppo is part of a "family of restaurants" (please don't say the word chain) run out of Minneapolis. The restaurant, however, manages to come across as fun and cute versus franchised and touristy, and the reputation of the other locations in Minneapolis and Palo Alto seems to pull even more diners in.

The fish are biting all over town at all-you-can-eat fish fries . . .

LAWRY'S TAVERN
1028 W. DIVERSEY AVENUE, (773) 348-9711
No, not the steak house. This is an unpretentious little tavern that serves big plates of unpretentious food to neighborhood regulars. Friday nights are all-you-can-eat fried sole, french fries, and coleslaw ($6.25). Wednesdays and Saturdays feature either chicken ($5.95) or pork chop ($6.75) specials. Other nights, all that's offered is orange roughy, shrimp, or pizza.
Open daily. Full bar. Street parking available.

THE DUKE OF PERTH
2913 N. CLARK STREET, (773) 477-1741
Chicago's premier Scottish pub with the Midwest's most extensive collection of single-malt scotch serves Wednesday and Friday lunch until midnight, all-you-can-eat beer-batter-dipped cod accompanied by peas and chips (that's fries to you colonials) for $6.95.
Open daily. Full bar. Patio dining. Street parking difficult.

24

Bagging It

WHAT'S COOKING IN AISLE 9?
GRABBING A BITE WHILE YOU'RE
BRINGING HOME THE BACON

Making a list, checking it twice. . . . If you're like me, you long ago identified the two things in life that are unavoidable and extremely unpleasant—laundry and grocery shopping. For most of us, it's probably easier to postpone shopping than to avoid laundry but at some point, the dirty deed is probably going to have to get done.

So, since Whole Foods is an expensive treat, you're off to the Jewel or Dominick's or, if you're particularly intrepid, the Cub or Costco. You, of course, only manage to get there on Saturday afternoon, ensuring a minimum number of parking spaces and the maximum number of carts in each line. Navigation is only possible through the back of the store, as the endless check-out lines have throttled any movement across the front. No matter how careful you are, no matter how much you try to stick to good intentions, next thing you know, your cart is overflowing, and

> **"Who killed the pork chops? What price bananas? Are you my Angel?"**
>
> —Allen Ginsberg,
> *A Supermarket in California*

there's no way you're going to be able to squeeze into the express line (no, four packages of Oodles of Noodles do not count as one big bundle of ramen).

It doesn't have to be this way. No, grocery shopping doesn't have to be an endless trudge up sterile aisles, of not finding ingredients for that recipe you've put off attempting for the last year, and instead buying all kinds of junk you don't need as your stomach rumbles, inexorably driving you to bags of salty snacks and cartons of fat-laden crackers, supplemented with prepackaged meals that practically cook themselves. No, shopping can actually be a relaxing culinary voyage into exotica, a leisurely opportunity to explore new worlds, both in the store and later in your own kitchen. (You do know where yours is, don't you?)

Once upon a time, going to market was a social occasion to look forward to, an opportunity to schmooze with the locals, actually learn how to tell whether a cantaloupe is ripe, and stock up on a little of this and some of that. Pockets of that experience can still be found among the faceless superstores that dominate our landscape. Treasure Island—the "TI," our own local retail magic kingdom, one of the first groceries with an in-store café (put off your purchases until you enjoy an espresso), the abundance of tasty samples (the constant supply of bread for dipping in olive oil or balsamic vinegar in the Italian section), and its stock of international paraphernalia—long ago recognized the value of enhancing the shopping experience. If you've got a specific food genre in mind, skip the chain stores with the mass-market Chun King, the Michelina, the President's Choice Memories of Bangkok. Go back to the neighborhood where you may discover an older world and a store proprietor who is also pleased to be your dining host.

EDEN, THE NATURAL BISTRO
1000 W. NORTH AVENUE, (773) 587-3060

More than just a juice bar, Whole Foods devotes an entire floor to Eden, a sit-down restaurant with a multi-course, healthy gourmet menu. The restaurant serves brunch (until 3 P.M. on weekends), lunch, and dinner—all of which is designed to showcase the foods and ingredients you can find in the store. Many of the dishes are vegetarian and have an ethnic flair, and entrées ($5.99–$12.99) span the gamut from Thai tamales to grilled ostrich fillets, with specials changing weekly. All are prepared with organic produce, and meat and dairy are free of growth hormones, pesticides, antibiotics, and other additives. Tables near the window offer an intriguing view from above of Whole Foods's shoppers. Fifteen-minute massages for $10 are good for an appetizer or dessert. You can park it in the spacious lot that also accommodates Best Buy customers.

Open daily. Full bar. Parking lot.

CZERWONE JABLUSZKO

3121–23 N. MILWAUKEE AVENUE, (773) 588-5781

"The Red Apple" is a fully stocked Polish mini-mart and deli, adjacent to a sit-down restaurant serving one of the most extensive and cheapest all-you-can-eat buffets in the Chicago area. The retail half of this operation stocks freshly baked breads, over a half-dozen different types of pierogis (including the old standards, cheese, meat, and potato, in addition to strawberry, rabbit, and duck), and kolacky (traditional Eastern European fruit-filled cookies), along with a full dairy case and extensive dry goods. One side of the store is taken up with a meat counter staffed by butchers who slice and dice various meats and cheeses in front of a fragrant, wall-length curtain of hanging sausages. Once you've filled your shopping basket with tasty Polish tidbits, you can swing across the hall and indulge in the all-you-can-eat smorgasbord, priced at $6.95, including drinks and ice cream! (For more details, see "Chowing Down: All-You-Can-Eat Meals That Will Stretch Your Waistband but Not Your Wallet.")

Open daily. Street parking available.

LUNA MEXICANA

3565–7 W. FULLERTON AVENUE, (773) 252-1MEX (639)

West of the Kennedy on Fullerton at Central Park is La Caridad, a brightly lit, piñata-festooned Mexican supermercado with a full-service diner attached. At La Caridad, loud and bouncy Mexican music accompanies the shopper on the trip down aisles lined with Goya and La Preferida staples, through the meat department where all the signs are in Spanish, around the plantain and banana tree, past the back wall that is completely covered with bags of assorted spices, and finally, to a quick stop in the bakery for some freshly baked cakes and pastries before check-out. Once you've picked up all your supplies to make your own tostadas, you can walk through the store into Luna Mexicana. Once a combination of a short-order grill and diner attached to the grocery store, the restaurant has blossomed into a full-blown, snazzy eatery with live music in one of its two rooms Wednesdays through Sundays. Typical Mexican specialties ($1.75–$8.95) with lots of seafood options ($8.95–$12.95) have made Luna a pricier option than its predecessor, although still well within most budgets.

Open daily. Street parking available.

WIKSTROM'S SCANDINAVIAN AMERICAN GOURMET FOODS

5247 N. CLARK STREET, (773) 878-0601

If you're craving some Viking fare, find yourself *vilkommen* at Wikstrom's, a Scandinavian deli located in the heart of Andersonville. You can enjoy a complimentary cup of coffee while you mosey through the refrigerated cases, selecting between the various tubes of fish roe, Norwegian flat potato bread, gallon cans of lingonberries, and small crates of salted cod. Pick up a couple bottles of Swedish glogg to mix up some festive beverages to wash down your purchases. After you've finished shopping, you can relax at one of the tables at the front of the store and enjoy a freshly made sandwich ($2.50–$3.50) with a bowl of homemade soup. *Ja!*

Open daily. Street parking difficult.

MOTI MAHAL

1035 W. BELMONT AVENUE, (773) 348-4393

If you don't want to go all the way up to California and Devon for authentic tandoori chicken, head to this Lakeview branch of one of Chicago's best-known Indian restaurants. A two-room storefront, one side has an Indian deli with cases of baked and fried temptations, along with well-stocked shelves of dry goods, including Indian tea, spices, burlap bags of rice, and other necessities imported from the land of the Raj. The retail side of the operation also has tables where you can enjoy your purchases immediately. The other room is a full-service, BYOB sit-down restaurant offering a large variety of good-sized, authentic Indian dishes. Share one of the large combination platters with a friend ($10.95–$13.95) if you don't know where to start.

Open daily. BYOB. Street parking difficult.

THE VIENNA CAFETERIA

2501 N. DAMEN AVENUE, (773) 235-6652

It's not exactly a hot dog stand, but a full-service cafeteria with a retail sales area. In a city where three-quarters of the hot dog stands are supplied by one source, when we're talking dogs, we can talk Vienna. The Vienna Cafeteria is located on the first floor of the building that actually houses the plant—the meat mecca where those little casings are stuffed with a variety of pork products. The Vienna line is deli heaven. You name your cold cut, and it's available between two slices of rye. But the real star attraction is the hot sandwich line. Step up for a hot dog and ask the lady who's been working behind that counter for the last 20 years to "drag it though the garden." Yes, that's secret meat speak for "the works." With that password, you'll get all the stuff, including the celery salt and the flourescent green relish. If you're not in the mood for something oblong nestled in a long, cylindrical bun, go for the barbecued beef—a mound of fragrant beef shavings smothered in a tangy sauce and heaped on a hamburger bun. Get there early—reliable sources say the barbecued beef is gone by 11 A.M. on Saturdays. Once you're done eating, stock up for home with extra product. Besides hot dogs by the case, you can buy entire slabs of corned beef and other deli items. Check out the "seconds" bin where slightly "damaged" merchandise is available at a discount. A good deal and (probably) relatively safe to eat.

Although it's there primarily to serve employees in hairnets, the cafeteria is open to the public every day, except Sunday, until 3 P.M.

L'APPETITO

HANCOCK BUILDING, 875 N. MICHIGAN AVENUE, (312) 337-0691
HURON PLAZA, 30 E. HURON STREET, (312) 787-9881

Tucked away at the base of the Hancock Building is one magnificent stop for all of your Italian needs. If you're after some pine nuts, prosciutto, or biscotti for that after-work soirée, L'Appetito is a quick stop that will fill all your needs before you jump on the Michigan Avenue bus to go home. While you're filling your basket with foccacia, Nutella, and Chianti, stop for a latte (L'Appetito uses Illy espresso) and a panino (Italian sandwich on traditional bread, $4.50–$7), a tostino (a grilled sandwich eaten as a snack, $4–$5.75), the daily pasta or pizza, or a scoop of the granita of the day. There's a spacious dining area or, on a nice day, you can sit at the tables in the Hancock Building courtyard. *Ciao, bella!*
Open daily. Street parking difficult; lots nearby.

VIRGIN MEGASTORE CAFÉ
(TORREFAZIONE ITALIA)

VIRGIN MEGASTORE, 540 N. MICHIGAN AVENUE, (312) 645-9300

It's a relatively recent phenomenon—the superstore where you can disappear and hide from the world with all the comforts of home, including food and beverages. Torrefazione Italia, the finest coffee currently exported from the city of Seattle, has set up shop at Virgin Megastore, supplying all the light bites and lattes you'll need to hang out indefinitely in the stacks of CDs, books, and videos. The usual muffins and cookies are available, as well as hefty sandwiches ($4.95) that fuel you to loiter away your day on Virgin's second floor. Tuna, turkey, and spicy Italian ham, among other options, are stacked on boomerang-size croissants or square slabs of foccacia bread the size of floor tiles. Wash it all down with a Torrefazione espresso, which is, according to an Italian friend, the closest brew to Italy that you'll get in Chicago, while you aimlessly thumb through books and magazines you have no intention of buying. Ignore the periodic interruptions from Virgin's deejay announcing blue light specials on today's greatest hits.
Open daily and until midnight on Fridays and Saturdays. Street parking difficult; lots nearby.

Cafés are popping up everywhere, not just in bookstores and record stores, but now in furniture stores too. While you can grab a cup of coffee and a scone at the **Crate & Barrel** in Lincoln Park (800 W. North Avenue, (312) 787-4775), you'll find more food and cheaper furniture prices at **Ikea's Chicago Restaurant** (1800 W. McConnor Parkway, Schaumburg, (847) 969-1400, ext. 1200). While the Bistro Café on Ikea's first level serves coffee, pastries, and sandwiches, the 350-seat, cafeteria-style restaurant on the third level offers Swedish specialties, as well as California-style cuisine, at bargain prices. Check out the meatballs with gravy, boiled red potatoes, and lingonberries (15 for $4.95), as well as the smoked salmon plate for $6.50. Finish off with Swedish apple cake and Swedish coffee.

Flying the Co-op

Hyde Park Co-op Spreads Its Wings

Among retail food cooperatives, Chicago's Hyde Park Co-op is one of the largest in the world with more than $33 million in annual sales and over 24,000 members. The Co-op believes its 55th Street location may rank as the busiest single co-op store in the country. In 1999, Hyde Park Co-op got even bigger with the opening of a third store in a shopping center at 47th Street and Lake Park Avenue in the North Kenwood neighborhood. Store Number 3 joined the

Co-op's other two locations, the original Hyde Park Co-op at 1526 E. 55th Street and the Mr. G Co-op, located on East 53rd Street (all of which have changed their names to "Co-op Markets" to reflect the group's focus on serving the larger South Shore community).

The original Hyde Park Co-op was founded as a buying club in an apartment above a bookstore near the University of Chicago in December 1932. The Great Depression was in full swing, and the Co-op's earliest members believed they could save money if they pooled their purchases and bought in case lots. After eight months, however, it was clear that savings weren't covering expenses.

Co-op directors consulted with Paul Douglas, a University of Chicago economics professor, who advised them to "either open a store at once or liquidate before you lose money." The Co-op subsequently expanded and opened its first store in October 1933 at 5635 S. Harper Avenue. As sales grew to $4,000 a week and the store became too small, the Co-op relocated to larger quarters at 1464 E. 57th Street in 1942. The new location had 100 grocery items and three checkout counters.

When the Co-op opened for business in October 1959 in its current 55th Street location, it was the largest supermarket in Chicago with 22,000 square feet of retail space. By 1962, sales had reached $10,000 a week for the first time and have continued to rise. The original store now offers one of the widest selections of goods in the Chicago area, as well as a liquor store, video rentals, a bakery, coffee bar, and an in-store café. In addition, branches of the United Credit Union, which any Co-op member can join, and a U.S. Post Office are located on the lower level of the shopping center.

The Co-op's newest store at 47th Street and Lake Park Avenue marked the organization's first foray into the North Kenwood area. The full-service store has 40,000 square feet, compared to 35,000 for the 55th Street store.

"We support the rebirth of the community in North

Kenwood, a neighborhood that has recently seen an influx of both affordable and market-rate housing, as well as new schools like the Ariel Community Academy and the new University of Chicago Charter School," noted Brian Berg for Co-op Markets.

"Our 47th Street location will represent the first full-service grocery store to open in North Kenwood in 50 years," added Berg. "We're striving to create a love affair with wonderful foods in a lively neighborhood."

Becoming a member and shopping at any of the three stores is easy. Just stop by the member services desk at a store and fill out an application (or online at www.coop-markets.com). A minimum one share purchase ($10) is required, although the co-op's bylaws allow for members to purchase up to 1,000 shares. The new member is issued a member number, which is thereafter presented at the checkout in order to get a year-end member's refund.

Member benefits include a voice in the management of the Co-op, as well as some more tangible and quantifiable perks, including:

- A patronage refund at the end of the fiscal year, the amount of which depends on the purchases made by the member and the profitability of the Co-op as a whole.
- Limited interest paid annually on your investment. The rate varies, but is usually slightly higher than the going rate on a commercial bank savings account.
- A five-percent discount on all purchases on Member Day, which is the third Thursday of every month. During October, which is Co-op Month, every Thursday is a Member Day.
- A subscription to *Evergreen*, the co-op's monthly newspaper, which contains an additional five-percent-off coupon that can be used any day each month. Members may also place free classified ads in the Evergreen.

Co-op Markets (7 A.M.–11 P.M. daily)

HYDE PARK SHOPPING CENTER
1526 E. 55TH STREET, (773) 667-1444

KIMBARK PLAZA SHOPPING CENTER
1226 E. 53RD STREET, (773) 363-2175

LAKE PARK POINTE SHOPPING CENTER
1300 E. 47TH STREET, (773) 268-4700

25

Organic Matters

GETTING DOWN TO EARTH
AND BACK TO NATURE

o, summer ends. You woke up back in April and realized the winter had left you pudgy and unfit to be seen in a tank top and shorts, let alone a bathing suit. You spent a good part of spring and the entire summer getting back into shape. You find yourself cruising into September, and you're looking good. Then, striding into fall, you're at your peak. But for most of us, it doesn't last long. As soon as cooler weather makes its inevitable move back, we start slacking off again. Like bears in hibernation, we sleep more and don't do much else. How do you break this vicious seasonal cycle?

Well first, you might look at what you're eating. Years ago, you had a

> **"Cheese: Milk's leap towards immortality."**
>
> —Clifton Fadiman, cholesterol-free and lactose tolerant

choice of being either a gluttonous carnivore or a smug total vegetarian, or a vegan. But, it has been said, the times they are a-changin'. These days, it's much easier to eat healthy, to eat natural, to eat free—fat-free, cholesterol-free, calorie-free, pesticide-free—than it has been in the past. In fact, the options to make your diet organically correct have become mind-boggling. You're no longer limited to tofu, beans, and greens. Eggs may be out, but prairie-raised, natural grain-fed lean meat is in. Cheese may now be a lactic death trap, but Italian turkey sausage is the topping du jour for non-dairy pizza all over the city. Please pass the tempeh.

Luckily for those of us who have embarked on a mission of culinary awareness, Chicago offers myriad opportunities to abandon our frankly corrupt bourgeois ways and eat like a fit Third World peasant. Ethnic eateries—especially Asian, Middle Eastern, and African—have always had a bonanza of healthy, protein-rich (courtesy of grains, beans, and the almighty tofu) options. But now, everywhere you look, there are a variety of healthy, natural alternatives ranging from the simple to the gourmet.

With all the options out there, "healthy eating" certainly does not have to be tofu, formerly regarded as a dreaded tasteless gelatinous cube. You, however, will notice as you get out and about that the lowly soybean, of which tofu is a by-product, is the foundation of much alternative eating. Tofu is now powering some of the most elaborate dishes around. Healthy burritos and pizza, whole-wheat with soy cheese, abound. Grilled tempeh, Indonesia's most popular soy protein food, is hot for burgers. With the rising cost of meat and the increasing emphasis on avoiding dairy due to cholesterol, lactose intolerance, and other arterial problems, we're just discovering what other cultures have known for centuries—the soybean is where it's at.

Not only is the soybean one of the cheapest sources of protein in the world, but it also provides more protein than any other known crop. In fact, the top five protein sources, of which tofu is one, are all derived from soybeans. Asians, way ahead of us in recognizing the value of the soybean, have so allowed tofu to permeate their lives that it has become part of their culture and language. In Japan, if a situation is hopeless, it's "as futile as trying to clamp two pieces of tofu together." Or, if someone wants you to get lost, he may say, "Go bump your head against the corner of a cake of tofu and drop dead."

Whatever your goal, fat and happy or lean and mean, there's a world of healthy opportunity out there. You can start slow, with an occasional lentil burger for your Big Mac, or once in a while foregoing a brat for a tofu dog. You are what you eat. It doesn't have to be a winter of culinary hibernation and discontent. Bean me up, Scotty.

THE HEARTLAND CAFÉ

7000 N. GLENWOOD AVENUE, (773) 465-8005

A Rogers Park mainstay for more than 20 years and probably the most extensive natural foods restaurant operation in the city besides the Blind Faith business, the Heartland Café offers not only a large restaurant with a colorful and large outdoor patio (great to view the interesting street life and interactions of the denizens of Rogers Park), but also live entertainment and an extensive store stocked with books and all sorts of garments and jewelry manufactured in some Third World country. The Heartland's menu includes poultry, fish, and seafood among its selections of entrées and sandwiches, which range in price from $4.50 for sandwiches, such as the Big Heart Lentil Burger or the Tempeh Burger ($5.95 with melted soy cheese), to $9.95 for the most expensive specials, usually a pasta with seafood. The Heartland also has an extensive breakfast menu and, unlike many healthy places, a well-stocked bar. Savor the tall, cold results of fermented yeast while you listen to some music and roll your own meal with the fried-bean plate.

Open daily. Full-service bar. Patio. Entertainment. Street parking difficult.

CHICAGO DINER

3411 N. HALSTED STREET, (773) 935-6696

Possibly the best-known vegetarian restaurant in the city, the Chicago Diner remains a magnet for the healthy and the out-of-town movie star, serving a long list of vegan and veggie options, including baked Grain Burgers ($6.25), reubens made with grilled tempeh ($6.95), lentil and tofu loaves ($8.25), and macrobiotic plates ($8.95). Even children can join the fun with their own menu of tofu dogs and grilled cheese (cheddar or soy on seven-grain bread).

Open daily for brunch, lunch, and dinner. Beer and wine. Street parking difficult.

VICTORY'S BANNER

2100 W. ROSCOE AVENUE, (773) 665-0227

If you think what the world needs now is more peace, love, and bliss burgers, check out the spiritual dining at Victory's Banner. Owner Pradhan Balter and his sari-clad staff subscribe to the teachings of Indian "Spiritual Master" Sri Chinmoy, who champions "a sincere inner life with an active outer life." The restaurant is vegetarian and offers to prepare dishes either for vegans or to meet special dietary requirements. Only hormone-free, free-range eggs are used in combination with marinated tofu, "fakin' bakin,'" and fresh fruit. The bent on health and spirituality doesn't dampen the popularity of chocolate chip pancakes ($5.75, offered in kid's portions for $3.95) or oat bran 'cakes served with toasted pecans, cinnamon baked apples, and real maple syrup ($4.55). Lunch features include the smoked Gouda chicken and the "Neatloaf" Dinner served with homemade mashed potatoes and gravy ($7.50). Wash it all down with a bottomless mug of homemade Chai tea ($2.45 single, $3.85 for the bottomless), so smooth and creamy, it's bliss in a cup.

Open daily until 3 P.M. No alcohol. Street parking available.

PATTIE'S

700 N. MICHIGAN AVENUE, 8TH FLOOR, (312) 751-7777

Pattie's offers a large variety of sandwiches, pizzas, calzones, and salads, all at $6.95 and under. Pizzas, made with nonfat mozzarella and whole-wheat crusts ($5.75–$3.95), are a good bet. The sausage is turkey sausage. For something pizza-like but a little different, try one of the four whole-wheat calzones (veggie and cheese, Spanish rice, spinach and mushroom, or eggplant parmesan, $3.75–$3.95), kind of a pizza turnover. Jerk chicken with red beans and rice ($4.95) is also a popular choice, as are the three kinds of burgers (veggie, $3.85, turkey, $3.65, and buffalo, $4.65) served with low-fat chips (add 3 grams of fat for the chips). As an additional plus, the menu lists the fat content of every item along with the percentage of calories from fat, and the entire menu has been approved by a registered dietitian.

Open every day except Sunday, 9 A.M. to 6 P.M. (Loop hours). Sidewalk seating. Street parking difficult.

THE LO-CAL ZONE

912 N. RUSH STREET, (312) 943-9060

Can it be fast *and* healthy? It can at the Lo-Cal Zone, a healthy little food shack behind the 900 North Michigan shopping center. Offering a wide variety of vegetarian and vegan options, the Lo-Cal Zone has pizzas, sandwiches, salads, chili, burritos, and Lo-Cal Zones (calzones, get it?). Check out one of the dozen burritos (all $5.75)—a 14-inch whole-wheat tortilla filled with everything from beans to turkey Italian sausage. The barbecue chicken burrito is particularly tasty, as are the corn tamales and homemade soups.

Open daily. No alcohol. Sidewalk seating. Street parking difficult; parking lot nearby.

TAQUERIA MAMASITA'S

3324 N. BROADWAY, (773) 868-6262

Mamasita's vegetarian burrito is the mother of all veggie burritos, the pinnacle that all vegetarian burritos aspire to. A huge mound of tortilla, Mamasita's burritos ($3.99) are stuffed with not only the standard beans and cheese, but also those standout ingredients—grilled carrots and broccoli garnished with a dollop of guacamole. *Olé*, sheer burrito vegetarian heaven. This Vegetarian Combination is also available in tacos ($1.65) and quesadillas ($3.50) or in all those forms in combination with chicken or steak. A boring bean burrito ($3.50) can also be had, but why? As an added benefit, Mamasita's prides itself on its fresh ingredients and true vegetarian cuisine. When was the last time you saw a Mexican establishment that advertised "No Lard"?

Open daily. No alcohol. Street parking difficult.

HEARTWISE EXPRESS

10 S. LASALLE STREET, (312) 419-1329

HeartWise Express provides a healthy alternative to the fast food you will find on practically every corner in the Loop. Each item on the menu is listed with its "vitals": number of calories, grams of fat, sodium, fiber, and cholesterol. The menu has a solid selection of salads, sandwiches, and vegetarian and chicken burritos, with nothing priced more than $5.95. House specials include veggie burgers and vegetarian sloppy joes served with potato wedges.

Closed weekends. Street parking difficult.

SUN & MOON

1467 N. MILWAUKEE AVENUE, (773) 276-6525

A café and catering operation, Sun & Moon serves world beat light bites and sandwiches ($3.50–$5.75), including a veggie melt on focaccia bread and a teriyaki turkey burger with grilled pineapple. Desserts, like the caramel-apple cake, are unhealthily American.

Closed Sundays. No alcohol. Street parking available.

SOUL VEGETARIAN EAST

203 E. 75TH STREET, (773) 224-0104

Seemingly an oxymoron, Soul Vegetarian East makes meatless soul food a possibility. Indulge in the Garvey veggie burger ($4.25), the barbecue roast sandwich ($4), or the Vegetable Combo Basket, a choice of protein or tofu tidbits and battered cauliflower or mushrooms ($8, pick three of four). Finish off with peanut-carob cookies while you relax on wicker chairs with kente-cloth cushions. When you're done, you can browse in the adjoining Boutique Afrika next door.

Open daily. No alcohol. Street parking available.

Raw Deal

The Skinny on Raw Food Guru
Karyn Calabrese

It helps if you start with good bones. Karyn Calabrese, in her mid-50s and a grandmother, looks better than most 22-year-olds. As a former model and actress, nature gave her a head start. But it's a nutrition and lifestyle philosophy that she's parlayed into a growing business that makes her a walking, talking, glowing advertisement for her personal mantra of living life raw.

Based in a city that relishes its history as "hog butcher to the world," Calabrese is a proponent of a lifestyle that includes a diet limited to raw vegetables. Raw foodies believe that heat destroys the natural vitamins, minerals, and, particularly, enzymes in food. According to the proponents of "green food," enzymes are the essential active ingredients in your body that break down chemicals, digest food, and assemble amino acids. While the medical community has failed to endorse a raw food diet, "rawists" counter that man is the only animal that cooks his food and maintain that we would all be far better off only eating food in its natural state.

Twenty years ago, the pursuit of a healthier lifestyle took Calabrese away from her former modeling and acting career. She says, "I didn't start out in this business to make money. In fact, I made ten times more money as a model and actress. But, as I was healing myself, things just evolved."

Calabrese's first health-oriented business venture was wheatgrass sprouts distribution, which she started from a greenhouse in Evanston and is a side activity she still maintains. Soon she was supplying the turf trays that serve as the raw ingredients for wheatgrass shots all over the city.

Eventually, she fell into the restaurant business and

opened **Karyn's Fresh Corner**—The Garden Café in 1995. "The restaurant wasn't planned," Calabrese says. "I had developed a nutrition counseling practice and had a client with multiple sclerosis and was making food for him, as well as others, at home. Soon I had six dehydrators in my house, and my husband said 'enough.'"

With no restaurant experience, Calabrese admits the restaurant's been one of her more challenging ventures. At her Fresh Corner, she sprouts, purées, and dehydrates, turning zucchini into spaghetti, making nuts into milk, and creating mock turkey, seasonally, from sunflower and pumpkin seeds. Patrons of all backgrounds have flocked to her indoor garden to savor the all-you-can-eat raw vegan specialties ($12.95 or $5.99 per pound), like crowd favorites Southern greens, gazpacho, "cream" pies and cheese from seeds and nuts, and, our personal favorite, almond paté.

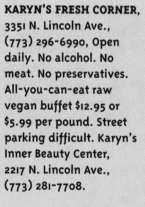

KARYN'S FRESH CORNER, 3351 N. Lincoln Ave., (773) 296-6990, Open daily. No alcohol. No meat. No preservatives. All-you-can-eat raw vegan buffet $12.95 or $5.99 per pound. Street parking difficult. Karyn's Inner Beauty Center, 2217 N. Lincoln Ave., (773) 281-7708.

On the heels of her restaurant's success, Calabrese opened her Inner Beauty Center to offer one-on-one counseling as well as, increasingly, group sessions. Inner Beauty services include private nutritional consultations, cleansing colon hydrotherapy, lymphatic drainage to clear the body's "waste pathway," massage, physical therapy with a licensed therapist, acupuncture, chiropractic treatments, and oxygen baths in a "sauna-like pod."

The sky's the limit these days for Calabrese. While she's negotiating the distribution of her raw culinary creations through retail stores, she's also working on a deal for a line of vitamin supplements and is talking to publishers about a book. She'd like to expand Karyn's Inner Beauty and open centers around the country.

On a Saturday afternoon, I was introduced to the power of Karyn first hand. I join a SRO crowd at Karyn's restaurant as they eagerly await their introduction to "Nature's Healing System," a four-week detoxification program that Karen keeps referring to as "thirty short days." We listen enthralled as Karyn explains how to change our lives with regular cleansing and detoxings to tune up our bodies like you'd tune up a car. We're shocked as she reveals we ingest 125 pounds of sugar and over 3,000 chemicals without so much as biting into a donut. We cringe as she visually illustrates the toxic effects of putrefying dairy, meat, chicken, and fish on our already overburdened colons.

By the end of two hours with Karyn, the class is fired up to put their decadent daily menus behind for "thirty short days" and ingest powders and potions with names like fenugreek, psyllium, and green kamut, plus as many raw fruits and vegetables as their colons can handle. I'm thinking, maybe I should get on the bandwagon and expel some of the excess mucus and dead wastes out of my own lymphatic systems. The stuff Karyn says makes sense and just look at her. Seeing is believing. Then I remember I'm suppose to have ribs for dinner. My colon is going to have to wait at least one more day for a tune-up.

26

Late for Dinner

MIDSUMMER NIGHTS' EATS

"It's a marvelous night for a moondance . . . with the stars up above in your eyes." Since ancient times, man has been fascinated by the darkness. Folklore revolves around tales pitting day against night, light against dark. Before the days of fluorescent bulbs, the setting of the sun made the familiar potentially unfamiliar. Unusual beings were thought to emerge in the darkness, in nature, and from within ourselves.

The moon has always played a preeminent role in the dark half of our lives and minds. We developed our calendars around the lunar cycle, and today we still celebrate holidays that are rooted in the seasonal celebrations of our ancestors. Although both the moon and the sun are responsible for the movement of the tides, the moon has twice the gravitational pull of the sun. Consequently, the cycles of the moon have a far greater

> "Where's a good place for . . . ? If I had a book for every time someone asked me that question, I could have written this book from aboard my yacht . . . instead of from inside my cab."
>
> —Chicago Jack, *A Cabbie's Guide to Chicago at Night: All Right, All Night and After Hours Fun Finder*

effect on tides and other natural movements. It is said that we even gain or lose slight amounts of weight in sequence with the 28-day lunar cycle.

Since the earliest days, people have attributed human action to the effects of natural phenomena. This philosophy continues in modern times. In spite of our enlightenment, mysteries that align themselves with the darkness still remain. Who can explain why hash browns snarfed well past the Witching Hour bring nearly a supernatural satisfaction never experienced in the morning? Who has ever rationalized the physical phenomenon of waking up starving with a concave stomach after pigging out at 3 A.M.? Some mysteries are better left unsolved.

For those seeking out late-night culinary excitement, Chicago truly is a second city. Unlike New York and other metropolises that offer nightcrawlers more opportunities to feed, Chicago is limited in late-night dining if you're not interested in a hot dog stand, a burrito house, or a greasy spoon. But, when it's well after midnight and you've worked up quite an appetite on the dance floor and your stomach is rumbling so loud that it's competing with the bass of the music, if you're resourceful, it's possible to search beyond the cheese fries, the beans and cheese, and the omelets to find a variety of establishments, from stylish spots to hangover hangouts, that are open until at least the stroke of midnight.

Stretch to discover a full "lunar cycle" of late-night options, including "new moons" (open just till midnight on weekends) to "full moons" (serving until at least 2 A.M.) to "lunar eclipses" (open 7 days, 24 hours). What's great about these late-night places is that they're unpredictable. With people super-loopy from the libations or simply high on energy, you'll never know what you're in for. It's like the afterset—with food. *Bon nuit, bon appétit.* "One more moondance with you in the moonlight . . . on a magic night . . ."

THE GOLDEN APPLE

2971 N. LINCOLN AVENUE, (773) 528-1413

Not quite as chic as the Nookies with their hordes of beautiful people, The Golden Apple, with its radiant neon apple sign, holds its own with any other diner in the city— any day, any hour. Over 200 breakfast, lunch, dinner, and dessert items, with most complete meals priced at under $8.99, should satisfy your cravings, no matter what they are, no matter what time. The menu has a Mexican twist, and the breakfast burrito ($5.50), a huge roll of beans, cheese, guacamole, tomatoes, lettuce, and "taco meat" accompanied by spicy rice, can be an excellent way to start your day or end your evening. One piece of advice—try to avoid the allure of the cream pies in the rotating glass dessert display. Stress tested at 3 A.M., these meringue-coated confections just couldn't stand up to the pressure.

Serving 24 hours, 7 days a week. Sidewalk café. Street parking available.

RIVER KWAI II

1650 W. BELMONT AVENUE, (773) 472-1013

Close your eyes, then open them and look around. You're not in Kansas anymore, Dorothy. No, with its low-slung ceiling, overworked window air conditioner cranking away, open kitchen piled with dirty dishes and red-faced, sweaty cooks, and five small tables, you could have easily been transported to any Chinatown in the world. You're at the River Kwai, one of the few Chicago restaurants that could have been plucked right out of New York. Opening at, say, 9 or 10 P.M., the River Kwai serves Thai and Chinese stir-fries, noodles, currys, soups, and rice dishes (priced $7.95 and under) until dawn the next day. Helpings are huge (liters of Thai iced coffee are served in soup carryout containers for $1.50), and all "house dinners" are served with a choice of "special" pork or chicken fried rice. Note, new siding has gone a long way to making River Kwai a lot less scary—on the outside.

Closed Tuesdays. Opens between 9 and 10 P.M.; closes 5 A.M. weekdays and 6 A.M. weekends.

EARWAX CAFÉ

1564 N. MILWAUKEE AVENUE, (773) 772-4019

This Wicker Park coffeehouse has relatively late dining with some extra perks not found in the average café. You can enjoy an extensive list of sandwiches and specials oriented to the healthy and the vegetarian, such as the eggplant chicken burger ($6.50), "Soul on a Roll" (shredded chicken with chipotle BBQ sauce, $7.75), and fresh tomato basil and potato rosemary pizzas (both $6.95). Earwax Café is combined with a video and record store, giving a new meaning to dinner and a movie.

Earwax serves late on weekends until 12:15 A.M., 45 minutes before closing. Street parking difficult; lot nearby.

TACO & BURRITO HOUSE

3946 N. BROADWAY, (773) 871-8988
548 W. FULLERTON PARKWAY, (773) 665-8389

The Taco & Burrito House, not to be confused with the Taco & Burrito Palace on Halsted, is a small, inconsequential establishment that's packed at all hours (until 5 A.M. on weekends) with devotées who worship at the altar of the almighty cheap burrito. Starting at $2.50, you can purchase a complete meal of a "Junior" vegetarian burrito filled with mounds of beans, cheese, tomato, lettuce, sour cream, and the secret sauce. For an additional $0.70, carnivores can upgrade to chicken, steak, marinated pork (al pastor), beans and bacon, and homemade Mexican sausage (chorizo). If you're really a glutton, skip over the "Junior" and go for the "King," the foot-long version weighing at least 20 pounds and starting at $3.50 for the veggie king. Of course, if you eat here as often as some hardcore fans, you may want to expand your options to the tacos, tortas, tostadas, quesadillas, or chimichangas. But, when it's all said and done, there's really nothing like wrapping your hands around a big burrito.

Open daily and late. No alcohol. Street parking difficult at both locations.

TECALITLAN RESTAURANT

1814 W. CHICAGO AVENUE, (312) 384-4285

Out on Chicago Avenue caught between rapidly gentrifying neighborhoods and ethnic enclaves is Tecalitlan, home of the one-pound-plus burrito. A formidable tortilla package that fills the entire plate, Tecalitlan's veggie burrito ($3.95) comes with cauliflower or broccoli, aguacate (avocado) optional. A full-service, sit-down restaurant, Tecalitlan also offers a complete menu with all the old favorites, including

14 flavors of soft tacos at $1.50 each, along with some specialty dishes to be savored by a certain palate, including the daily caldo de birria (lamb soup) and menudo (tripe soup), which is only served on weekends. Tecalitlan is one of the *Sun-Times* restaurant critic Pat Bruno's favorite places when he's hankering to leave the white tablecloths behind and take it to the streets. **Open daily until midnight during the week and 3 A.M. on weekends. Full bar. Street parking available.**

EL PRESIDENTE

2558 N. ASHLAND AVENUE, (773) 525-7938

Resembling a Denny's spruced up with Marvel Comic-like pictures of Indian warriors in feather helmets rescuing bosomy Aztec maidens, it's a rare item on El Presidente's menu that tops the $8 mark. The food is acceptable Mexican, and at 4:30 A.M., well, beans rarely taste so good. There are plenty of *huevos* selections on the menu for those who feel the wee hours should be reserved for and are sacred to breakfast. Try the machacado con huevos, scrambled eggs with dried beef, rice, and beans, $5.95, served "hot" for a really good feeling the following morning.

Open 24 hours, 7 days a week. Street parking available.

KAMEHACHI CAFÉ

1400 N. WELLS STREET, (773) 664-1361

Do you find yourself with a yen for raw fish in the wee hours? Well, at Kamehachi Café, you can satisfy your sushi cravings until 2 A.M. An attractive, blond-wood sushi place that's graced with a neon martini glass and chopsticks, Kamehachi caters to the Old Town yuppie crowd with its "Beginner Sushi 101" ("all cooked food . . . nothing raw!"), including California roll, an ebi (shrimp), and tamago (egg) omelet for $5.50. Standard sushi combo of six pieces and cucumber roll is $9.95.

Closed Mondays. Serving beer, wine, and sake. Street parking difficult.

PICK ME UP CAFÉ

3408 N. CLARK STREET, (773) 248-6613

Open nightly from 5 P.M. from 5 A.M. on week-nights and 24 hours on weekends, Pick Me Up serves an assortment of Italian options, sandwiches, good vegetarian chili ($3 cup/$4 bowl with thick slices of honey wheat bread), and big breakfasts ($5.25). It's never too late (or early) for the Pick Me Up's brownie sundae.

Open nightly. No alcohol. Street parking difficult.

HARMONY GRILL

3159 N. SOUTHPORT AVENUE, (773) 525-2508

You can listen to good American rockabilly at Schubas and then head next door for good American comfort food until 2 A.M. on Fridays and 3 A.M. on Saturdays. Sandwiches are $7 to $9, and entrées, including pastas, fish, and meat dishes, are $8 to $12.

Open daily. Full bar. Limited parking lot; street parking available.

THIRD COAST CAFÉ

1260 N. DEARBORN STREET, (312) 649-0730

One of Chicago's classic coffeehouses with a limited menu and bad service.

Open late Monday–Wednesday; 24 hours a day Thursday–Sunday. Beer, wine, and single malt scotch. Street parking difficult.

After-Dark Delights

Sample the Creative Appetizer Menu at this Clubby Newcomer

Whatever your taste, the West Loop's nightlife offerings are diverse, from posh, chill-mode lounges to rowdy party places. The problem, however, is that pickings are slim when it comes to a nice budget-friendly spot for a late night bite or two. The area is bustling with the fine-dining establishments on the Randolph Street strip, including the highly praised Blackbird, the French-flavored Marche and the overrated Nine. But other than Bar Louie, there's not much else as far as inexpensive beyond a greasy chicken shack and a hot dog stand in the area.

4 TASTE,
415 N. Milwaukee Ave.,
(312) 226-7850,
4 P.M.–2 A.M.
Tuesday through
Friday; 4 P.M.–3 A.M.
Saturday. Closed
Sunday and Monday.
Street parking is
available.

If you're just looking to grab something fast before you head out or wind down, these options are fine, but if you're looking to sit down with a nice meal in a hip and happening hangout, thank god for **4 Taste**. The lounge-like atmosphere attracts a young, professional crowd, most of whom are getting a late start on their night out at the clubs. You'll see them in big groups or huddled together on dates. The pace is definitely set for late-night dining; the music system is cranked way up with progressive house and techno music.

4 Taste makes eating cheap chic. A stylish yet small spot with about 10 tables and ample bar seating, it offers hot and cold appetizers until about 1:30 A.M. The biggest selling point is that everything on the menu is $9.95. But we're not

talking chicken wings and mini pizzas here, we're talking creative fare with flair. And though they're appetizer portions, you'll certainly get your money's worth.

On the cold menu, standouts include the buffalo carpaccio with mustard curry mayo, arugula, shaved parmesan, and crushed black pepper; roasted maple leaf duck breast with rice wine–cured purple cabbage and tamarind sauce; and the asparagus and roasted bell peppers with balsamic sesame seed oil vinaigrette.

The hot list, however, is where things really get interesting. It's easy to get greedy-eyed when perusing this menu, so be careful. We, nevertheless, ordered almost everything. Cooked to perfection were the roasted New Zealand baby lamb chops with sautéed grapes and red wine reduction; grilled shrimp with black beans, chipotle, cream and cumin oil; grilled free-range Australian beef tenderloin with caramelized onions and dijon cream; the seared ahi tuna with oven-dried tomato wasabi cream and soy reduction; and the apple-stuffed raviolis with smoked chicken, sundried tomatoes, walnuts, and cream.

There's only one dessert offering, the crème brûlée. But again, this is no ordinary crème brûlée. For $6, customers get six mini crème brûlées—in flavors such as chocolate chip, amaretto, Grand Marnier, banana, and Kaluha. It's a sweet send-off for a nice night out on the town.

27

Early to Rise

IF YOU'VE GOT TO GET
OUT OF BED . . .

Breakfast, brunch, *petit déjeuner*, *zaofan*—whatever you call it, your first meal of the day is critical. By morning, if you haven't had a little snack during the night, your blood metabolism will have dropped down to 64 degrees, and you'll need to eat again to raise it to a properly functioning 98.7. Whether it's something simple on the

> **"Love and eggs are best when they are fresh."**
>
> —Russian proverb

go (a hot cup of coffee, a steaming mug of tea, a squirt of warm goat's milk) or a more substantial sit-down repast (French toast or waffles, kippers and eggs, lox and whitefish), this is the meal that sets you in motion, whether it's off to work or just down to your Sunday paper.

Like much of what we eat, breakfast foods have evolved under the influences of different cultures. The pancake became a johnnycake when European settlers used cornmeal borrowed from Native Americans to make their *pannekoeken*. As people moved around, johnnycakes became griddlecakes and then became flapjacks. 'Cakes, crêpes, tortillas, or wonton wrappers, the distinctions sometimes blur, but we like them all.

Even with all the borrowing and sharing, typical breakfasts still vary around the globe and even within our own U. S. of A. If we were to zip around the world in 80 words, here's what we would find as we follow the sun:

• Nippon, land of the rising sun, where Tokyo businessmen in badly-fitting blue suits sip steaming green tea and slurp down miso soup, natto (fermented bean), nori (seaweed), shake (grilled fish), and fried eggs.

• The bustling port of Hong Kong, also bustling with dim sum carts serving assorted dumpling-ized foods to hungry hordes.

• Viva Roma, where stylish Italians dash into uno caffé for a couple sips of cappuccino and a few bites of panino.

• Ah, Paris—city of light, café au lait, and croissants. Nothing sets that Gallic nose a twitchin' like the smell of fresh baked pain au chocolat.

• Back in the U.S.A., a quick streak through the time zones may find the denizens of Gotham City chowing on pillow-sized bagels with cream cheese and lox; Southerners sipping chicory-laced coffee with their hoppin' john or grits and cheese; residents of Seattle, espresso capital of the world, shaking off the morning damp with a steaming double latté; and college students everywhere snarfing cold pizza.

So, what do you have to get up for in Chicago? You've got your *Tribune* and your *Sun-Times*, and you don't know where to go. Well, wake up and read on.

KITSCH'N ON ROSCOE
2005 W. ROSCOE AVENUE, (773) 248-7372

Years ago, there was a breakfast place in Roscoe Village called the Planet Café that was packed with memorabilia and catered to patrons in their pajamas. The Planet later expanded beyond out of its original snug space and went out of business. Now there's Kitsch'n on Roscoe, a cozy breakfast spot that's heir to the Planet's legacy, but is a whole lot cleaner and brighter, and serves immensely better food. With its crayon-bright formica floors, linoleum tables, and multihued vinyl chairs, Kitsch'n pays homage to the Brady kids and those of us who watched them the first time around, but the menu is definitely weighted in the new century. Breakfast includes creative selections like the French Toast Tower ($7) and Green Eggs & Ham with Pesto ($6.50). Lunch and dinner offer gussied up options like southern-fried chicken club ($7.50), served with a choice of chips, french fries, or mashed potatotes; Not Your Mother's Meatloaf ($12), made with portobello mushrooms and roast pepper sauce and served with garlic mashed potatoes; as well as three different kinds of pot pies, garlic and seared veggies ($8), chicken and fennel ($9), and shrimp and ginger ($10). The waitstaff is some of the best in town, whether they're hunting down pieces of Mr. Potato Head for some shrieking kids, gently organizing a long, still-half-asleep line characterized by a bad case of bed-head, or making friendly small talk at the counter—a refuge when it gets really crazy here and the best way to avoid the long line. If you're looking to sink your teeth into some nostalgia, try a bite at Kitsch'n. Pajamas optional.

Open daily. Patio dining in the front, beer garden in the back. Street parking available.

JIM'S GRILL

1429 W. IRVING PARK ROAD, (773) 525-4050

Jim's, a nondescript, tiny diner at Irving Park and Southport, offers the ultimate dining dollar in a congenial atmosphere. Tables are few, and stools at the small counter, where you can slip into various esoteric discussions between regulars and strangers, can also be hard to come by. But squeeze in 'cause the food is great and the prices are better. Choose between a variety of your standard diner breakfast options, such as an omelet, toast, hash browns, and coffee, or two eggs, bacon/sausage, toast, hash browns, and coffee (each $2.75). Or, branch out to the more exotic Korean selections on the menu. Try the vegetarian pancakes for $3.95, mounds of vegetables stir-fried in a rice-based batter served with a tangy sauce. Or, try one of the $4.95 Korean specials that vary daily—maybe some hot, spicy noodles or vegetarian maki rolls. If you're leaning toward an even more substantial start to your day, try the Bi-Bim-Bop, a kind of Korean fried rice served with a fried egg and stir-fried vegetables (chicken, beef, or pork optional). Go easy on the hot sauce unless you really want to wake up.

Closed Sundays. Open Monday–Friday 7 A.M.–3:30 P.M., Saturday 9 A.M.–3 P.M. No alcohol. Jim's sister restaurant, the Korean Buddhist vegetarian Amitabul, is open daily (see "Organic Matters").

FURAMA RESTAURANT

4936 N. BROADWAY, (773) 271-1161

So, maybe you get up, and you're still in the mood for something just a little exotic. The run-of-the-mill eggs or pancakes just aren't going to cut it today. Furama may be the answer you're looking for. Seven days a week, dim sum carts wield their way among the countless hungry (both Asian and gwailoh) diners occupying tables with rotating lazy Susans at Furama's cavernous establishments. Choose from a variety of steamed or fried dumplings and rolls costing only $1.75 to $1.90 for a plate. Don't skip the barbecue pork buns ($1.75) or the sweet fried rice ($3.25). Huge plates of roast duck, soy sauce chicken, curry squid, or jellyfish with sesame are $5.25. Polish it all off with an egg custard for dessert ($1.75). Then go home and nap.

Dim sum served daily from 11 A.M.–3 P.M.

BONGO ROOM

1470 N. MILWAUKEE AVENUE, (773) 489-0690

In its new location on Milwaukee Avenue, the Bongo Room is now able to seat three times as many early risers as would fit in its former cramped quarters under the Damen El stop. Although lacking the tiny, jumbled charm of the former location, the new Bongo Room still offers one of the city's best reasons to leave the comfort of the comforter. With a changing menu executed with creativity and flair, the Bongo Room turns breakfast and lunch into a decadent culinary affair—possibly as sinful as anything you might have found between the sheets. Calypso French toast stuffed with banana mascarpone cheese and drizzled with mocha cream ($9.50), snow crab Benedict with saffron-watercress hollandaise ($10.75), and bittersweet cocoa espresso pancakes topped with butter finger–cashew butter ($7.95) are just some of the Bongo Room's treats. Even a simple bowl of cereal, granola served with fresh fruit and raspberry-mint yogurt ($6.50), has more snap, crackle, and pop than most of us are used to handling before 6 P.M.

Open daily, brunch is weekdays 7 A.M.–3 P.M., weekends 9:30 A.M.–2:30 P.M. No alcohol. Street parking difficult.

S&G

3000 N. LINCOLN AVENUE, (773) 935-4025

A typical diner/breakfast establishment, Sam & George's, the S&G, has two standout redeeming features. First, in a dueling diners scenario with its neighbor the Golden Apple across the street, it's open 24 hours on the weekends, serving coffee in brown mugs around the clock. Second is S&G's selection of twenty-five different egg casseroles, meals that combine fried potatoes, eggs, and a variety of fixin's, along with a side of toast, for a real meal for real people (all ranging in price from $5.95–$7.95). A real favorite of pork patrons (or those with a wicked hangover), the Gypsy has potatoes buried under a layer of eggs, ham, cheese, mushrooms, etc. Those ordering the Sparta—potatoes and eggs with feta cheese and vegetables— might get served the Athenian (add gyros meat).

Open daily, 24 hours on the weekends. No alcohol. Street parking available.

BRETT'S RESTAURANT

2011 W. ROSCOE AVENUE, (773) 248-0999

Brunch is your opportunity to enjoy the dishes of one of the city's most talented and creative chefs for less than one-third of what you might spend on dinner at Brett's in Roscoe Village. A cozy bistro with wrought-iron seating that helps set the atmosphere of eating out on the sun porch, Brett's serves a creative brunch on Sundays with most dishes priced $9 and under. Pumpkin waffles with maple syrup ($6.50) and spinach pancakes with corn salsa ($7.75) are both regular breakfast items. If you're not feeling quite so creative, a number of omelets, including one with goat cheese, mushrooms, sun-dried tomatoes, and a fried potato cake ($7.75) are also options. Specials vary by season. A children's menu is also available.

Brunch served Sundays from 10 A.M. to 2 P.M. Full bar. Street parking available.

BREAKFAST CLUB

1381 W. HUBBARD STREET, (312) 666-2372

A small bungalow has been converted to a pink dining room and the Breakfast Club. Packed with regulars at close-set tables, the Breakfast Club serves breakfast and brunch specialties, along with burgers, sandwiches, salads, and some main dishes like pasta and meat loaf (all priced under $8). Morning specialties include Swedish pancakes with lingonberries ($6.25), potato pancakes with apple sauce ($5.75), French toast stuffed with cream cheese, cinnamon, and walnuts ($6.75), apple-cinnamon oatmeal with honey ($3.95), and omelets like sundried tomato with onions and cheese ($5.75). Note: Service can be very slow on weekends.

Brunch served daily from 6 A.M.–3 P.M. (from 7 A.M. on weekends). Full bar. Sidewalk dining in nice weather.

ANN SATHER

5207 N. CLARK STREET, (773) 271-6677

929 W. BELMONT AVENUE, (773) 348-2378

2665 N. CLARK STREET, (773) 327-9522 (CARRY-OUT ONLY)

3416 N. SOUTHPORT AVENUE, (773) 404-4475 (CARRY-OUT ONLY)

Ann Sather has been serving Swedish breakfasts (and some pretty bodacious dinners) since 1945. Skip the wait at Belmont by heading north to the spacious Andersonville branch. Don't miss the thin Swedish pancakes with the lingonberry preserves ($4.95, add $0.50 for either ice cream or strawberries) and order a side of Swedish potato sausage ($1.75). Cinnamon buns are $7.50 a dozen to go.

Belmont is open daily. Full bar, including Swedish glogg. Parking lot. The Andersonville location is closed on Tuesdays.

Rasher Decision

Seeking a Magically Delicious Irish Breakfast

Try saying top o' the morning on St. Patrick's Day by starting off with a traditional Irish breakfast. No, not your first beer of the day, but the fabled Irish grill.

My friend Fergal, who recently moved back to Dublin after eight years in Chicago, is my authority on everything Irish. I sent him an e-mail asking about his breakfast preferences, and he replied that real Irish really do eat Irish breakfasts—they're not a figment of the American imagination, like so many other things said to be from the Emerald Isle. Says Fergal, "You can't beat a nice greasy fry up. Black and white pud(ding) is a must. Definitely no hash browns though. A standard breakie might be the aforementioned pud, a few fried eggs, rashers (a.k.a. "bacon" stateside), sausages, mushrooms, etc."

As Fergal noted, the traditional Irish breakfast is a plate of fried eggs, sausages, rashers, black and white pudding, bangers (sausages), brown bread, and optional sides of fried tomatoes, mushrooms, and potatoes. There's no mystery about fried eggs and mushrooms, but some of the other standard parts of a traditional Irish breakfast are less familiar to American stomachs.

The pudding, for example, is nothing like what you mix up from the Jell-O box. Puddings look like fat sausages, but their particular meat and spices give them a distinctive taste and distinguish them from regular sausages. Packed into long rolls, the puddings can be sliced and then grilled or fried until crisp. Black pudding, which is also known as blood pudding or blood sausage, is pork sausage made with pig's blood (when the real thing is to be had). White pudding is a similar sausage made without blood.

Puddings are an ancient Irish dish. According to Reay Tannahill, author of *Food in History*, blood drinking and eating has been common in most pastoral communities throughout history. Irish peasants, it was noted by a French traveler in seventeenth-century Ireland, "bleed their cows and boil the blood with some of the milk and butter that came from the same beast; and this with a mixture of savoury herbs is one of their most delicious dishes." This preparation was a version of *drisheen*, a kind of black pudding still known in Country Cork and elsewhere today.

The best rasher is a piece of Shannon Traditional Bacon, one of Ireland's top exports, which is right up there in popularity with McCann's Oatmeal, Baileys Irish Cream, Guinness, and Irish whisky. In contrast to American bacon taken from pork bellies, Shannon bacon is cut from the loin, making it a leaner and more expensive cut of pork. Shannon bacon resembles Canadian bacon but is cut long with "the streak" of American bacon. It's never cooked hard like American bacon. The bacon fat is then used to fry the bangers, puddings, tomatoes, and other vegetables.

At the **Hidden Shamrock**, which bills itself as the "best Irish breakfast in town," breakfast is served with fresh tomatoes, mushrooms, black and white pudding, two basted eggs, sausages, rashers, homemade brown bread, and potatoes. The restaurant prides itself on preparing every Irish breakfast fresh to order, "not cooked two hours ahead of time and put on a hot plate." A spokeswoman for the Hidden Shamrock notes, "We get a lot of people who come in for our Irish breakfast, but usually later in the day, because it's so filling. Americans typically eat it at dinner, while local Irish tend to come in around noon and have an Irish breakfast for lunch."

Traditional Irish breakfasts can also be ordered daily, all day, at **Chief O'Neill's**, **Fado**, and the **Abbey Pub**. Start your day off with the luck of the Irish. *Bain taitneamh as do bheile* (a little Gaeilic for *bon appétit*).

ABBEY PUB

3420 W. GRACE AVENUE, (773) 463-5808

CHIEF O'NEILL'S PUB

3471 N. ELSTON AVENUE, (773) IRELAND (473-5263)

FADO IRISH PUB

100 WEST GRAND AVENUE, (312) 836-0066

HIDDEN SHAMROCK

2723 N. HALSTED STREET, (773) 883-0304

Fresh Toast

Pop Into a Perky Brunch Spot

I believe there's an inverse relationship between parking and meal prices. The less parking, the higher the prices—which is one reason I rarely eat out in Lincoln Park. So many places in those neighborhoods are over-hyped, overpriced, and it can take as long to park as it does to stand in line for a table. An attractive eatery locates itself conveniently within a four-block walk of public transportation or in some neighborhood that offers a legal, albeit small, street parking opportunity, say within in a three-block radius.

Given this philosophy, it's not often that I'm found in DePaul's Oz Park neighborhood hungry. So, imagine my surprise one night as I strolled west on Webster, and **Toast** popped out at me. Returning the following morning (after successfully wrestling into a tiny space just shy of a crosswalk and only a block away), I found Toast to be the East side's answer to Wicker Park's breakfast and lunch hot spot, Bongo Room. Both are cozy, sponge-painted fantasies to wake up to. But where the Bongo Room is a cramped and artfully dilapidated little storefront serving brunch fancies to artfully disheveled, black-clad Wicker Park patrons, Toast is a bright piece of real estate dishing up early day taste treats to shiny, happy Lincoln Park people.

Owned by the operators of the oh-so-hip Iggy's and Harry's Velvet Room, Toast offers culinary depth to a surface motif of cute little toasters, sprinkled throughout the restaurant, and cute waitstaff. In spite of this insinuation of gustatory backwardness and motivated by savory, steaming plates piled high and garnished with exotic cheeses and vegetables—names of which the waitstaff should really learn to pronounce properly to maintain that aura of chic superiority—my dining partner and I jumped the table line and snagged counter seats where apparently, in spite of long waits, a hostess blithely confirmed for us that possession is nine-tenths of the law.

After admiring the spunky toaster magnets on the refrigerator behind the counter, we brushed the crumbs left behind by the former occupants of our stools off our perky "eat" placemats and debated our options. Should it be breakfast or lunch? Door Number One or Two? On the breakfast side, while my eyes gave an enthusiastic thumbs up to both the eggs Benedict with prosciutto and white truffle hollandaise ($7.95) and the French toast filled with either strawberries or mascarpone cheese and topped with seasonal berries ($6.25), my stomach waved a cautionary flag at such indulgences. Omelettes ($6.95) offered a choice of vegetarian (shitake and oyster mushrooms oozing in Gruyère cheese), asparagus and blue cheese, three cheese, or Tijuana jalapeños with onions, toma-

TOAST, 746 W. Webster Ave., (312) 935-5600, is open Tuesday through Friday from 7 A.M. until 4 P.M. and weekends from 8 A.M. to 4 P.M. Other Toasts are located at 228 W. Chicago Ave., (312) 944-7023 and 2046 N. Damen Ave., (773) 772-5600.

toes, Chihuahua cheese and cilantro. Going bare basics, "steel cut" oatmeal with brown sugar and apples struck me as an option for no-nonsense simplicity.

While my partner waded into the rich danger of white truffle hollandaise and slightly dry chicken sausage, I opted for lunch. Although mango chicken chutney and warm couscous shrimp salad (both $5.95) both sounded attractive, I was after something more substantial. I wasn't sure I could do the steak and Gorgonzola sandwich ($8.95), served with sweet potato chips, before at least 3 P.M. on a weekend. Wasn't feeling nostalgic enough for banana peanut butter and jelly ($3). No, I made a beeline for one of the hottest menu segments out there—the wrap. These days, doesn't it just seem like everybody's wrappin'? I eliminated the vegetarian wrap ($5.95) and the paella wrap ($6.95), narrowing it down to the Thai chicken or the spicy, blackened shrimp and asparagus with red pepper butter in a chile tortilla (both $6.95). Assured by our waitress that "everybody really loves the Thai chicken," 15 minutes later I wrapped both hands happily around about a pound of Thai fixin's and happily munched away while peanut sauce, coconut, and cilantro oozed down over my wrists. I took the other pound home in a doggy bag for a second banquet later.

"It's not what's eating you—it's what you're eating," notes the restaurant. Toast, I'd recommend a slice or two.

Indexes

ALPHABETICAL LISTING BY RESTAURANT NAME

ALPHABETICAL LISTING BY RESTAURANT TYPE

Mirabell Restaurant & Lounge /
  Wrigleyville, 70
Resi's Bierstube /Lakeview, ix, 70, 189

Global

Bite /Ukrainian Village, 146
Bongo Room /Wicker Park, 272
Brett's Restaurant /Roscoe Village, 273
Café Selmarie /Lincoln Square, 223
Caffé De Luca /Wicker Park, 147
Chef's Station /Evanston, 178
Co-op Markets /Hyde Park, 247
Corner Bakery /Mag Mile, 138
Cru Café & Wine Bar /Mag Mile, 135
Eden, the Natural Bistro /Lincoln Park,
  242
Flying Saucer /West Side, 147
Foodlife /Mag Mile, 132
404 Wine Bar /Lincoln Park, 192
Grillers Café /Mag Mile, 136
Ivy at the Oak Tree, The /Mag Mile,
  132
Jane's /Bucktown, 223
Leo's Lunchroom /Wicker Park, 145
Lo-Cal Zone, The /Mag Mile, 255
Lucky Platter /Evanston, 178
Lula Café /Logan Square, 11
Map Room, The /Bucktown, 148
Oak Street Beachstro /Mag Mile, 136
Potbelly/Evanston /Lincoln Park /Mag
  Mile, 140
Puck's at the MCA (Museum of
  Contemporary Art) /Loop, 200, 205
Tilli's /Lincoln Park, 188
Toast /Lincoln Park, 278
Zoom Kitchen /Mag Mile /Lakeview,
  137

Greek

Athena Restaurant /Greek Town, 188
Cross Rhodes /Evanston, 183
Grecian Taverna Restaurant & Lounge /
  Lincoln Square, 225

Guatemalan

El Tinajon /Lincoln Square /Roscoe
  Village, 5

High Tea

American Girl Café, The /Mag Mile, 26
Seasons of Long Grove /Long Grove, 26
Villa Kula /Lincoln Square, 159

Indian

Gaylord India /West Rogers Park, 45
Ghandi India /West Rogers Park, 42
India Garden /West Rogers Park /Mag
  Mile, 41, 135
Kanval Palace /West Rogers Park, 41
Moti Mahal /West Rogers Park /
  Lakeview, 244
Patel Brothers Groceries /West Rogers
  Park, 42
Raj Darber /Lincoln Park, 42
Sabrinihari /West Rogers Park, 41
Sher-A-Punjab /West Rogers Park, 41
Standard India Restaurant /Lakeview,
  42
Star of India /Lakeview, 43
Tiffin /West Rogers Park, 44
Udupi Palace /West Rogers Park, 41
Viceroy of India Restaurant /West
  Rogers Park, 41

Irish

Abbey Pub /Lakeview, 23, 207, 276
Chief O'Neill's Pub /North Center, 23,
  276
Fado Irish Pub /River North, 27, 211,
  276
Hidden Shamrock, The /Lincoln Park,
  25, 276
Irish Oak, The /Wrigleyville, 212
Joy of Ireland /Mag Mile, 25, 26
Tommy Nevin's Pub /Evanston, 24

Israeli

Hashalom /West Rogers Park, 107

Italian

Al's #1 Italian Beef /Taylor Street,
  91
Anna Maria's Pasteria /Lakeview, viii,
  86
Babaluci /Bucktown, 144

Flying Chicken, The /Lakeview, 159

Stir-Fry
Flat Top Grill, The /Lincoln Park /
  Evanston, 234
Mongolian Barbeque /Wrigleyville, 234

Swedish
Ann Sather /Andersonville /Lakeview /
  Lincoln Park, 172, 274
Erickson's Delicatessen /Andersonville,
  173
Ikea's Chicago Restaurant /Schaumburg,
  247
Svea Restaurant /Andersonville, 172
Swedish Bakery, The /Andersonville,
  173

Thai
Always Thai /Lakeview, 79
Dao Thai Restaurant and Noodle Palace /
  Mag Mile, 190
River Kwai II /Roscoe Village, 263

Tibetan
Tibet Café /Lakeview, 45

Turkish
A La Turka Turkish Kitchen /Lakeview,
  111, 115

Café Demir /Lakeview, 157
Café Zam Zam /Lakeview, 157

Ukrainian
Ann's Bakery /Ukrainian Village, 37
Old Lviv Ukrainian Food Restaurant /
  Ukrainian Village, 37
Sak's Ukrainian Village /Ukrainian
  Village, 36

Vegetarian
Amitabul /North Park, 64
Blind Faith Café /Evanston, 180
Chicago Diner /Lakeview, 253
Heartland Café, The /Rogers Park, 253
Heartwise Express /Loop, 256
Karyn's Fresh Corner/Roscoe Village, 258
Soul Vegetarian East /South Side, 256
Sun & Moon /Wicker Park, 256
Taqueria Mamasita's /Lakeview, 255
Victory's Banner /Roscoe Village, 254

Vietnamese
Hoang Mai /Argyle Street, 80
Le Colonial /Mag Mile, 187
Nhu Hoa /Argyle Street, 81
Pasteur /Edgewater, 226
Song Huong /Argyle Street, 80
Vietnam Little Home Restaurant /
  Ravenswood, 79

ALPHABETICAL LISTING BY NEIGHBORHOOD